P9-CRO-345

Seventh Edition

Making Sense

A Student's Guide to Research and Writing

Social Sciences

Margot Northey
Lorne Tepperman
Patrizia Albanese

OXFORD
UNIVERSITY PRESS

OXFORD
UNIVERSITY PRESS

Oxford University Press is a department of the University of Oxford.
It furthers the University's objective of excellence in research, scholarship,
and education by publishing worldwide. Oxford is a registered trade mark of
Oxford University Press in the UK and in certain other countries.

Published in Canada by
Oxford University Press
8 Sampson Mews, Suite 204,
Don Mills, Ontario M3C 0H5 Canada

www.oupcanada.com

Copyright © Oxford University Press Canada 2018

The moral rights of the authors have been asserted

Database right Oxford University Press (maker)

First Edition published in 1986
Second Edition published in 2002
Third Edition published in 2007
Fourth Edition published in 2009
Fifth Edition published in 2012
Sixth Edition published in 2015

All rights reserved. No part of this publication may be reproduced, stored in
a retrieval system, or transmitted, in any form or by any means, without the
prior permission in writing of Oxford University Press, or as expressly permitted
by law, by licence, or under terms agreed with the appropriate reprographics
rights organization. Enquiries concerning reproduction outside the scope of the
above should be sent to the Permissions Department at the address above
or through the following url: www.oupcanada.com/permission/permission_request.php

Every effort has been made to determine and contact copyright holders.
In the case of any omissions, the publisher will be pleased to make
suitable acknowledgement in future editions.

Library and Archives Canada Cataloguing in Publication

Northey, Margot, 1940-, author
Making sense in the social sciences : a student's guide to research
and writing / Margot Northey, Lorne Tepperman, Patrizia Albanese.
— Seventh edition.

(The making sense series)
Includes bibliographical references and index.
Issued in print and electronic formats.
ISBN 978-0-19-902678-4 (softcover). —ISBN 978-0-19-902671-5 (PDF)

1. Social sciences—Authorship. 2. Report writing. 3. English
language—Rhetoric. I. Tepperman, Lorne, 1943-, author
II. Albanese, Patrizia, author III. Title. IV. Series: Making sense series

H91.N67 2018   808.06'63021   C2017-906686-2
                      C2017-906687-0

Cover image: Suttipong Sutiratanachai/Mopment/Getty Images
Cover design: Laurie McGregor
Interior design: Sherill Chapman

Oxford University Press is committed to our environment.
Wherever possible, our books are printed on paper which comes from
responsible sources.

Printed and bound in the United States of America

1 2 3 4 — 21 20 19 18

Contents

Preface

Good writing takes time. It usually follows the old formula of 10 per cent inspiration and 90 per cent perspiration.

Writing in university or college is not fundamentally different from any other writing. But each piece of writing has its own special purposes, and these determine its particular substance, shape, and tone. *Making Sense in the Social Sciences* examines both the general principles for effective writing and the special requirements of social science research. It also points out some common errors in student composition and suggests ways to avoid or correct them. Written as a set of guidelines rather than strict rules, this book aims to help you escape the common pitfalls of student writing, and develop confidence in your work. It outlines some basic principles, and simple and sound techniques to help you do this.

We intend this book to teach you how to share your work with others, through clearly written term papers, examinations, presentations, and research reports for your social science courses. Writing well in the social sciences demands not only a good writing style but also a good understanding of research design, theory, measurement, argument, and communication. All of these qualities must be present for you to get your ideas across clearly and persuasively.

Much of what appears in the following chapters is written to help you conduct and describe a research project of your own. Nevertheless, the same principles apply, with equal force, to understanding, describing, and criticizing the work of others.

One of our goals is to show you how to conduct and present your own research—research that will make sense to someone who may not already be persuaded of your views. Our second goal is to show you how to make sense of the work of other researchers, so that you can use and evaluate their findings in essays, book reviews, and examination answers.

Making sense in the social sciences is similar to making sense in the physical sciences and humanities. However, some of the issues and challenges described here are more marked in the social sciences, which use more varied research methods than the physical sciences and humanities. Some problems are unique to particular disciplines of social science, but others are not. We discuss some of the common problems, and how to avoid them, using examples from across the social sciences.

In writing this edition, we relied on reactions to previous editions and suggestions for change and improvement. We updated examples and material in the chapters. We especially focused on removing unnecessary overlap across chapters, and expanded discussion of how to present your work. Overall, we tried to reflect the current state of this changing academic field.

As in the previous editions, we have noted the diminishing importance of a distinction between quantitative and qualitative methodologies; the value of all methodologies, each having its particular area of competence and pertinence; and the usefulness of multi(mixed)-method analysis in obtaining stable results and opening up communications between sub-disciplines.

In this edition, we have also addressed some newer and currently pressing concerns. For example, we have more to say about the latest standards around Internet citations; the need to evaluate website and Internet resources, including social media, for currency and veracity; current thinking about citations and plagiarism; and the use of less-traditional sources in building a bibliography. In this last respect, we consider the role of peer review in the context of selecting valid sources for research. We also address proposal-writing as a type of project; and in the chapter on writing essays, include a sample essay outline.

Today, no single model of analysis dominates social science; instead, many approaches are used for exploring data and the links between macro and micro levels of reality. We discuss some methodological developments of the last few decades and contrast them with older methods. We provide illustrative examples of the way different types of analysis contribute to social science knowledge in different areas, including sociology, anthropology, demography, criminology, women's studies, and political science. However, in the midst of variety, we find a few simple themes that are repeated throughout the book: particularly, they are the connectedness of research methods and the connectedness of the social sciences.

Statistics typically address generalities: the characteristics of large populations and large trends, for example. These generalities are so large that they rarely help us to picture the individual people who personify them. For this reason, statistics often leave people cold. Yet they capture broad "truths" about a population because they are usually based on scientific sampling of that population. So, like it or not, we need to gather statistics.

At the same time, we need to gather stories. The best stories about social experience are particular, not general: they sketch particular people caught in particular dramas at particular times and places. Stories capture our interest in a way that statistics usually do not. Stories also tell "truths" about the human condition, despite their particularity. In the end, every population is just the sum of the unique stories that make it up. Statistics and stories are just two sides of the same coin, the forest and the trees respectively. Both accounts are true, but each speaks to a different part of our need to know the truth. We aim to show the connections between big and small truths in the chapters that follow.

Just as statistics have a logic, so too do stories. Stories have logical structures in the same sense that sonatas and symphonies do. Good authors (and composers) know these standard forms and genres of exposition. The skillful manipulation of formal elements is what makes people respond to accounts emotionally. Perhaps these forms are, in some sense, essential and universal: perhaps every successful love story will have the same structure, wherever and whenever it is written, for example. Likely, every story will also reflect particular features of a time, culture, or civilization. In both cases, successful stories have a structure: they are no more random than the social statistics describing a crime rate or a population of families. Good writing needs order, just as society itself needs order. In this book, our goal is to help you better understand and accomplish this orderly storytelling in your own work.

These points may sound unnecessarily abstract, but we are making them for two reasons. First, this book is about good writing and about the analysis of society; and we hope to show you that these two goals are related and compatible. They fit well in one book, and you can learn about both at the same time. Second, this edition of the book emphasizes—as some earlier editions did not—the essential compatibility of statistical analysis and storytelling, of quantitative and qualitative analysis, and of *scientific* and *interpretive* approaches to reality. More than ever, social scientists in every discipline recognize the need to bring these approaches together in their research. Students, for their part, need to know this important change is taking place; and our book makes a small contribution to this change in thinking.

The value of this book is not limited to helping you write good term papers, exams, and research projects. More sensible communication in the social sciences is useful outside of school too: in education, government, business, and journalism, for example. We hope you will use the principles learned from this book long after you have stopped writing papers that only a professor or teaching assistant will read. Dip into the book as a quick reference, or read it through, then email us (palbanes@soc.ryerson.ca or lorne.tepperman@utoronto.ca) to tell us what you think.

Acknowledgements

Much of the work on this edition involved general editing, updating examples and references, trimming down sections where material overlapped across chapters, and adding a few new sections. In the process, we have enjoyed working with Jodi Lewchuk, the Oxford University Press editor who advised us on changes the book needed and supported our efforts along the way. Finally, we were guided through a smooth and speedy copy edit by Jessie Coffey who made everything (seem) effortless.

Appropriately, this book is dedicated to all of the undergraduates who struggle daily to understand how social science is different from common sense and armchair speculation on the one hand, and jargon-filled data juggling on the other. We hope this book will make sense of social science for them.

We would like to acknowledge the use of the following diagrams: "Deductive and inductive approaches to the relationship between theory and research," from Alan Bryman, Edward Bell, and James J. Teevan, in *Social Research Methods, Third Canadian Edition*; "Hypothesized path model with wishful identification and comprehension as mediators," from Andrew J. Weaver, Jakob D. Jensen, Nicole Martins, Ryan J. Hurley, and Barbara J. Wilson, "Liking Violence and Action: An Examination of Gender Differences in Children's Processing of Animated Content," in *Media Psychology*; "Theoretical model of place-based voluntary participation," from Vernon D. Ryan, Kerry A. Agnitsch, Lijun Zhao, and Rehan Mullick, "Making Sense of Voluntary Participation: A Theoretical Synthesis," in *Rural Sociology*; "Early universal marriage and polygyny among women in a traditional economy and a stationary population," from Helena Chojnacka, "Early Marriage and Polygyny: Feature Characteristics of Nuptiality in Africa," in *Genus*; and "The qualitative and quantitative paradigms compared," from Charles S. Reichardt and Thomas D. Cook, "Beyond Qualitative versus Quantitative Methods," in *Qualitative and Quantitative Methods in Evaluation Research*, edited by Thomas D. Cook and Charles S. Reichardt.

A Note to the Student

Everyone knows a tough job market faces students when they graduate from college or university. So what, then, is the "use" of a book like this one, which proposes to teach students about research and writing? What is the use of knowing about research if you're not going to be a paid, full-time researcher? What's the use of knowing about writing if you're not going to be a novelist or speechwriter?

You've probably thought about these questions yourself, so here are a few tentative answers. First, jobs in the modern work world are increasingly "white collar" or non-manual jobs that require you to read, write, and answer questions systematically. These may be service jobs, sales jobs, managerial or supervisory jobs, or professional jobs. Each of these requires a discrete set of skills, but reading, writing, and question-answering are important in all of these jobs. Equally important in this fast changing world of work is the need to constantly learn new skills and develop occupationally: again, learning and changing call for reading, writing, and posing and answering questions.

Second, jobs in the modern work world require "critical thinking" skills that can only be acquired through reading, writing, and question-answering. "Critical thinking" doesn't mean criticizing the boss and co-workers: most bosses and co-workers don't like that very much. Critical thinking means learning to think creatively, and learning to think "outside the box." That's where new ideas come from, and in the work world new ideas often bring success, promotion, and even fame.

Third, putting aside the demands of the modern work world, we all need critical thinking skills and the related skills that we aim to hone in this book, in other areas of our lives. Without these skills, in this rapidly changing technological age, we cannot hope to be well-informed citizens, good parents, or helpful friends and neighbours. Our need to know and understand the world, to live in it safely, is important and growing all the time. Paraphrasing Shakespeare, ignorance is *not* bliss, for it is *not* folly to be wise in our modern world. It is folly to ignore the world around us, in all its complexity.

So, for these large and almost grandiose reasons, we have authored this slender book. We think it will help you to write and do research yourself, and in those ways, to get good grades in your postsecondary classes. But it will do much more than that, if you think deeply about what you are learning and continue to put what you learn into practice.

1 Writing and Thinking

In this chapter we will examine

- strategies you can use first to think and then to write about your research topic;
- tactics to help you consider the purpose of your writing, its intended reader, and its tone;
- the thesis statement; and
- the rule of equal thirds when managing your time thinking, writing, and revising.

Introduction

You write all the time! Think about the amount of time you spend texting and writing emails. Writing is a powerful tool for sharing ideas and demonstrating what you know. You use information to accomplish a purpose. Academic writing is no different. Fear and anxiety about academic or other formal writing is common and can create barriers to success at school, work, and in other aspects of everyday life. It gets easier with training and practice (Price, 2010). Nobody is born a good writer, but you can pick up strategies and skills along the way to make writing easier and even fun.

Good formal writing requires solid research. Research is a game, played largely in people's heads—with players, rules, and goals. It is a game of thinking and then transferring thoughts onto paper or into a computer. Winning is accomplished by producing superior thoughts that are written in a clear and persuasive manner. This requires planning and training. Nowhere is this more obvious than in the writing of essays, tests, and research papers, where writing and thinking are everything.

You are not likely to produce clear, persuasive writing unless you have done some clear thinking, and thinking cannot be hurried. Psychologists have shown that you can't always solve a difficult problem by determined reasoning alone.

Sometimes, when you're stuck, it's best to take a break, sleep on it, and let the unconscious or creative part of your brain take over for a while. Relaxation may help you produce a new approach or solution. Keep the research in mind and keep your eyes open for new ideas. Remember that leaving time for creative reflection isn't the same as sitting around, hoping inspiration will strike out of the blue.

Starting Strategies

Writing is about making choices: about which ideas you want to present and how you want to present them. Practice makes these decisions easier, but each piece of writing involves making choices.

You can narrow the field of choice if you realize that you are *not* writing for anybody, anywhere, without any particular reason. It's sound strategy to begin by asking yourself three questions:

- What is the purpose of this piece of writing?
- Who am I writing for?
- What does the reader expect?

Your first reaction may be, "I'm writing an essay for my instructor, to satisfy a course requirement," but obviously this won't help. Your answers have to be more precise. Thus, a better answer might be, "I want to study X using research method Y to prove Z for course A." Here are some suggestions for finding precise answers to these questions.

Think about your purpose

Your purpose may include one (or more) of these possibilities:

- to show that you understand certain terms or theories,
- to show that you can do independent research,
- to apply a specific theory to new material,
- to show your knowledge of a topic or text,
- to demonstrate your ability to evaluate secondary sources, and/or
- to show that you can think critically or creatively.

An assignment designed to see if you have read and understood specific material calls for a different approach than one meant to test your critical thinking or research skills. If you don't figure out the exact purpose of your assignment, you will likely not have positive results.

Understanding the purpose of your assignment will help you to determine how much of your own ideas and assumptions you are expected to bring into your writing. Different purposes lead you to taking different steps and approaches, and these different steps and approaches lead you to different kinds of conclusions, outcomes, and types of knowledge. As a result, we are reminded that knowledge is socially constructed (see Ghassib, 2012). This means that in most cases, what we come to accept as knowledge is based on culturally and historically specific assumptions about how the world works (Pascale, 2010). This is very exciting because it means that there is a growing acceptance that knowledge is not a simple, clear, and fixed set of facts, established by a privileged set of experts (Pascale, 2010). It means that there is room to challenge the existing ways of thinking about the world, and that there are different ways of knowing (Creswell, 2013; Briggs, 2013; Ghassib, 2012; Pascale, 2010). In other words, knowledge can be the product of reflexivity and interpretation, and is complex and variable depending on a large number of factors (see Creswell, 2013; Flick, 2006). If the purpose of your assignment allows it, you then have the ability to explore new and exciting ways of thinking about the social world. So to start, you must understand what you are being asked to *do* or *show* through your piece of writing.

Think about your reader

To convince a person that your views are sound, you have to consider his or her way of thinking. If you are writing a paper on youth unemployment for a sociology professor, your analysis will be different from the analysis you would use if you were writing for an economics or history professor. You will have to decide which terms to explain and what background information you should supply. In the same way, if your reader does not support the idea of a common currency between Canada and the United States, and you intend to propose that Canadians use American money, you should anticipate any arguments that your reader may raise, and address them in advance.

If you do not know who will be reading your paper—your professor, or your tutorial leader or marker—just imagine someone intelligent and interested who is skeptical enough to question your ideas, but flexible enough to adopt them (and assign the paper a good grade) if your evidence is convincing.

Think about the tone

When texting with friends, you use a casual tone, but academic writing is more formal. Just how formal you need to be will depend on the instructions you have been given. If your anthropology professor asks you to express yourself freely and personally in a journal, you may be able to use an informal style. Essays and reports, however, require a formal tone. Here are some examples that may be too informal for academic work.

Use of slang
Although the occasional use of slang may be used to achieve a special effect, frequent use is not acceptable in academic writing. Slang expressions are usually regional and short-lived: they may mean different things to different groups at different times. (Just think of how widely the meanings of *hot*, *cool*, and *sick* can vary, depending on the circumstances.)

Frequent use of contractions
Generally speaking, contractions such as *can't* and *isn't* are not suitable for academic writing, although they may be fine for informal writing—for example, this handbook. This is not to say that you should avoid using contractions altogether: even the most serious academic writing can sound stiff without any contractions at all. Just be sure that when you use contractions in a college or university essay you use them *sparingly* because excessive use makes formal writing sound weak and informal.

Finding a suitable tone for academic writing can be a challenge. The problem with trying to avoid informality is that you may be tempted to become too formal. If your writing sounds stiff or pompous, you may be using too many high-flown phrases, long words, or passive constructions (see Chapter 7). For example, it is better to say "a growing number of women are becoming self-employed" than "an escalating quantity of women are entering more flexible arrangements in the form of entrepreneurial endeavours." When in doubt, a more formal but simple style is usually most effective.

Develop a thesis statement

Some have argued that what a novice writer lacks most is focus or unity of thought, and what is required to keep a writer on track is a *thesis statement* (Raymer, 2010; Haluska, 2006; Jortner, 2003). A thesis statement is typically a single sentence that expresses what your essay or paper is about—a big idea boiled down to one thought (Frank, 2005). The thesis statement is the writer's promise to the reader that focuses and controls the essay (Carroll, 2012). In other words, good thesis statements not only set out what your piece of writing is about, they indicate your views on the topic and the direction you will take in your work (Raymer, 2010).

Carroll (2012: 18–19) explains that you should become familiar with the ABCs before tackling a thesis statement:

- "**A**—The thesis ASSERTS." This means you need to "get an angle on the topic, an aspect about which [you] feel confident." Avoid being wishy-washy and/or waffling.
- "**B**—The thesis writer must BE AN INSIDER." This does not mean writing about your personal experiences. It means "choosing an angle—your angle—as an expert on one particular aspect of the topic." And,
- "**C**—The thesis statement must be CLEAR." We often want to sound profound in our theses, but profound ideas can and should be written in clean, clear, and simple language. A simple, straightforward, and knowledgeable assertion is much more effective than something that attempts to sound (but isn't) profound and philosophical.

Carroll (2012: 19) notes that: "[t]he thesis should pop and crackle with precise word choice, not ambiguity." The thesis statement drives the structure and content of your paper (Montante, 2004). It should show what the work will say on a topic but also what you, the writer, think that it means (Duxbury, 2008). For example, Haluska (2006: 52) gives the following example: imagine that you have been asked to write a short report on one journal article. Judging by each of these thesis statements, which would produce the most effective essay?

A. The article talks about _____ and _____.
B. This is an excellent article because of how clearly it explains _____ and _____.
C. This article seems pretty uneven; although the author explains _____ well, his main points, _____ and _____, are presented in such a confusing way that I could hardly keep track of them.

If you selected either B or C above, you would agree with Haluska (2006: 52), who explains that in both cases, the student has "read the article with enough mental vigour to have formed an intelligent opinion about it." The essay will be focused and unified if the writer then gives specific details demonstrating the validity of each claim (also see Carroll, 2012).

Budget your time
Think about the length and value
Before you start writing, or even researching, you will need to think about the assignment in relation to the time you have to spend on it. If your instructor has assigned a topic and specified a length, it should be easy for you to assess the level of detail needed and the amount of research you will need to do. If only the length is prescribed, that limit will help you decide how broad or narrow the topic you choose should be (see Chapter 8 for more on this). You should also think about how important the assignment is in relation to the rest of your work for the course. A piece of work worth 10 per cent of your final grade will not demand as much attention as one worth 30 per cent.

How long will it take? The rule of equal thirds
There is no such thing as a question that *must* take a week, a month, or a year. Any question can be answered in the time you have available, whether that's three minutes, three hours, or three months.

Other things being equal, however, an intelligent answer that takes three hours to complete will be better than an intelligent answer that takes three minutes. If you have only three minutes to answer, do your best in the time available and you will be respected for the result. However, if you have three hours to answer, by all means use that three-hour period to its fullest. Your instructor will be expecting more from a three-hour answer than from a three-minute one.

Many students who struggle with their writing do so because they do not make effective use of their time. Often, students spend too little time revising their work. Research by Levy and Ransdell (1995) found that writers who revised the most got the highest grades.

If you have trouble budgeting your time for an assignment, consider using the "rule of equal thirds," suggested by Sanford Kaye in his book *Writing under Pressure* (1998). He recommends that whatever you're writing, you should always spend about one-third of your time thinking, reading, and preparing to answer; another third of your time writing the first draft; and the final third cleaning up and revising (for research on writing and revising, see Peñuelas, 2008).

So, for example, if you have three months to write an essay, spend one month thinking about the problem and collecting information and whatever other data you may need. Spend your second month writing a first draft of the essay, and spend your final month rereading, reorganizing, and revising, checking it for errors and typos. Let's consider each step in more detail.

The first third

You should spend the first third of your allotted time doing background reading, designing your research, identifying and/or measuring your variables and arguments, and collecting and analyzing your information or data.

Before you can start writing, you need to find out what you don't know. You also have to develop strategies for limiting what you need to know. If, for example, you decide to write something on modern family life in Canada, you will find hundreds of books and articles on that topic. You cannot read all that material; you need a strategy to narrow the question you are going to answer and a way to decide which things you have to read and which you can ignore. (We discuss ways of limiting your topic in Chapter 8.)

The second third

Once you have narrowed your question, and read and thought about your topic, you are ready to start writing. Force yourself to obey the *equal thirds* rule: if you look at your calendar and it's the first day of the second month of your three-month essay, put aside your research and start writing. Eventually, when you have more experience writing, you will know how and when to relax this rule. At the beginning, however, try to follow it carefully.

Some people insist on making a detailed plan of their essay before they start to write, but an outline might not help if you are one of those people whose greatest problem is anxiety about starting to fill a blank page. If you are one of these people, don't worry about making a detailed outline before you begin writing. After all, you have thought and read about your problem for a month. In the second third of your time, sit down and start filling that first blank page/screen. Following some of the rules listed below will make the writing much easier and more systematic.

What distinguishes a good three-hour answer from a good three-minute answer is *not* whether the answer is "right"; it's how clearly you present your argument and how thoroughly you explore your reasons for giving the answer you do. Developing strong arguments is the main purpose of this second third of your assignment. In fact, learning to make good arguments is what post-secondary education is all about. A well-developed argument should contain the following:

- **A beginning.** What is the question to be answered? What does it mean? What do I have to show? What is my tentative answer to the question? What is my thesis statement?
- **A middle.** Many *because* clauses arguing on one side of the question; many *because* clauses arguing on the other side.
- **An ending.** What is the final answer to the question? Overall, what did you find? What are the implications of the answer, if any, for theory, for social policy, and for everyday life? What new directions and questions emerge since we now know what you found?

As an estimate, in a 10-page, 2,500-word essay, no more than 2 pages (or 500 words) should be spent on the beginning and no more than 2 pages should be spent on the ending. The remaining space—6 pages or more—should be spent on the middle part, in which you develop your arguments with *because* clauses.

Because clauses are central to good writing and should make up at least two-thirds of anything you write. *Because* clauses explain your reasons for answering the question in one way rather than another. They are the means through which you present your evidence, that is, the data collected to support your argument.

You must review opposing positions and discuss them fairly and thoroughly in your essay; otherwise your work will appear one-sided. After reviewing the opposing *because* clauses, you will have a chance to rebut the opposing views to show why you do not find them persuasive—why they do not lead you to support their position, instead of the one you declared in your thesis statement.

There is no one model you must follow for presenting your argument and challenging opposing views. We often prefer to present the opposing argument first, show why we think it is unsound, and then give the argument that supports our position. Our 10-page essay might look like this:

Beginning (1 to 2 pages)
(1) What is the question, and what is your tentative answer to that question (your thesis statement)?

Middle (6 to 8 pages)

(2) Arguments against your answer (1 to 2 pages)

(3) Arguments against those arguments (1 to 2 pages)

(4) Arguments for your answer (2 to 4 pages)

End (1 to 2 pages)

(5) What is our final answer? (This includes return to your thesis statement, making refinements, and adjustments, and identifying implications.)

You should proportion your time to this use of space. Remember, the central portion of your essay—in which you present your *because*—should receive at least 60 per cent of your writing time and space.

As you are giving your *because* clauses, you may find that there is reading you should have done, and data you should have collected or analyzed. Go ahead and make these adjustments to your database, but remember: this stage of work—the middle third of your time—is mainly a writing stage. If you find you are spending a lot of time doing extra reading or data collection, you have organized your time poorly. Most of that work should have been done in the first third of your time.

The third third

You may wonder why we have allotted a third of our writing time to cleanup. It's because this is an important stage, and many students rush through it—producing surface edits rather than revisions that improve writing quality dramatically (Santangelo and Olinghouse, 2009; Peñuelas, 2008). Some even skip over it altogether. As a result, they turn in essays that are disorganized, messy, full of grammatical and spelling errors, and lacking a careful reference section. Once read carefully for content, these essays tend to have glaring holes in the logic and large gaps in the evidence presented.

All of this can make a marker think that the student wrote the entire essay in a single evening when, in some cases, the student may just have failed to do a proper cleanup. You should never hand in the first draft of an essay. Once you have written the first draft, there are several things you can do to improve your work:

- Submit your essay to the "laugh test." Imagine reading your essay out loud to your parents, friends, or a public audience. If the thought of this makes you cringe in horror or feel embarrassed, it may be because what you have written does not express the thoughts for which you are willing to take responsibility. Think of your essay as a conversation with the grader and rewrite it so no part is embarrassing, no matter who might read it.

- Read your revised essay *out loud* to yourself. Does it flow? Are you stumbling on words and sentences? Do sentences and paragraphs flow from one another or are there large gaps? If the words, sentences, and paragraphs are not clear and flowing to you, they won't be to anyone else.

- Read the revised essay out loud to your family or friends, or ask a friend to read it carefully and criticize it honestly. Nobody likes criticism, but when you are handing in something for a grade, you may prefer to get criticism from a friend first. You may receive a more accurate assessment of your work if someone who is not familiar with the material you are studying can follow your reasoning and find your argument convincing. Just make sure that your reader understands that you want honest criticism and not reassurances intended to boost your confidence.

- Once you have reviewed your work and received criticism, you can begin to revise your essay. Rewrite the passages in question, adding new information or clearer explanations so that an average reader will be able to follow and accept your argument. When you are writing something, you cannot control what ideas your reader will bring to your work. Even though you may be writing your essay for a professor with a background in the area, you should develop your terms and ideas clearly.

Remember, writers are *always* at the mercy of their readers and should prepare for the worst. It's always safer to add clarification to something that might be ambiguous than to assume the reader will understand what you are trying to explain. It is best to try to anticipate what readers might say and what questions they might have. This way, you can deal with their criticisms before they have a chance to make them.

So, submit your work to the laugh test, undergo friendly criticism, and rewrite and rethink as in the final third of your time. Then take care of the details by looking for typos, spelling mistakes, and grammar problems. Never rely solely on a spell-checker though, since it will find only misspelled words and not words that are spelled correctly but used incorrectly (such as *they're* for *their* or *it's* for *its*—see Chapters 12 and 14 for common errors in grammar and word usage).

The essay you are going to write

Suppose the essay you are going to write is worth 20 per cent of your final grade. If so, you should spend about 20 per cent of the time you have allotted for this course's workload writing it. If you spend eight or nine hours a week on *each* of your courses, you will spend about 220 hours on a full-year/two-semester course. Therefore, you should spend about 44 hours on an essay worth 20 per cent of your final grade for that two-semester course. Let's make this 45 hours, to keep the calculations simple. (Cut these numbers in half if you are taking a one-semester course.)

When you write your essay, keep a log of the hours, and force yourself to follow the time budget you have established. If you are following the model we have presented above, your schedule should look like this:

- **First third.** 15 hours. Think, read, make notes, and prepare to answer.
- **Second third.** 15 hours. Write the first draft of your essay. This comprises the following:
  - *The beginning.* State the question and a rough answer that your essay will give: 2.5 hours.
  - *The middle.* Write the *because* clauses of your essay: a total of 10 hours, comprising
    - 2.5 hours to state the case against your argument;
    - 2.5 hours to rebut the case against your argument; and
    - 5.0 hours to support your own case.
  - *The ending.* Refine and change your opening position. State the implications of your conclusion: 2.5 hours.
- **Third third.** 15 hours. Do the laugh test. Clean up and revise your essay. Add new evidence, where needed. Fix spelling and typing errors. Make accurate footnotes (if necessary) and references.

Writing an Exam Answer

When you are answering an exam question, things are different, but not much. Suppose you are writing an essay test in which you have to answer two half-hour questions. Once you have read through the test and have decided which question you are going to answer, try the following:

- **Prepare.** Spend 10 minutes thinking about the question and making notes. Make sure you understand all parts of the question and that you have decided on an answer by the end of the first 10 minutes.
- **Write.** Spend 10 minutes writing an answer: about 1 or 2 minutes to open the discussion; 6 to 8 minutes for *because* clauses; another 1 or 2 minutes for closing statements.
- **Clean up.** Spend 10 minutes reading your answer to check for errors, things you have left out, spelling mistakes, and so on. Make the appropriate corrections.

Leaving two or three blank lines between each written line makes it easier to clean up your answer; the extra space allows you to add details or make corrections neatly if necessary. If you have studied, argued your *becauses* convincingly, and cleaned up neatly, you should impress your reader and get a good grade.

Is This Approach Too Mechanical?

Writing anything according to a formula, like the rule of equal thirds, is stilted and mechanical. This is not how famous authors write bestsellers. Good authors know the "formulas" of writing so well that they can depart from them creatively, and in time, you too will be able to do this.

However, much of what you do as a student is learning "the forms"—the rules of writing within your discipline. These rules both constrain and empower you; like traffic rules, they keep you moving and make wasteful detours and dangerous accidents less likely. Learn the rules in this book, follow them, and when you are ready, relax the rules and set your own course. Meanwhile, let the rules guide your early efforts at making sense.

Summary

Academic writing may seem strange and difficult at first, but with practice, it does get easier. Keep things simple and ask yourself a few questions before you begin: What is the purpose of this piece of writing? Who am I writing for? What does the reader expect? Plan your time and your thoughts. To start, stick to the rules you set out. You will see that with practice, you can relax and begin to enjoy the process.

2   Designing a Project

In this chapter we will examine

- the forms of argument you can make in an academic paper or essay;
- their application to "real-world" research projects, outside school; and
- how independent and dependent variables help to locate the centre of interest.

Introduction

Once you have thought about your target audience, the purpose of your work, and how you plan to budget your time, the next step is to think about design. In this chapter, we introduce another set of rules and choices available when doing research. These rules and choices, which build on those discussed in Chapter 1, apply to particular kinds of arguments you are making. The rules offered in Chapter 1 still apply, but here we show you how to shade or nuance those rules to make your case more effectively.

Good design is fundamental to good research. By *good design*, we mean planning a project in advance to produce results that are persuasive. Good design is just as important to a social scientist as it is to an architect or an engineer. Without it, the project you're building will not stand up for long. A poorly designed project cannot produce a clear, sensible report or exam response, because its results will not answer the question you are trying to address. Knowing the question you are trying to answer, and the types of data and analysis that would best answer it, is the essence of good design.

The principles of good research design are valuable not only in conducting and reporting good research, but also in interpreting and criticizing the work of others. We have written some suggestions that you, the student, can follow as though you were designing your own project. They can also be used to understand, describe, and criticize research someone else has done. In this way, they can improve your ability to make sense in a book report, as well as in an essay or exam answer.

This chapter examines four main types of research design and points out some pitfalls of mixing them or ignoring design outright. Some of the material may seem difficult because it is unfamiliar and uses an unfamiliar vocabulary; therefore, we have provided a glossary of key terms at the end of the book.

Starting Points

Choose a good problem

The first step toward doing good work is choosing a problem that is worth working on. The topic you choose should be of theoretical or practical importance, yet small enough to be studied in a skillful way in the time available. Overreaching yourself—starting more than you can finish or spending too much effort answering a question that is, when looked at objectively, not worth answering—will not produce worthwhile results. Above all, the topic you choose should be one that interests you because you will be investing a lot of time and energy to complete the task. You will find it easier to dedicate yourself to a subject that interests you instead of one that does not, and you will do a better job as a result.

Know the type of design you are using

Different designs have typical patterns, and if you deviate from the prescribed pattern for your chosen design, you may not be able to answer the question that is of central interest. For example, if your goal is to understand the *causes* of alcoholism, describing the *effects* should take a secondary place. (Distinguishing between causes and effects is sometimes difficult; we will say more about this in discussing systemic design.) So, knowing the design to use is closely tied to understanding the question you are trying to answer.

Types of designs

We can classify research designs in many ways. Courses on theory and research methods will introduce you to other useful classifications, but the methods below will help you make sense of your research goals and those of others.

Before we go further, let's take a moment to distinguish between two types of study that we will refer to as descriptive and explanatory studies. An *explanatory study* explains or gives reasons for why something occurs: Why do Aboriginal youth have higher-than-average suicide rates? Why do the mass media oversimplify and dramatize violent news events? Why did people vote Stephen Harper's Conservative government out of office?

Descriptive studies encompass everything else, ranging from an exploratory study in which we merely put "things to consider" on the table, to an inventory of interesting facts about some situation. So, for example, descriptive studies might include the following topics: what it feels like to be excluded from a group because of your race or sexual orientation; or, five things you notice when you first get off the plane in the Republic of Congo; or, what is likely to happen when you tell a "white lie" rather than the truth in a difficult social situation.

As you might imagine, each of these topics has a characteristic thesis statement. As we discussed in the previous chapter, your thesis statement outlines the case you, the author, intend to make in an essay or report. It clearly and briefly sketches the argument you will present in your work and is usually found at the end of the introduction of your paper. In an explanatory study, this will be a statement of the theory that will be put forward as a premise to be proved. In a descriptive study, the thesis statement expresses the author's position on the subject and can be supported with evidence. In every instance, a thesis statement is clear and concise, and needs proof in the form of evidence or documentation.

Typically, in an explanatory study, the thesis statement will make clear the main hypothesis to be tested and that more than one hypothesis will be considered. For example, here are some possible thesis statements for the topics identified above:

- Aboriginal youth today have higher-than-average rates of suicide because of their historical subordination by white society, including repression in residential schools.
- The mass media oversimplify and dramatize violent news events, not because people have become so desensitized to violence that any moderate portrayal will be ignored, but because violence increases viewership.

- People voted Stephen Harper's government out of office for three reasons: usual feelings of voter disappointment with a government in power for two terms or more; the rise of a new and charismatic Liberal leader, Justin Trudeau; and a suddenly diminished (and unexpected) popularity of the NDP leader, Thomas Mulcair.

As you might expect, the thesis statements for descriptive essays are much less pointed and merely suggest the variety of topics the essay will consider. Here are some thesis statements for the descriptive topics mentioned above:

- When you are excluded from a group because of your race or sexual orientation, your first feelings are sadness and outrage, followed by a vague sense that perhaps you deserve to be treated badly.
- When you get off the plane in the Republic of Congo, the first things you notice are an explosion of sounds, colours, and smells, and, more than anything, the boiling, humid air.
- When you tell a "white lie" in a difficult social situation, you first imagine you have gotten away with something, but gradually you realize that keeping up the fiction you produced is harder than to have told the truth.

Devising a thesis statement requires some brainstorming. Once you have a topic or general area of concern, ask yourself: What is interesting about this topic? Why did I think of it? How could I keep someone's attention by talking about this topic for one minute? Five minutes? Twenty minutes? In short, your first step is to think of something that would interest you and interest—or at least, not bore—your friends and your instructor. Then, you have to find a "nugget": a short phrase or idea that will be the key, the core, the payload for your interesting discussion.

This process might sound vague, but it will become clearer through practice. Developing a topic takes hard work, just as writing about it does. Your main goal may be to explain or to describe something, but you will find it most useful to think about research design in a more complex way, with (at least) four alternatives, rather than two. Once you have decided on a thesis statement, it's time to consider the causes, effects, and mitigating factors—or variables—of your problem.

Before continuing, therefore, we must define different types of variables; once we have done this, we will move on to consider how the number of variables will affect the design you choose.

Types of variables

A *variable* is a characteristic or condition that can differ from one person, group, or situation to another (we call the people being described *units of analysis*). For example, we might select 20 political science majors (our units of analysis) at a university and from each collect such information as gender, grade point average, socio-economic background, and participation in campus politics. These characteristics are variables in the sense that they can vary among the people we are studying.

An *independent variable* is a causal or explanatory variable: a condition or characteristic that we presume to be the cause of change in a dependent variable. A *dependent variable* is a characteristic or condition that is altered or affected by changes in another variable: we assume that it is the effect of an independent variable. For example, participation in campus politics is the dependent variable we are hoping to explain through reference to three independent variables: gender, grades, and socio-economic background. Our thesis statement might be, "Men are more likely to participate in campus sports, while women are more likely to take part in all other campus activities, especially if they have a high grade point average and come from a high-income family."

Using the information we collected, we could examine whether variations in gender, grade point average, or socio-economic background influence campus political participation. In other words, we could find out whether one gender engaged more than the other, students with higher grade point averages more than students with lower grades, or students from wealthier backgrounds more than students from poorer backgrounds.

A third type of variable is the *intervening variable*. As its name implies, this variable intervenes between the independent and dependent variable. An independent variable affects the dependent variable by means of the intervening variable. For a variable to be considered intervening, it must be influenced by the independent variable and must influence the dependent variable. Thus, it must be both an effect of the first cause (independent variable) and a cause of the later effect (dependent variable).

A fourth type, the *conditioning variable*, controls whether the independent variable will have a strong or weak, positive or negative effect on the dependent variable. Unlike the intervening variable, the conditioning variable is not an effect of the independent variable, nor is it a cause of the dependent variable. The conditioning variable may suppress, magnify, or distort the relationship between an independent and dependent variable. Said differently, it sets the conditions under which causes will influence effects.

To see how this works, consider some research on the relationship between domestic equality and marital satisfaction. The results of research in this area seem contradictory. Some research says that marital satisfaction (the dependent variable) increases when spouses share responsibility for household duties equally (the independent variable); other research finds it makes little difference. We resolve the confusion when we introduce a third variable—attitudes toward gender equality—as a conditioning variable. Among wives with traditional ideas about marriage and gender relations, an unequal division of domestic labour does not affect marital satisfaction. Among wives with modern ideas about marriage and gender relations, an unequal division of domestic labour decreases marital satisfaction.

In short, independent variables are *causes*, and dependent variables, *effects*. The numbers of presumed causes and effects define the type of research design to be followed. Because any piece of research can examine one or many causes and one or many effects, four types of design are logically possible. We depict them in Figure 2.1. For our present purposes, the four main types of research design are *relational, predictive, explanatory*, and *systemic*. We define these four types by how many dependent and independent variables each is examining. We will consider these types of designs in order, going from the simplest (the relational) to the most complex (the systemic).

Relational Studies

Relational studies examine one cause and one effect, and the conditions under which the relationship between them is strong or weak, positive or negative. In a *strong relationship*, a large change in one variable produces a large change

		Number of "Causes," or Independent Variables	
		One	Two or More
Number of "Effects," or Dependent Variables	One	Relational Study	Explanatory Study
	Two or More	Predictive Study	Systemic Study

Figure 2.1 Types of research design

in the other; in a *weak relationship*, a large change in one variable produces only a small change in the other. In a *positive relationship*, two variables increase or decrease together; in a *negative relationship*, one variable increases as the other decreases.

The purpose of a relational study is to examine the conditioning variables that decrease or increase the effect of the independent variable. For example, take the classic social science concern, suicide rates. Researchers have long known that suicide rates differ according to gender and marital status: one gender seems more suicide-prone than the other; and one marital status, more suicide-producing than others. Taken individually, these independent variables do not produce strong effects; taken together, however, they do. Some researchers have shown the suicide rate is highest for married women and single men, but much lower for single women and married men. Thus, the relationship between suicide rate and gender is mediated by marital status. Marital status is the conditioning variable here. Marriage suppresses the likelihood of suicide in men and increases it in women. To discover why, we must then study the nature of marriage.

This investigation, which identifies and explores the context within which an independent variable has the effect it does, is a standard example of a relational study. Nevertheless, within this group we find various subtypes. One of the most important is the deviant-case analysis.

Deviant-case analysis

Deviant-case analysis is a research design that studies one or more cases that fail to conform to an expected pattern and explores potential conditions affecting this failure. In the deviant case, a cause that usually produces a particular effect produces a different effect (or no effect at all). By failing to support a given hypothesis, the deviant case forces us to revise and enrich the original hypothesis. The purpose, as in the suicide-rate study above, is to discover what additional variable is changing the usual effect of the independent variable.

We start a deviant-case analysis by conceding there are exceptions to the theory we are testing. For example, consider the topic of problem gambling. Many children inherit their parent's addiction, whether that parent is an alcoholic, a drug addict, or a compulsive (or problem) gambler. This may or may not reflect biological inheritance of specific genes that influence addictive behaviour; much remains to be learned about the genetic factors in addiction. However, we do know that many different social processes increase the likelihood that a child of an addict will also become an addict.

These biological and social factors are the processes through which a child is likely to inherit his or her parent's addiction. However, not every child of an addict becomes an addict. In fact, the proportion inheriting an addiction may be only 10 or 20 per cent at most (good figures on this are hard to come by and the available estimates vary widely). Also, many people become alcoholics, drug addicts, or problem gamblers without having had a parent who is addicted in the same way. These cases, then, deviate from expectations.

This is precisely where *deviant-case analysis* comes in. Where the prevailing theory would predict that problem gamblers will have problem-gambling parents and non–problem gamblers will not, we need research to find out the reasons many people deviate from this general rule. For example, doing research might show how and why someone becomes a problem gambler without having had a problem-gambling parent. Research along these lines might explain that a person can have traumatic childhood experiences without having an addicted parent. It might also show that some people begin gambling without having learned how to gamble from a parent. Likewise, we can find many reasons to explain why people grow up without an ability to forge good adult relationships or deal effectively with their stresses. In short, deviant-case analysis enriches our understanding of problem gambling (and other addictions). It also makes our original theory about the "inheritance" of addiction more complex and nuanced than it was originally.

Predictive Studies

All predictive studies examine one cause and two or more effects. However, the two main types of predictive studies differ in whether the independent (causal) variable is identified by a theory, as in *pure research*, or by a policy, as in *applied research*.

Predictive studies with causes defined by theory

Pure, or basic, research is theoretical and includes *speculative studies, experiments*, and *quasi-experiments*.

Speculative studies

Speculative studies imagine the effects of an independent variable on many dependent variables. Because they are imaginative, we sometimes call them *thought experiments*. We carry out speculative studies by applying loose theory or intuition to a combination of imagined and real data. Plato's *Republic*, Thomas More's *Utopia*, or Michael Young's *Rise of the Meritocracy* could all fall into this category. Such studies might try to answer questions like the following: How would Canadian society change if no one ever died? What would have happened in the Second World War if the atom bomb had not been invented? How would people use their time if no one had to work? Would people still have children the old-fashioned way if they could clone "genetically perfect" children? Will Facebook make it unnecessary for people ever to meet in person?

These varied speculations have common features. First, they all examine one independent variable and try to predict, or speculate about, its many likely effects. Second, they can be informed by observable data, but they cannot be tested. Third, they all need the researcher to understand, theoretically, the connections between independent and dependent variables in the real world.

Good speculation must consider what is already known. For example, we can partly predict the likely effects of people living forever, given the already observable effects of a longer life expectancy. The effects of people not having to work at all can be partly predicted by the observable effects of increased leisure on modern lifestyles. No one knows whether the condition speculated about will continue what is already happening, or whether, after a certain critical point, relationships between the independent and dependent variables will change in dramatic, unforeseeable ways.

This kind of thought experiment has led to what are sometimes called "alternative histories." Here, scholars ponder what might have happened if the Nazis had won the Second World War, if the Catholic Church had prevented the rise of Protestantism, or if the United States, under President George W. Bush, had not gone to war in Iraq.

Experiments

Experiments study observable effects of interventions to test predictions made by a carefully reasoned theory. Often researchers try to anticipate the direction and approximate size of the outcomes. They may predict whether a particular intervention will increase the dependent variable by 10 per cent or cut it in half. Doing this research requires laboratory work (to reduce outside influence); controlled data collection (including random or unbiased sampling of the people to be studied, and precise measurement); and quantitative data and analysis. Real experiments differ from thought experiments both in the precision with which researchers perform them and in the possibility of verifying predictions.

Many consider the classical experiment the ideal means of testing a relationship between dependent and independent variables. Though experimentation is not possible in most of the social sciences (because of difficulty reducing outside influences in a controlled setting), familiarity with this approach will give the reader a better sense of what experimental researchers are hoping to achieve.

In experiments, we typically find two groups, or *conditions*. In the *experimental condition*, subjects are manipulated in some way that researchers predict will have a certain effect on their behaviour; and in the *control condition*, subjects are *not* manipulated. To see how much the experimental manipulation changes behaviour, we need a *baseline*—a measure of the behaviour before the experimental manipulation takes place. This is the purpose of the control group, which is identical to the experimental group in all important respects except that it does not receive the experimental manipulation. If the experimental group changes more than the control group, we can credit that change to the experimental manipulation.

Consider the following example. An experimenter wants to test the theory that drunken behaviour is not the result of a drug or alcohol acting on body chemistry. Her thesis statement is the following: "People behave as though drunk mainly because they think they have consumed alcohol and therefore can get away with behaving drunkenly." Her thesis statement is the following: drunken behaviour is a result of people's expectations about the effects of drugs and alcohol and a wish to take advantage of the deviance that intoxication legitimates.

The hypothesis is that people who *think* they have consumed a depressant drug will act more drunkenly than people who think they have consumed a stimulant drug (who, we hypothesize, will behave in a more sober manner). We expect people who know nothing about the expected effects of the substance they consumed (i.e., the control group) to behave more soberly than the first group and less soberly than the second.

Three groups of undergraduates, randomly sampled from a psychology class, agree to take part. We test individual subjects on a simulated automobile driving task for five minutes to show their baseline driving skills. Then each is given a placebo, a chemically inert substance, in this case a sugar pill. We give each participant false information about the expected effects of the capsule he or she has taken. Some are led to believe they will feel energized, others that they will feel drunk. Subjects in the control group are given no hint of what effect they should expect. Twenty minutes later, each participant is directed to drive the simulated automobile for another five minutes.

We measure the change in driving skills for each subject, and then calculate an average change score for each of the groups. The finding? Subjects in the group that believed they received a depressant felt drunk, and those in the group that believed they had taken a stimulant did not. However, the experimenter found no significant difference noted in their driving skills. The depressant group did not drive worse, nor did the stimulant group drive better than the control group after taking the capsules. The experimenter therefore rejects the hypothesis as invalid.

Random sampling (and random assignment into the three groups) is important in this case, and in other types of research, because it increases the likelihood the results are unbiased and can be generalized to the population at large. The use of a control group is important because it provides a baseline against which to compare the experimental group. We assume that people's attitudes or behaviours remain constant over time unless purposely varied by the experimenter.

Quasi-experiments

Like experiments, quasi-experiments study the observable effects of interventions. Typically, we carry out quasi-experiments in situations where true experiments cannot be done because we cannot control the selection of subjects or the conditions in which they will be studied. This is not to say that quasi-experiments are sloppy or merely speculative; they often involve precise data collection and can be useful in analyzing how behaviours change over time. Yet they are not true experiments.

Quasi-experiments may also use control groups for comparison. Consider this example. It seems obvious the student funding at colleges and universities affects how long it will take students to complete their course of studies, or even whether they will complete their studies at all. In universities or programs where more fellowships and scholarships are available, or where tuition is low or free, more students enter their desired programs of study and leave them with degrees in a reasonable period of time.

Noting this, an imaginary provincial government decides to run a quasi-experiment. Their thesis statement might be, "Free tuition significantly increases the college and university attendance of students from poor families who might otherwise feel they could not afford higher education." In this study, tuition will be free in one university, and every full-time student will receive $10,000 toward living expenses. In another, tuition will be free, but no living expenses will be provided. In a third university, the old conditions, whereby students pay tuition and receive no repayment for living expenses, continue to prevail. We let the system run for four years and then measure the proportion of students in each university who have completed their four-year degree program. If our hypothesis about student funding is correct, University *A*, with no tuition costs and full funding, will have graduated a greater proportion of students than University *C*, with regular tuition costs and no funding. By the same reckoning, University *B* will fall in between.

The problem with this study is the researchers would not be able to select the experimental or control groups randomly, nor could they prevent other changes in these communities that might also contribute to an observed difference. For example, if the students at University *A* came from significantly wealthier families than students at University *C*, the resulting differences would be smaller than if students in these two universities came from equally wealthy families. (The differences would be greatest if we applied the experimental condition—free tuition and full funding—to the poorest students in the province. Then, we would measure whether that condition brought their completion rate up to par with the richest student body in the province.)

In short, without systematic matching or controls, a quasi-experiment yields a weaker conclusion than an experiment. That conclusion is nonetheless more secure than one provided by research without the before-and-after measurement, the control group, and the rigorous collection and analysis of observable data.

Predictive studies with causes defined by policy

The group of policy, or applied-research, studies includes social-impact assessments, demonstration projects, and evaluation studies.

Social-impact assessments
Social-impact assessments predict the likely effects of a policy intervention, using a combination of thought experiment, expert opinion, and surveyed

public opinion. They are not testing a hypothesis. Instead, they are trying to predict how people would react to interventions and, given their likely extent and seriousness, what course of action should be pursued: this one, another one (similarly analyzed), or none at all.

Researchers have conducted social-impact assessments in many oil-producing regions of the world (including Alberta, Newfoundland, and Scotland) to predict the probable impact of oil extraction on the surrounding area. Such assessments have paid attention to likely effects on the environment, local economy, community organization, and way of life. Such predictions are influential in deciding where and how quickly to develop the oil industry.

More recently, research has been done to evaluate the effect of casinos on the local communities in which they are situated. Casinos have been found to increase tourism and spending, increasing local revenues. On the other hand, they increase social problems (problem gambling, for example), which force a community to spend more of its revenue on social and health services. As a result, some believe there should be no further opening of casinos until social-impact assessments are conducted on the communities in which casinos will be built.

If you were asked to carry out this research, what data collection methods would you use?

Demonstration projects

Demonstration projects resemble quasi-experiments, but they are motivated by concerns about a policy that has already been adopted, as opposed to one under consideration. They study the effects of interventions in a field setting. Here, too, political and organizational feasibility decides the choice of intervention. Deciding whether to continue and/or increase the scope of intervention is based on observed, not expected, impacts.

For example, suppose that a government ministry decides to keep fewer inmates in prisons. Their thesis statement might be, "Releasing prisoners into halfway houses reduces the risk they will reoffend, compared with releasing them directly into the general population." Obviously, the ministry believes that a halfway house may help released prisoners reintegrate into society better than if they are released directly into the community. So, an experimental halfway house is set up and a sample of inmates is released into it. The behaviour of inmates is observed for 24 months following release and compared with the behaviour of similar inmates released directly into the community. Levels of adjustment to life outside prison—for example, rates of re-arrest and unemployment, or levels of psychological well-being and social integration—are measured for the two groups and compared. If the group released into the halfway house does much better, the ministry may decide to extend this arrangement to larger numbers of released inmates. The demonstration project may also call attention to parts of the original plan that need fixing before widespread adoption.

Ideally, inmates will be randomly selected to enter the halfway house (the experimental condition) or take part in the control group. Practical considerations may make a strict experimental design impossible, but the aim is to learn from trial and error, not (as in the social-impact assessment) from speculation.

Evaluation studies

Evaluation studies examine projects and programs to decide whether they have had the predicted effects, and if not, why not. One type, *process evaluation*, often uses qualitative data (to be discussed in Chapter 5), to find out whether the new arrangement—for example, the halfway house—has worked as expected. A second type, *outcome evaluation*, discovers whether the new arrangement has produced the desired result (in this case, better-than-usual adjustment).

All three types of studies in the applied-research group—social-impact assessment, demonstration project, and evaluation study—are predictive in the sense that they focus on the effects of a real or anticipated intervention. Remember that every predictive study is characterized by only one independent variable—here, the intervention—and many dependent variables, or outcomes. Whether we can reasonably risk the intended intervention in the real world largely guides the choice between a social-impact assessment and a demonstration project. Only a demonstration project can be evaluated because only it produces real, not expected, results.

Explanatory Studies

Explanatory studies seek to explain why something happens or has happened. A dependent variable (or effect) is to be explained by two or more independent variables (or causes). Many student papers and professional research projects are of this type.

We might use an explanatory study to examine divorce. We may study it on a macro-social level—that is, trying to explain what social conditions produce high divorce rates—or on a micro-social level—trying to explain under what kinds of family conditions couples break up. Either way, we find ourselves having to deal with many variables. Often, economic circumstances provide opportunities for divorce (for example, both spouses have an income) or stresses that increase the chance of divorce (for example, both spouses are tired from overwork and resent coming home to more demands). Some cultural variables influence people's openness to the idea of divorce, including religious beliefs about divorce, beliefs about what a "good marriage" or "marital satisfaction" is, and beliefs about the social acceptability of divorce. And don't forget the legal aspects: whether divorces are easy or hard to get; cheap or costly; fast and clean or messy and dragged out. Thus, we cannot explain the rate of divorce without taking all of these variables into account.

Trying to explain a dependent variable with only one independent variable will produce unsatisfactory results, no matter how promising the independent variable you select. This is because most social effects are produced by a combination of causes. Further, working with only one independent variable provides no basis for judging how important a cause is in explaining the effect under study. You should, therefore, plan to include two or more promising independent variables in your explanation.

The social sciences differ in their adherence to this rule. Psychology and economics, for example, are much more likely to examine the effects of one independent variable at a time. The rule (of multiple independent variables) applies much more to the remaining social science disciplines. The rule is also often defied by amateur social scientists—people who write social science books for mass audiences. For example, books claiming to show that violent television programs cause juvenile violence or that liberal values destroy family life often make the mistake of examining only one independent variable in an effort to explain one dependent variable.

Applied explanatory studies

Researchers can also use explanatory design in applied research, which is action- or policy-oriented. Three examples are the needs assessment, the market survey (or political poll), and the Royal Commission. The first two are used by a large variety of organizations, the third, only by various levels of government. Still, they share common features: all three are used to study one effect of interest by examining and weighing many (potential) causes to see which of these causes has the greatest bearing on the effect.

Needs assessments

Needs assessments are explanatory studies that begin with a thorough description of some social problem (e.g., alcoholism) or social group (e.g., alcoholics) and aim to find out how widespread and how harmful the problem is. A needs assessment is often used by governments (as a smaller, less formal alternative to a Royal Commission) or other service-providing, non-profit organizations. We call such a study a needs assessment because it attempts to assess whether a policy or program is needed to reduce the problem.

After describing the problem, the needs assessment typically theorizes about its causes. Finally, it recommends whether the organization that has commissioned the study *should* take action, given its findings about the extent of the problem, its likely causes, and the organizational resources for influencing these causes. Such a study usually precedes other types of research—namely, the demonstration project and the social-impact assessment—that focus on possible interventions.

Market surveys and political polls

Market surveys and political polls are typically concerned with selling something to someone, be it a refrigerator to a homeowner or a political candidate to a voter. In each instance, the researcher is concerned with finding out the support for the product, the characteristics of respondents who are the strongest supporters or worst detractors, and the reasons for support and non-support.

Often, the goal of such research is to change marketing strategy to produce more effective sales. This is done in any of three ways: first, the company can advertise the product more directly to those the study found to be its greatest supporters; second, it can change the product, in fact or in appearance, to make it more appealing to its detractors; and third, it can change the sales pitch to make it capitalize more effectively on the secret fears and wishes of consumers—their *real* reasons for support and non-support.

Royal Commissions

Governments in Canada, the United Kingdom, and other Commonwealth countries commonly appoint Royal Commissions to study a social problem and find out what people think is causing it. (Governments in other countries conduct similar inquiries under other names.) As explained by Library and Archives Canada (2014),

> Royal commissions, or commissions of inquiry, are appointed by Cabinet under the terms of the Inquiries Act in order to carry out full and impartial investigations of specific *national* problems. The terms of reference for the commission and the powers and the names of the commissioners are officially stated by an Order-in-Council. When the investigation is complete, the findings of the commission are reported to Cabinet and the Prime Minister for appropriate action.

The report of a Royal Commission differs from the smaller needs assessment in that it examines broad issues of major concern to the public. It also pays attention to both expert opinion and public sentiment about the problem and its possible solution(s). In a sense, a Royal Commission is a politicized needs assessment, aimed as much at improving the government's image as at solving the problem.

Royal Commissions held in Canada, especially those over the past 50 years, have covered various important topics, and sometimes, they have resulted in important policy changes. They have produced a great deal of descriptive research, theorized about the cause of present problems or issues, and suggested legislation to deal with them. Reviewing an online list of Royal Commissions in Canada can be a great starting point for research ideas.

Systemic Studies

Systemic studies try to explain two or more effects by two or more causes. Such studies are common in all the social sciences. The subject under study typically comprises many people and many parts: it may be a group, an organization, a community, or a society. The ultimate goal of this research is to understand how a system of interlinked parts works: how the parts affect one another, often in indirect, reciprocal, and self-modifying ways.

Explaining the causes of the Second World War would need a systemic study. Not only did the war have many causes, but the war itself also had many effects (economic, diplomatic, military, and social, among others). All of these influenced one another and jointly kept the war alive. Even more obviously, it would be impossible to explain the violence that has broken out in the last 30 years—in the former Yugoslavia, Rwanda, Congo, Afghanistan, Iraq, Angola, Sudan, and Syria, to name only a few—without a systemic design. Only such a design could consider historical patterns of ethnic, religious, regional, economic, and political conflict, as well as external influences (e.g., the role of the United States, the United Nations, China, the European Union, and various multinational corporations).

Therefore, any thesis statement that opens a report on a systemic study would have to make clear that many themes will be introduced and that they are all related to one another in complex ways. A systemic design is necessary when you have embarked on an explanatory design and have found too many interlinked causes and effects for a neat solution. Try shifting to a systemic design, and then focus your attention on how these linkages uphold one another. (Some might even say that a systemic design is always right if you are explaining how or why something happens, because you are always interested in knowing the reciprocal links among all variables.)

A good example of where systemic design may be useful is in the study of family conflict and family secrecy. In this case we need to understand families as systems of roles, in which each person and each role keeps the others in check. Here, our thesis statement might be something like, "Every family is a complicated world of truths, lies, and secrets, where people say one thing but do another. In this way, family relations can be as complicated as diplomacy between neighbouring countries." Every family has problems, and every family has special ways of recognizing, containing, or dealing with its problems. Families often work hard to keep problems hidden from outsiders to preserve the appearance of calm conformity to the outside world. If they succeed, no one but the family will know about their hidden secrets, conflicts, and strains. Still, that does not mean they do not affect the family.

Family secrets are so common and persistent that we must allow for the possibility that they contribute to the way the family works and to the survival and well-being of family members. For example, secrets help the family develop without feeling its identity is shamed or threatened. They preserve intimacy that is related to love, closeness, and emotional commitment. Secrets shared among family members also strengthen internal cohesion and solidarity. Finally, keeping secrets protects the family from outsiders.

However, keeping secrets may have negative effects on the family and its members. Secrets also foster a tolerance for deception and lying in close relationships. People who keep secrets may develop an inability either to take responsibility for their own actions or to force others to take responsibility for theirs. Most importantly, power imbalances increase when one person knows more than, or something harmful about, another. This may result in threats or blackmail. At the least, anxiety about the unwanted disclosure of the secret is likely to harm family relations. As a result, we can infer that families are better off solving their problems than hiding them.

This example shows that a study that starts as a simple analysis of a small family problem may end up exploring the links among many variables that support and intensify one another's effects. We may finish by learning a lot about the relationships between unemployment, drinking, spousal abuse, and child truancy, for example. Examining an issue such as why abused spouses and children do not reveal their secrets to teachers, employers, friends, or the police is too complicated a matter for an explanatory study and much better suited to a systemic design.

Summary

An explanatory study focuses our attention on one dependent variable. It measures and compares the influence of many causes on one effect. A predictive study, on the other hand, focuses attention on one independent variable and examines or speculates on its many effects. The relational study is unlike either of these: it focuses attention on conditioning variables that change the effect of one independent variable on a dependent variable. Finally, the systemic study focuses attention on the interdependence of all causes and effects, and is, therefore, concerned with analyzing an entire system of independent, dependent, intervening, and conditioning variables.

It should now be clear why, as a beginning researcher, you are wise to avoid mixing research designs. After all, different designs answer different questions, focusing attention on different variables or relations between variables and drawing attention away from the rest. (There is one exception to this general rule: sometimes mixing relational and explanatory designs is permissible, and we'll address this strategy in Chapter 3.)

Given the limited time you have to do everything well, you should first attend to the central question in your paper. That will be the dependent variable in an explanatory study, the independent variable in a predictive study, and the most important conditioning variable(s) in a relational study. And, in a systemic study, you will be interested in the relations among all variables. Remember that erring on the side of saying too much about your central concern is always best, even if it means saying too little about other matters.

Mixing designs can be effective if the researcher is aware of doing so. However, the average student researcher has limited time and money, and limited expertise in research design. Therefore, we call for modest goals. Do what you can do well. Choose one task—one design—and take it to completion. You will not need to apologize for what you have not done if what you *have* done is excellent.

3   Theorizing about a Project

In this chapter we will examine

- basic ideas in theory-making, including the ideas of explanation, paradigm, theory, and prediction;
- the importance of always keeping sight of your main and secondary questions; and
- the eight "deadly" theoretical pitfalls to avoid.

Introduction

As we discussed in Chapter 1, there are several possible purposes for any piece of writing. In some cases, you will be expected (or will choose) to explain why something is the way it is. A well-substantiated explanation of a specific set of social or natural phenomena—or a set of logically related statements about those phenomena—is called a *theory*. You may be interested in applying a specific theory to new material, or you may be interested in testing a theory you have developed. Both require you to understand and engage with some basic ideas in theory-making.

Basic Ideas in Theory-Making: Explanations

Most types of writing in the social sciences contain explanations. An explanation is a clear and thorough account of the problem or situation being studied. The process of explaining has at least two parts: developing a theory to help the researcher think about relationships between variables, and collecting data to test the correctness (validity) of that explanation. It is important to note that you can start with a theory and then collect data to test its validity, or you can begin with observations or data and then build a theory (for more on this, see "The Research Cycle" on page 39).

There are at least six kinds of explanations in social science:

- a *causal explanation* identifies the immediate cause of a particular event (for example, how European diseases helped conquer the Indigenous peoples of North America);
- a *probabilistic explanation* identifies the causal effect on a series of events (for example, how exposure to magazines and television containing idealistic body imagery affects self-esteem among female adolescents);
- a *meaningful and purposive explanation* identifies the causal effect of actors' motives, aims, and goals (for example, how beliefs about strangers in small towns contribute to how they are treated by locals);
- a *functional explanation* identifies the systemic effect (or outcome) of one event as the cause of another (for example, why the drive for social cohesion is likely to promote capital punishment, war, or scapegoating);
- an *evolutionary explanation* identifies the survival instinct as the cause of the event (for example, why younger women may marry older men); and
- a *deductive explanation* provides an account that can be deduced from established general laws. Here, the explanation is an account of a *particular* event or relationship that is deducible from *general* principles of social life acting in *particular* circumstances.

Consider this example of a deductive explanation of why women do more housework than men in most heterosexual North American households:

General principle:
People try to improve their well-being.

Particular circumstance:
In our society, most men continue to earn more than women.

Deductions:

- Men will lose more potential pay than women by doing unpaid housework.
- Housework by men will reduce family income.
- Income loss will reduce family well-being.
- Therefore, women should do more housework than men.

This is an observation (which may not be correct) about domestic inequality explained by general principles. This explanation also points to theoretically interesting anomalies (or deviant cases). For example, why, in some heterosexual families,

- male partners do *less* housework although their female partners earn more than they do; or
- male partners do *more* housework although their female partners earn less than they do.

A study of deviant cases produces more variables for our explanation. To explain the first deviant case, where men do less housework than expected, we need to understand *patriarchy*: a cultural belief in the legitimacy of gender inequality and male dominance underlying all circumstances, however irrational. To explain the second deviant case, where men do more housework than expected, we need to understand *companionate* or *egalitarian unions*: a cultural belief in equality and task-sharing between men and women. Now, the explanation runs as follows:

General principle:
People act to improve their well-being.

Particular circumstance:
In our society,

- most men earn more than most women;
- some couples value a companionate or egalitarian union; and
- some couples value traditional gender roles.

Deductions:
Domestic work will reflect the ways couples choose to improve their well-being:

- In couples who seek to improve their financial well-being, men will do less housework than women only if they earn more than their female partners do.
- In couples who seek to improve their marital satisfaction, men will do the same amount of housework as their female partners, regardless of what each earns.

- In couples who seek to adhere to traditional gender roles, men will do less housework than their female partners, regardless of what each earns.

We continue this way to study anomalies and deviant cases until we understand all the principles that yield the various types of household work arrangements we have observed. Every explanation is thus a series of *because* clauses repeatedly answering the question *why?* Thus,

- *Why* do women do more housework than men do?
  Because families forgo more income if men do the housework.
- *Why* do families forgo more income if men do the housework?
  Because our society does not assign great value to the traditional work that many women do—household work and care work. And,
  Because we pay women in the labour force less than we pay men for work of equal value.
- *Why* does our society value women's work—whether paid or unpaid— less than men's work?
  Because in a society dominated by men, the work of women was traditionally done for free. The culture taught that women were more generous and nurturing than men were.
- *Why* were women believed to be more generous and nurturing than men were?
  Because that cultural belief supported male dominance.

Thus, every explanation can lead to *infinite regress*. Each effect has many causes; each cause has many effects. Therefore, every explanation must be a continuously edited story—a model, rather than a final snapshot, because all explanations involve simplification. However, explanations also require notions of causation. Here are the general qualities of a good explanation, no matter what is being explained:

- **logical consistency.** In a good explanation, the *because* clauses make sense.
- **parsimony.** A good explanation makes the fewest untestable assumptions.
- **agreement with the evidence.** In a good explanation, the logical deductions can be tested with empirical evidence, and the evidence confirms them.
- **predictive power.** A good explanation predicts what we can expect to find when we study other cases.

- **falsifiability.** A good explanation could be proved wrong by contrary evidence, if researchers were to find such evidence.
- **persuasiveness.** A good explanation is more believable than any other explanation.

What makes any account or explanation persuasive varies historically and culturally. Some explanations are hard for a society to accept; others are easy. For example, at certain points in western European (and North American) history, even well-informed people were ready to accept witchcraft as an explanation for many natural events; today, few are willing to do so. Yet even within Western science, some explanations are easier than others to accept. Most scientists accept evolutionism and the big bang theory; few accept extrasensory perception, UFOs, and telekinesis. Explanations of natural events that rely on these factors are unlikely to persuade. What follows is an examination of the ways to ensure that your explanation will make sense. Many points made below will apply just as readily to the predictive, systemic, and relational designs discussed in the last chapter. Bear in mind also that these points will be just as useful in evaluating and criticizing the explanations of others as in building your own.

Paradigms

In every social science there are different *paradigms*—ways of thinking about the same question. They are founded on various basic assumptions about how the world works, and they lead to different conclusions about important questions to ask and appropriate data to collect. In other words, support for one paradigm often points a researcher toward some plausible explanations and away from others. Recall the brief section in Chapter 1 on the social construction of knowledge. We noted that knowledge is based on culturally and historically specific assumptions about how the world works (Pascale, 2010), and that knowledge is complex and variable depending on a large number of factors. Let's see how this plays out when we think about different paradigms.

For example, two competing paradigms in sociology and anthropology are the *structural-functionalist* paradigm and the *conflict* paradigm. A functionalist interprets criminal behaviour as evidence of inadequate upbringing, psychopathology, or membership in a deviant subgroup. A conflict theorist, by contrast, interprets such behaviour as evidence of alienation, economic inequality, or protest against the ruling interests of society.

Each way of interpreting criminality leads a researcher to ask different questions, collect different kinds of data, and reach different conclusions. You can collect data that address *both* paradigms simultaneously—in fact, some philosophers believe that the advancement of scientific knowledge continues by this adversarial process—but social scientists often work within one paradigm at a time.

Know how your question relates to your paradigm

If your explanation relies more on one paradigm than another, be sure of the assumptions you are making and the larger questions that your approach suggests. Collect data that will clearly connect your research to other research within the same paradigm.

For example, suppose you are arguing that there is no drug problem in Canadian society today—that concerns of a nationwide drug problem are the product of a group that is promoting the idea because it is in their interest to do so. Such an argument would fall into the category of a conflict theory of law and deviant behaviour. To be consistent, you should also hold the following views, which are central to conflict theory:

- that people hold unequal wealth and power in Canadian society;
- that those in power act to preserve or increase their wealth and power; and
- that widespread social beliefs, especially those that are spread by the mass media, are aimed at preserving the position of the wealthy and powerful.

A criticism of this position is that though the wealthy and powerful act in their own interests, as do other people, not every act or belief contributes to their well-being. The belief in a widespread drug problem, for example, may not seem to work in the interest and well-being of the powerful; it is up to the researcher to show that it does.

Once you are aware of the general and particular criticisms of your position, be sure to address them. Even if you cannot collect all the information needed to challenge them, at least show that you are aware of the criticisms and suggest further research that would adequately deal with them.

Remember you are looking for explanations and answers

As important as it is to situate your work within a paradigm, you should not get carried away. Your real purpose is to answer a question, not to prove that one paradigm is better or worse than another. A paradigm will prove its usefulness by guiding you in certain directions and helping you answer the question at hand.

You may find that more than one paradigm contributes to your understanding of a particular problem. Many perspectives may contribute to a good answer. If so, admit that fact, even if it means using a paradigm you had not previously accepted. Theories are to be used by researchers, not researchers by theories. Denying the weaknesses in your own paradigm and the strengths in another is bad research practice. Findings and interpretations produced in this way will not hold up for long and will do little to advance social science.

Theories

The research cycle

The process of creating and testing a theory often follows a research cycle, such as the one depicted in Figure 3.1. In the research cycle, you can begin with a *theory* (though "*inductive research*" begins with observations and moves toward constructing theories): a set of logically related statements about some phenomenon of interest. From this theory, you logically *deduce* hypotheses. To deduce something is to infer it on purely logical grounds from a set of earlier conclusions or assumptions. For example, if February in Winnipeg is always cold and snowy, and people are eager to avoid getting sick, it follows by deduction that a high proportion of Winnipeggers will likely be wearing coats and boots next 15 February. (This also yields a piece of practical advice: if you're travelling to Winnipeg for a romantic Valentine's Day getaway, bring warm clothing.)

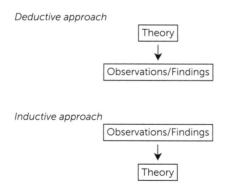

Figure 3.1 Deductive and inductive approaches to the relationship between theory and research

Source: Bryman, Bell, and Teevan (2012). Reprinted with permission of Oxford University Press.

However, this deduction about Winnipeg and Winnipeggers in February is merely a hypothesis. *Hypotheses*, sometimes called *propositions*, are statements about presumed relationships between two or more variables. They give rise to specific predictions that no one knows to be true, but that can be proved true or false, valid or invalid, by the collection and analysis of data. Next 15 February, you may find most Winnipeggers in shorts. This is very unlikely, but possible: we need evidence to test our original hypothesis.

To take a more plausible example, consider whether children who watch violent cartoons end up acting in more violent or aggressive ways, and whether boys in particular are more likely to prefer to watch violent cartoons and so grow up to behave more aggressively than girls. You start with the premise—suggested by your theory—that people are shaped and motivated by what they see—social learning theory—rather than being predisposed to behave in particular ways (Bandura, 1977; 1973).

Next is the process of *operationalizing* the concepts in your hypothesis so you can test it for accuracy. An operational definition is a practical or working definition of a concept (like aggression, social class, or education), attached to specific measures of that concept. Operationalization involves identifying and/or creating empirical measures of the key concepts (we will discuss measurement at length in the next two chapters). The measurement procedures produce *observations* that either support the hypothesis or prove it wrong. Thus, we should be able to agree on the meaning of a term—for example, *social class*—define that meaning, specify ways to measure it (by wealth, income, occupational status, education, and so on), and show that the measurements behave similarly in different contexts. Even a seemingly obvious notion like "education"—used often in social science research, and among the most effective predictors across a wide variety of models—hides many conceptual and measurement issues that need careful consideration.

Assume, however, that we have managed to operationalize the key variables to carry out observations. From these specific observations come *generalizations*: conclusions about the general significance of the observations for the hypothesis that we stated.

The last stage of the cycle is *induction*, the process of fitting the generalized results (that are derived from observations) together with the theory as originally stated. If these two fail to fit together, we need a reformulation of the theory. Then the cycle begins again, with another study and new hypotheses.

Let us follow up on a previous example. It is widely assumed that some children like violence in cartoons (and thus, viewing violent cartoons will lead to aggressive behaviour), but Weaver et al. (2011) note that this assumption has not been supported in existing studies. Weaver et al. (2011) conducted a study that contributed to media violence research by testing whether violence and action (independently manipulated) influenced children's liking of cartoons. They proposed a model to test potential effects of violence and action on children's enjoyment of cartoons. They used animation software to create four versions of a cartoon that varied in terms of violence (present, absent) and action (high, low). Their main research question asked the following: Will non-violent versions of the cartoon be liked more than violent versions of the cartoon?

Following a review of the existing literature, they came up with eight hypotheses, three of which were:

- H1: The high-action version of a televised cartoon will be liked more than the low-action version.
- H7: Males will like the violent version of the cartoon more than the non-violent version, whereas females will like the non-violent version of the cartoon more.
- H8: Males will like the high-action version of the cartoon more than the low-action version, whereas females will not differ in their liking of the low- and high-action versions.

If we focus on the second hypothesis, the empirical (i.e., observed or measured) data may reveal any of the following:

- (a) that male children are more likely than female children to prefer watching violent cartoons;
- (b) that there is no difference between the preferences of male children and female children; or
- (c) that female children are more likely than male children to prefer watching violent cartoons.

If result (a) is achieved, the hypothesis is considered to have been supported or confirmed, so the theory that produced the hypothesis is also considered confirmed (for now). If result (b) or (c) is achieved, the hypothesis is not considered confirmed, and neither is the theory that gave rise to it. Result

(b) would probably lead the researcher to look for reasons and factors that may be at play in this particular circumstance. Result (c) might lead him or her to rethink the theory.

It is important to stress that we can never prove a theory finally and decisively correct. We speak of a theory being proved true or false, or more valid or true than another theory about the same phenomenon, only for the time being. A new theory or a better test may prove it invalid tomorrow.

Getting to know your own theory

Using flow charts

Reaching a clear understanding of what you are arguing is more difficult than you might think, but following some easy steps will help. Start by listing all your variables. Then lay them out in a diagram connecting the variables influencing one another using labelled arrows, with a plus sign (+) showing an expected or assumed positive relationship between two variables and a minus sign (–) showing a negative one. (Remember that in a positive relationship, the connected variables increase and/or decrease together, while in a negative relationship, one variable increases as the other decreases.) Some pairs of variables may not be connected at all.

Diagramming an explanation forces you to deal consciously with what you think is going on: What are the key variables? What are the important relationships and non-relationships? What parts of the overall theory can be analyzed separately from the others? And therefore, how must you analyze the data to test your theory?

A typical explanatory diagram (or *flow chart*) displays the dependent variable on the right-hand side and the independent variables on the left. Thus, the order of supposed causation flows from left to right, through intervening variables that come into effect after (or occasionally at the same time as) the independent variables. We depict one version of such a flow chart, called a path model, in Figure 3.2.

This flow chart, from Weaver et al.'s (2011) study of whether the extended enjoyment of media violence influenced children's liking of cartoons, uses a path model to test potential direct and indirect effects of violence and action on liking of cartoons. The model depicts the hypothesized or assumed relationships between the independent variables of interest—violence, age, action (and gender, not shown in this figure)—and the dependent variable, liking (of the cartoon). According to the model, the hypotheses are depicted by the

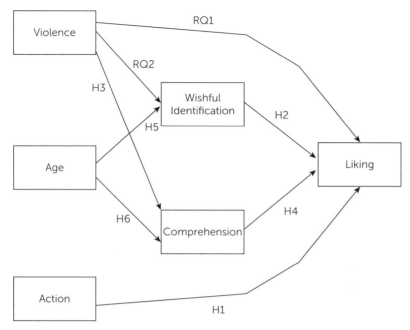

Figure 3.2 Hypothesized path model with wishful identification and comprehension as mediators

Source: Weaver et al. (2011). Republished with permission of University of Illinois, from "Liking Violence and Action: An Examination of Gender Differences in Children's Processing of Animated Content," *Media Psychology*, Volume 14 (1), 2011; permission conveyed through Copyright Clearance Center, Inc.

letter *H* and a number—for example, H1 was drawn to depict "action" affecting "liking" (Weaver et al., 2011: 51).

Interestingly, after controlling for other variables—wishful identification and comprehension—it was found that violence had no direct effect on the liking of the cartoon, but did indirectly decrease liking for males by decreasing boys' wishful identification with the anthropomorphized characters. Action increased liking for males but not for females (Weaver et al., 2011).

The same left-to-right convention cannot be used in depicting a systemic model, in which many independent and dependent variables affect one another simultaneously and even feed back on one another repeatedly. Figure 3.3, which aims to explain the influence of community attachment on voluntary citizen participation in rural community improvement projects, is an example of a systemic model (Ryan, Agnitsch, Zhao, and Mullick, 2005). Ryan and his co-authors were interested in understanding what distinguishes citizens who volunteer on behalf of the public good from those who fail to volunteer at all. Try tracing the argument that the model charts.

A. Systemic Model of Community Attachment

B. Elaboration and Extension of the Systemic Model

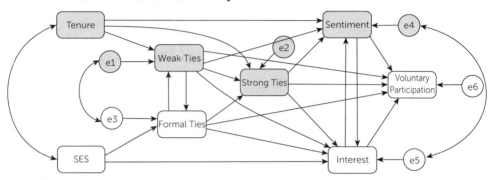

Figure 3.3 Theoretical model of place-based voluntary participation

Source: Ryan et al. (2005). Republished with permission of John Wiley & Sons, from "Making Sense of Voluntary Participation: A Theoretical Synthesis," by Ryan Vernon, Kerry Agnitsch, Zhao Lijun, and Rehan Mullick, in *Rural Sociology*, Volume 70 (3); permission conveyed through Copyright Clearance Center, Inc.

The researchers found that a person's local social ties are important for explaining his or her level of attachment. They also found that the form and level of local ties of individuals are accounted for by their socio-economic status and community tenure, such that higher socio-economic status leads to a greater number of local formal ties, while longer tenure results in more both weak and strong informal ties (Ryan et al., 2005).

Consider, finally, an even more complex systemic chart (Figure 3.4) showing factors that go into explaining the survival of *polygyny*—the rare arrangement in which one man is married to multiple women at the same time. As the chart shows, any explanation of this practice must take into account such economic factors as the scarcity of labour; traditional cultural practices that affect social status, mating, and sexuality; and demographic factors such as high mortality (owing to poor health) and high fertility (owing to strong pro-natalist attitudes).

Nothing shows more clearly than this chart why it would be almost impossible to legislate an end to polygyny without also changing the social, economic, cultural, and demographic factors that support the practice. Specifically, the author (Chojnacka, 2000: 194) predicts and observes a decrease in polygyny as a result of:

(a) increasing rates of population growth, which lead to an increased supply of labour;

(b) increasing role of capital (and machinery) in agriculture—leading to higher labour productivity; and

(c) increasing productivity of labour, connected to out-migration of redundant labour from agriculture to urban areas.

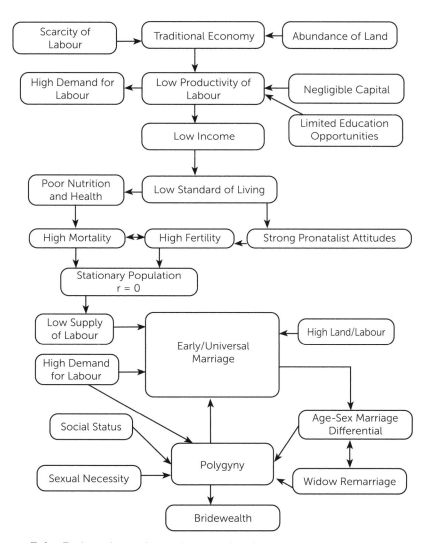

Figure 3.4 Early universal marriage and polygyny among women in a traditional economy and a stationary population

Source: Chojnacka (2000). Republished with permission of John Wiley & Sons, from "Early Marriage and Polygamy: Feature Characteristics of Nuptuality in Africa," *Genus*, Volume 56 (3–4), 2000; permission conveyed through Copyright Clearance Center, Inc.

Drawing upon what you know about (sub)cultural diversity in Canada, though it is still illegal, can you think of any factors that may contribute to an *increase* in polygyny in this country?

Get a friend to help you theorize

Identifying and diagramming your own theory is not easy. You sometimes need a disinterested person to remind you why you are doing this project and what you expect to learn from it.

Find someone who is willing to listen. Then try to explain what you are arguing and why. If you can make the main pieces of your argument fit together for this person, you probably know what you're doing. If you have trouble making sense to your listener—or to yourself—make changes and try again, with the same or another person. If you can't make sense to others, this suggests that your argument is not sound or that you are not comfortable with your explanation.

Know your main question and stick to it

So far, we have been looking at the big picture: placing your explanation in a larger body of research and ensuring that you have taken account of the relevant variables. Nevertheless, we should not lose sight of a key point: making sense means always knowing your main question, the main point you are trying to make. It's easy to get lost in the details, so be careful not to lose sight of the forest—your main question or thesis statement—for the trees.

Sometimes you lose sight of your main goal when chancing into a treasure trove of data that are only indirectly related to your original research question. You may forget to use the data to answer your original question and end up reporting on interesting but unrelated nuggets instead. This information may be interesting, and you may have redirected attention to other possible explanations about which you have no theory, but often you cannot easily move back from an unstructured exploration into a coherent explanation. Exploration is not bad in itself, but you should be wary if you have strayed towards unrelated exploration or description.

Know how your main question relates to secondary questions

You can never go too far in thinking about your main question and its secondary questions. You should address these questions with data, or at least admit that these related questions deserve further research. Examples might include explanations of why particular intervening or contextual factors are important, or discussions of other paradigm-related issues.

Imagine, for example, that research on television sitcoms found that the central characters were often middle-class people living a prosperous, urban lifestyle, and that this portrayal implied to viewers that such a lifestyle was desirable, easily obtainable, and a reward for social conformity. You might then analyze the component parts of this portrayal. What does it mean that these characters hold certain kinds of jobs, wear certain kinds of clothes, or have certain kinds of furniture? What meanings do viewers attach to specific roles or material objects, and where do these meanings come from? Why, for example, are doctors portrayed as heroic, unselfish, and helpful? What is the social meaning of "doctor" in our culture, how did it arise, and how is it maintained despite our first-hand experience that doctors, like everyone else, are just as likely to be unheroic, selfish, and unhelpful? These secondary questions will help you draw some conclusions about the initial research.

Explore at different levels of analysis

The social sciences involve research at several levels of analysis, as the examples in this book suggest. Social scientists study societies, organizations, communities, and individuals—social formations characterized by different levels of complexity. We should make two points about levels of analysis.

Avoid reductionism

Although some theorists have argued to the contrary, events at one level of analysis (at the organization level, for example) cannot be easily broken down, or reduced, to a larger number of smaller events at a lower level of analysis. Such a strategy, called *reductionism*, is not acceptable.

Take, for example, an examination of the reasons people form social movements: Why do people join together to protest discrimination or inequality? This question cannot be answered simply by moving to the individual level of analysis and studying the psychology—the attitudes and motives—of participating protesters. A sense of outrage at the individual level may be *necessary* for a social movement to form, but it is not *sufficient*. For protest to occur, outraged people must mobilize: there must be leadership, communication, a shared consciousness, and material resources—money, food, an office, and increasingly, social media (see DeVriese, 2013). Therefore, the rise of a protest movement does not prove that people have only just become outraged: they may have just mobilized. Also, the absence of protest does not prove people are not outraged, but possibly that they are not organized.

This example suggests that a social phenomenon is best examined at various levels of analysis simultaneously. We may discover that forces working at different levels of analysis are pulling in opposite directions. For example, at the individual level people may feel outraged at their own and other people's unemployment. Yet unemployed people tend to be politically inactive: they often do not publicly protest their condition to demand a broader remedy. Part of this problem is organizational: a shortage of leaders, resources, and communication. However, part of it is cultural: our value system holds people responsible for their own fate. In Canada we are brought up to believe that what happens to people, particularly around employment, is their own fault: they have earned their successes and failures and must live with them. Thus, on the psychological level, all the conditions may be met for social action against unemployment, but on the cultural level, the opposite conditions prevail. Here we see that with problems at the social-organizational level, cultural (or ideological) factors work against the behavioural expression of forces working at the psychological, or individual, level.

Test theories at different levels of analysis

To say that we should test theories at diverse levels of analysis may seem to contradict what we have just said about opposing forces at different levels. Indeed, analyses at different levels will often yield different results. But this is not always the case.

Consider the issue of punitiveness—how severely we punish wrongdoers. Societies vary in their degree of punitiveness. Canada is, and has been, much less punitive than many societies, in that people in this country are not banished, tortured, or executed for minor (or even major) offences, as is the case in some other societies. Yet Canada does imprison a higher proportion of convicted criminals than many other modern nations. What accounts for Canada's punitiveness compared with that of other countries?

We might think that this punitiveness is the result of internal instability: societies (as well as groups, communities, and individuals) that feel insecure are more likely to punish severely to increase their internal cohesion by reaffirming moral boundaries.

This hypothesis can and should perhaps be tested at multiple levels of analysis. If the hypothesis is valid, we should find that individuals who are most socially or economically marginal or insecure will express the most punitive sentiments toward wrongdoers. At the societal level, rates of punitiveness (i.e., prison terms for convicted criminals) should increase in times of war, economic depression, or internal unrest, in response to perceived threats to the society. At the cultural level, racism, nationalism, xenophobia, and other declarations of preference for people like oneself should, along with punitiveness, increase when the culture is being threatened by massive immigration or foreign domination.

If we find that these changes occur as predicted, there is reason to believe that we have found the basis for a general theory of punitiveness. Our work is far from done, however. Without examining the process by which punitiveness increases at each level under conditions of internal instability, we run the risk of two grave methodological errors, both connected with improper movement between levels of analysis: the ecological fallacy and the fallacy of misplaced concreteness (for a detailed discussion of these, see "Pitfalls to Avoid," p. 57). If we can avoid these fallacies, our multi-level theory will be more compelling than a theory that holds at only one level of analysis.

Predictions
Know what new ideas your theory suggests

The purpose of a theory is to explain, or clarify, how variables are related to one another. One way to test the accuracy of a theory is to make predictions based on the theory and to test them with data.

Prediction is not always the perfect test of an explanation, yet it is desirable. People often accuse social scientists of merely restating the obvious in difficult jargon. To get past this criticism, researchers should aim to show that their theories can produce ideas, understanding, or findings that are not possible using common sense alone.

Consider the question of how families deal with the stresses produced by chronic illness. Common sense tells us that different families will deal with their difficulties in different ways—a logical prediction, but vague. Systematic observation and theory show us *which* families cope better and *which* coping strategies work better than others. They show that adjustment goes on through a series of stages, each with its own problems and resolutions, before people can attempt the next stage. If we are trying to understand why a particular family is coping in the way it is and how we can help it to cope better, we are far better off with a theory than with common sense alone. With theory we can hope to predict the future course of a family's problems and to predict which interventions will work best at given times for a given family.

State your expectations in advance

Creating a flow chart is perhaps the best way of stating your expectations, but it is not the only one. Even without a flow chart, you should be clear about what you expect the data to reveal and why. This will help to clarify your theoretical assumptions, suggest appropriate research methodology needed to test your theory, and point to missing variables that might help explain or interpret your results.

Anticipating specific findings means you win whichever way the data turn out. If the expected result occurs, you can reasonably claim that this supports your theory, because that theory was able to make the correct prediction. If unexpected results show up, the analysis becomes even more interesting. If you have developed your theory carefully, linking your explanation to questions and findings in the literature, you are right to have expected what you did. The fact that your result is unexpected points to a need for rethinking, or for considering other variables you and others have overlooked. We ignore many useful findings in social science because they fail to support our theories. However, finding a negative relationship where you had expected a positive one or a weak relationship where you had expected a strong one might lead you to a conclusion that is even more interesting than your prediction.

Moving into a relational design

When unexpected results occur, your analysis should move out of an explanatory design into a relational one. This means that the search is on for intervening variables that make sense of the unexpected relationship between the independent and dependent variables. A deviant-case analysis may be in order, for example (see Chapter 2).

Suppose you had predicted that in a particular election, immigrants would vote for Party *A* and not for Party *B*, based on the belief that different parties protect different interests. The results, however, show something different:

many recent immigrants voted for Party *B*. Your theory of immigrant voting may indeed be wrong, but other key variables may also play a part in making the theory correct. For example, some immigrant voters may have *believed* that Party *B* would protect their collective interests. If so, you should modify, not discard, your original theory of immigrant voting. We find that people will vote for their interests as they *see* them and as they *see* the platform of the party they're voting for. In this way you come to focus on a new, interesting problem of political misinformation or manipulation, and you can collect new data on people's *perceptions* that you had not previously considered.

In Canada, we find a complicated relationship between "class voting," "ethnic voting," and "regional voting." Oddly, higher education and income tend to predict votes for the New Democratic Party (NDP), while lower income predicts votes for the Conservative Party. This is mediated by whether the voter is a union member (which increases the likelihood of voting NDP at any education or income level). Medium levels of income predict votes for the other parties: for the Liberals if the voter lives in Ontario or is an immigrant or a member of an ethnic minority; for the Bloc Québécois if the voter lives in Quebec; for the Conservatives if the voter lives west of Ontario.

This example shows that, even with a seemingly simple activity like voting, the explanation may require you to understand how many variables interact with one another.

Know the conditions under which your theory holds true

All explanatory studies contain elements of a relational design. None can ignore the context within which the data are collected, or the factors likely to make the explanation stronger or weaker.

The most obvious examples are historical and cultural contexts. A social fact or social law can be shown to hold true in a particular time and place, but not in others. Showing that something is universal or timeless requires a great deal of data and even then, may be impossible to prove. For instance—in one factory, social relations on the job may influence job satisfaction, but we cannot automatically generalize this to all factories. This relationship may be stronger in unionized factories than in non-unionized ones, where concerns about job security, working conditions, or pay are greater. It may be stronger in a period of prosperity than in one of mass unemployment, for similar reasons. It may be stronger in small-scale, traditional workplaces or in newly industrializing societies than in modern, highly bureaucratized or mechanized workplaces in industrialized societies.

Specifying the conditions under which your theory holds true is important. First, it helps you clarify what is going on in the situation you are examining, and why. Second, it helps you judge the generalizability of your findings and their applicability to other situations.

Generalizability is often important in applied research, where decisions affecting one group are based on research findings from another. Imagine a project to decide how we might improve relations between citizens and the police in a particular city. Someone theorizes that such relations are improved when citizens with inquiries have easier, less formal access to the police. The theorist suggests taking some police out of a centralized police station and putting them into a storefront "mini-station," where people can come ask questions, lodge complaints, and interact with police officers in an informal way. Such a mini-station is set up for a trial period of six months, and then community members are surveyed to learn whether their views of the police have improved. The data show no change in views.

What conclusion can we draw? Should we continue the study or even extend it to other neighbourhoods? Our answer depends in large part on the characteristics of the neighbourhood in which the mini-station was situated: for example, on whether the community members had originally been fearful of the police, had tended to misinterpret their motives and behaviours, and had felt reluctant to make initial—let alone subsequent—contacts. The results have a different meaning if found in an unreceptive community than in a receptive one.

Preparing to Make and Test Theories: The Literature Review

Science as a cultural and social institution has norms or rules. One of the most important of these is public disclosure of results. Researchers are expected to disclose fully the findings of their work to their colleagues and to submit these findings, in the form of journal articles or books, to qualified referees who will then assess and/or challenge the work. This is known as peer review. Only if the work passes this testing process will it find its way into reputable publications. From there, the work is abstracted—boiled down—for inclusion in professional databases, which are increasingly available in electronic form. In practice, a researcher in Calgary or Kolkata can go online and find out, almost instantaneously, which researchers around the world have been studying a particular problem and what they have found.

Of course, published knowledge may be a little outdated by this time (often by as much as two or three years, owing to delays in peer review and publication), which is why serious researchers attend conferences, where they can hear the most up-to-date findings from the people who have done the research. But outdated or not, published research is the best record of what is known in a particular field about a topic; that is where all new work has to begin.

There are many reasons for doing a literature review before setting out to make and test theories. First, someone may have already discovered the answer to the question you are asking. Or, other researchers may have taken steps to answer the question, and you can build on their work. Second, someone may have demonstrated that it is almost impossible to answer the question you are asking. For these reasons, no serious scholar or student would fail to review and interpret the literature before embarking on his or her own project (see Price, 2010). Jaidka, Khoo, and Jin-Cheon (2013) explain that literature reviews are surveys of previous studies that aim to identify research gaps and help researchers place their own work in the context of previous findings. They cite Hart (1998: 27) who notes that a literature review can serve the following functions:

1. To distinguish what has been done from what needs to be done.
2. To identify important variables relevant to the topic.
3. To synthesize earlier results and ideas, and gain a new perspective.
4. To rationalize the significance of the problem.
5. To identify the main methodologies and research techniques that have been used.
6. To place the research in context with state-of-the-art developments, and so on. (Jaidka et al., 2013: 304)

The literature review found in any scholarly work is an interpretation, synthesis, and critical analysis of published literature relevant to a study. A researcher who does not conduct a review of relevant literature risks focusing on a trivial problem, duplicating a study that has already been conducted, or repeating others' mistakes (Merriam, 1988: 61). Kellsey (2005: 526) reminds us that engaging in academic writing means you are joining a scholarly conversation, and therefore "just as you would not jump into a conversation with a group of people without listening long enough to know what the conversation was about, you do not want to jump into the scholarly conversation without relating what you are doing to what has been done before."

Searching for articles

Before discussing how to write a literature review, it is important to know where to look for relevant material published about a topic and how to assess it. Researchers can find books and articles about their topics in libraries and on the Internet (for more on searching for trustworthy sources on the Internet, see Chapter 8). Most university libraries have subscriptions to online databases. You are likely able to access the online databases via the Internet by logging on to your library's computer system from home. For specific information on how to access the resources at your school, visit your library or check its website.

Fraenkel and Wallen (1996: 65–6) suggest three sources of information to draw on for literature reviews: general references, primary sources, and secondary sources. They describe *general references* as the starting point because these references tell researchers where to look for similar and related studies. Examples of general references include indexes and abstracts (for example, Sociological Abstracts, MEDLINE, or PsycINFO). *Primary sources* are the complete recorded findings of individual studies, sometimes found in monographs or scholarly journals. *Secondary sources* mainly consist of authors' analyses and reports on other people's work. A textbook is an example of a secondary source: it discusses and describes the research of other, often primary, sources. A literature review, like you'll find in a textbook or the first half of a journal article, includes a summary and interpretation of other people's research and sources (use these summaries sparingly and strategically—look up the references that they refer to).

A researcher who has only a vague sense of the published literature about a topic is well advised to start with an overview by making use of general references. "Looking backward" through relevant encyclopedia articles, handbooks, and abstracts of journal articles will help the researcher identify major theories and studies (Timmins and McCabe, 2005). But before searching even for general references, it is wise to spend some time thinking about what search parameters to set. Using appropriate keywords is the cornerstone of an effective search. Before starting, and while searching, it is important to consider all possible keywords, including synonyms and alternative terms linked to your topic (Timmins and McCabe, 2005). The researcher might also look for articles in specific publications or published within a certain time frame. Another strategy is to begin with articles by the best-known scholars in the field, and to expand the search to include authors cited by those scholars. Be aware that if the topic is too narrowly defined, the search may result in very few articles. A better way to start is by conducting a broad search of all the different terms and variables relevant to the topic. A structured, thorough, and systematic approach to the search produces the best results. Keeping a record of the search strategy and process is useful (Timmins and McCabe, 2005). In compiling material for the literature review, the researcher should always work backward, reading the material from this year first, then the material from last year, and so on. Often material more than five to ten years old is outdated. It is equally important to know when to stop searching. When a search turns up familiar results or when you do not find new significant studies, it is time to stop searching and start synthesizing and writing.

Assessing whether an article is "scholarly"

Many of your library's databases will include both scholarly and non-scholarly articles. How do you know which to use, if you are instructed to use only scholarly or peer-reviewed sources? To start, many of the databases allow you to check off a box on the website ("[ ] – scholarly/peer-reviewed articles only"), which instructs the system to filter out non-academic sources. It also prudent to ask yourself a few key questions:

- Does the article have an author/authors? If the author is identified as "anonymous," it is likely not scholarly/peer reviewed (authors want their name on articles, and are evaluated and rewarded/praised for how often their names are cited in other people's research).
- Are there photographs or advertisements surrounding the text of the article? This may be an indication that the article was published in a "popular" magazine rather than a scholarly journal.
- Does the article include a bibliography, or a reference or citation list? Not having one may be an indication that the article is not scholarly,

because as noted above, it is important for researchers to cite, situate themselves in, and/or build upon the work of others (in other words, they too have a body of literature/literature review that they are required to identify and cite).

While these are not surefire ways to determine with full confidence that the articles that you have selected are scholarly or peer reviewed, they provide helpful hints to assist you in making more informed choices about what to include in your literature review.

Writing up the literature review

Like any other scholarly piece of work, a literature review is composed of three parts: an introduction, a body, and a conclusion. The introduction to a literature review gives a brief description of the problem and a short outline of published literature about the topic. The body of the review consists of a detailed discussion of relevant published studies. It is here that similar studies are grouped according to common themes or variables. In this way, literature reviews can be used to summarize the current thinking about a particular topic or problem. For prime examples, see the *Annual Review of Sociology*, the *Annual Review of Anthropology*, the *Annual Review of Psychology*, and so on. These publications contain articles by leading figures, synthesizing the knowledge in particular problem areas of the field. In analyzing the literature and pointing out strengths and weaknesses, the researcher will be able to identify gaps in the literature that can be filled with further research. Thus, the body of the literature review leads the reader to a new research question, which is usually stated at the end of the review in a closing paragraph.

According to Jaidka et al. (2013: 310), the information that you focus on for inclusion in your literature review can address the following aspects of past studies:

1. research objectives;
2. research methods;
3. research results; or
4. critiques.

Remember that a proper review should integrate, synthesize, and critique the relevant literature. A list of articles with summaries is no more than an annotated bibliography. Cooper (1984) identifies three types of literature reviews:

1. the *integrative* form, which is a summary of the published literature;
2. the *theoretical review*, in which the researcher highlights theories related to the problem that is being studied; and
3. the *methodological review*, in which the researcher focuses on methods that have been used. A good review of literature should contain aspects of all three types.

A good literature review is organized around ideas, not sources. Organizing the literature around themes and trends is the proper approach. With quantitative studies, both dependent and independent variables can work as organizing themes. Too many paragraphs that begin with the names of researchers ("Ludwig and Martin report . . ., " "Johannes and Mutabo have found . . .") is a hint that the review is organized too much around sources and not enough around ideas.

Pitfalls to Avoid

Once you have identified a problem and the main theories and queries surrounding that problem, you are ready to make and test your own theory. The process of making and testing a theory is full of pitfalls. Some pitfalls are so common that they have become classic social science problems with names to identify them. Social scientists have spent a great deal of time discussing these pitfalls, and you can read more about them in the literature. What follows is a brief account of classic problems to avoid.

The ecological fallacy

The ecological fallacy is the mistake of drawing a conclusion at one level of analysis and applying it to another. Social science analyzes data at several different levels of complexity: those of the individual, the group, the institution, the society, and the culture. Moving between levels of analysis can lead to errors.

For example, imagine that research has found that juvenile delinquency rates are highest in those parts of a city where the average household income is lowest. This does *not* necessarily prove that children from low-income families are more often delinquent than children from higher-income families. Children from high-income families may be the delinquents in both parts of town, but in the wealthier parts, their delinquency less often results in detection, arrest, or conviction.

Also, we are not justified in doing what Émile Durkheim (1951) did in his classic study of suicide. He studied suicide rates for various countries and, noting that the rates were higher in countries that were predominantly Protestant, inferred that Protestants were more suicide-prone than Catholics. However, he did so without any direct evidence that Protestants, not Catholics, were committing the suicides in question.

In sum, we run a serious risk of error when we infer individual behaviour from ecological or aggregate data (i.e., rates of behaviour in entire neighbourhoods, cities, or nations). Usually, aggregate data merely *suggest* relationships that we can test with other data. They may also be used to explain other aggregate data. We cannot automatically assume, for example, that people who live in modern cities will have "modern" ways of thinking. Nor can we assume that modern ways of thinking will automatically give rise to modern institutions. Please note, however, that research by Heckelman (1997) shows that under some circumstances, estimated coefficients from aggregate data can be directly related to true underlying micro-coefficients, so interpretations can be made. Though this is not always the case, it is becoming clear that in certain situations, the ecological fallacy does not pose a problem (see Subramanian, Jones, Kaddour, and Krieger, 2009, for more on this debate).

Multicollinearity

Often many independent variables are correlated with one another: that is, they vary together. We call this phenomenon *multicollinearity*.

Consider the problem of explaining the dramatic decline in average family size noted throughout the Western world in the late nineteenth and early twentieth centuries. The decline is correlated with many changes that are also correlated with one another: the spread of literacy, urbanization, industrialization, increased standard of living, reduced child mortality, and so on. These variables tended to change together (and to change one another), which is why we often lump them together under the general term of *modernization*. To say which of these was the key influence on child-bearing is difficult. It is therefore arbitrary to identify one of these variables as *most* important in producing the observed effect. As a researcher, then, you should avoid making any strong claims about the causal influence of any one particular variable in such a situation.

The fallacy of misplaced concreteness

You commit the fallacy of misplaced concreteness if you assign to some abstract entity (for example, "society" or "the community") thoughts or behaviours of which only individual humans are capable. Like the ecological fallacy, this mistake results from confusion about the proper level of analysis.

For example, to characterize some societies as more warlike or militaristic than others is both implausible and imprecise. Societies do not make wars; people do. "Society" is an abstract idea and therefore incapable of acting. When we say that a society is warlike, we are implying that all its citizens like wars, or that its major institutions or dominant classes are filled with people who are itching for a fight. More likely than not, it is only a few people who are promoting military activity, and often for practical reasons (such as profit making, broadening their power, or increasing their prestige) rather than because they like war for its own sake.

Misplaced concreteness combines several serious errors. It assigns actions and motives in a way that is sloppy and too general. It reduces social structure to individual traits, as though each member of society were identical. It fails, in this example, to identify who is militaristic and why; and further, it fails to identify why these people are often successful in causing wars. Finally, it leads us away from an analysis of distinct conflicting individuals, groups, and classes, toward a nearly mystical belief in an acting, consensual society.

This error is common even in simpler social units. Some would argue, for instance, that the notion of "family" results from misplaced concreteness, particularly when we use it in a way that suggests a common will, goal, or interest. We can easily identify the members of a particular household, and even which members of that household are related. But when we use the term *family* for such a group, we make certain assumptions about dependency, love, sexual relationship (or lack of it), commitment, and identification that may or may not be present in the particular household or kinship group. We should be careful not to assume a group forms a family without studying the relationships involved.

Tautology or circularity

Relationships that are true by definition are not worth researching because they tell us nothing new and cannot be falsified by data. Exploring such circular— or *tautological*—relationships adds nothing to our understanding of an issue.

Obvious tautology is rare, but other kinds are more common. Consider the theory of status attainment that says that in modern societies, a person's adult job status will be determined mainly by his or her educational attainment, whatever class he or she is born into. This theory proves largely tautological when we discover that *job status* here is measured in part by the average educational attainment of people in a particular job. Thus, the theory states the following: "Attaining a job with a high average educational requirement will be accomplished by gaining a high level of education." This is tautology.

Unmeasurables

Theorizing about things you cannot measure—*unmeasurables*—is often not useful. Variables are more complicated than you imagine. You should avoid theorizing about variables you cannot measure clearly and meaningfully because there is no way of telling whether you are right or wrong. You worsen this problem if your theory contains "escape clauses" to explain away results that are opposite to what you had predicted.

Consider two classic examples: Marx's theory of alienation and Freud's theory of repression. Marx argued that in a capitalist society, workers lack control over the labour process—over what they make, how they make it, and to whom the profits flow. The result is a sense of alienation or estrangement from work, from the product of work, from oneself, and from others. This leads to the prediction that as we vary worker control over the labour process, the expressed sense of alienation should vary. Yet studies have shown that many workers in (objectively) alienating work settings do not feel (subjectively) alienated. They do not express feelings of estrangement from themselves or from others. A Marxist would counter that such workers show a false consciousness (a false view of the class situation) that causes them to deny their true feelings. Because we cannot discover their true feelings, we must conclude that this theory is unprovable, at least right now.

Freud's theory of repression is similar. He argued that people have certain natural or inborn drives (the id): for example, drives toward expressing sexual or aggressive impulses. However, most societies have prevented or repressed the free expression of these drives, some especially strongly. The theory seems to predict that people will sublimate, or redirect, these impulses in ways that would not result in punishment; express the impulses in fantasy (for example, dreams or art); or suffer neurotic symptoms if they do not express the impulses at all. However, many people show low levels of sexual or aggressive impulse in any form and yet do not appear neurotic. A theorist from a contending school of psychology would say that the existence of these exceptions proves Freud wrong, arguing instead that we learn aggression and sexuality; that it is not instinctive; and that low levels of such expression are proof of learning, not repression. A Freudian would respond that the apparent absence of expression shows denial, and that the instinctive impulses find their outlet in another way—in smoking, overeating, loud laughter, or a strong devotion to work. Nevertheless, the Freudian theory cannot be proven as it stands because it contains no limit on the number of possible exceptions to the rule.

Methodological and conceptual problems such as these lead to poor predictions that are either untestable or, when tested, proven wrong.

Misuse of constants

Constants are, as their name suggests, unchanging: they never vary. Thus, a constant can never be used to explain anything; only variables can explain one another. More bluntly, no one can explain a variable by a constant, or a constant by a variable, or a constant by a constant. A constant just *is*.

The uselessness of constants in explanations should be obvious. Unfortunately they enter many explanations nonetheless. A prime example is the use of *human nature* to explain things, whether wars, divorces, discrimination, or the production of art. The statement, "Wars are caused by human nature" is untestable as it stands. It seems likely, at first glance, that data could disprove this statement because wars come and go but human nature presumably remains constant. However, someone might respond that wars are caused by a combination of human nature and another factor (for example, a shortage of agricultural land, resulting in population pressure). In this event, the researcher might just as well treat the other (variable) factor as the true explanation. In the end, referring to human nature is never a useful way of making a social science theory, and you should ignore human nature as an explanatory variable.

Non-events

Non-events did not happen. Yet researchers try to study them all the time: why countries did not have revolutions; why cities are not situated in particular places.

There are two reasons why you should be cautious when studying non-events. One is that there are no data because nothing happened. If it is true that people did not evolve to look like ostriches, we can have little to say about the conditions under which they would or could evolve to look like ostriches. (This is the unlikely example the philosopher Thomas Malthus used in his *Essay on the Principle of Population* [1798] to discourage idle speculation about the future.) Or, if Canada has never had a revolution, we can say little about the circumstances under which it would or could have one, except under conditions we will specify shortly.

You are in a better position to explain why things *did* happen because data can be plausibly arranged in an explanation. Take the example of young people who run away from home. We have many convincing theories about what makes family life pleasant and what makes parenting better or worse. Children flourish in loving and cohesive homes, with parents who are supportive, consistent, moderate, and caring. Our theory would be that children run away from homes that are the opposite of this. We should expect to find an under-representation of children from happy homes on the streets of our major cities engaged in begging, prostitution, and crime. The research finds the following to be the case: most runaways are children escaping difficult family situations. Running away is often a response to neglect, abandonment, and physical or sexual violence (Berman et al., 2009). Running away is an example of an event that does happen (and happens often). We can develop explanations and even try to find the causes of runaway behaviour because we can collect data on this situation.

Non-events do not produce data, so we cannot study them in the same way. The only way we can make a non-event the subject of our study is if we have a similar event to compare it with. Success must be compared with failures to see what factors are always present in the successes and always absent in the failures. Failing that, we must study non-events in relation to a general theory about events. For example, understanding why Canada has not had a revolution requires us to start with a general theory of revolutions, specifically a theory about the conditions needed to produce one. Making such a theory requires, as we have already noted, an investigation of both revolutionary and non-revolutionary societies: a comparison of non-revolutionary Canada with revolutionary Russia, France, or the United States, for example.

You should not study a non-event for purposes of explanation without either a general theory about corresponding events or data on corresponding events.

Non-findings

We stated earlier that the unexpected discovery of a non-finding may be cause for rejoicing. If a predicted result fails to appear, this may motivate the researcher to refine a theory, not discard it. However, consider research by Daily and Near (2000) that explored the relationships between various measures of CEO satisfaction and firm performance to determine if happier bosses build more profitable businesses. They found that every predicted relationship but one was significant in the predicted direction. The one exception was the relationship between CEOs' overall satisfaction (as opposed to various individual measures of satisfaction) and firm performance. In the end, we did not find out what influences firm performance using their model. In this sense they produced a non-finding. What conclusion should we draw?

One possibility is that a bad theory led the researcher to measure the wrong variables. If so, we must reject the initial theory as unhelpful. Another possibility is that the researcher failed to consider contextual or intervening factors, and that a good explanation will be much more complex than originally thought. Instead of adding up in some simple way, the various influences may interact or multiply together in any of what might be thousands of different ways. Such a conclusion, while conceivably correct, may in the short run lead to despair. No one is able to study thousands of possible combinations among dozens or hundreds of independent variables. The researcher is, in effect, reduced to starting over—making a new, simple theory—or giving up the problem altogether.

The final, and perhaps best, explanation of a non-finding—and its most disappointing meaning—is that the researchers did not measure one or more key variables correctly. If this is the case, they did not manage to predict firm performance because they did not know what the term was supposed to mean, or because what the researchers meant was not what other people mean, or finally, because the questions asked of respondents were badly chosen.

If so, the theory may be right or wrong, but there is no way of telling from the data available. Bad measurement has defeated us. Ultimately, developing any scientific discipline rides on the quality of its measurements. Much of scientific work is taken up with devising and refining measuring instruments and then reporting on the observed measures: At what temperature does water boil? How many children are born per mother? At what income does a family fall into "poverty"? While these issues may seem boring to some, in the end they are the essentials of science, including social science. That is why the next two chapters of this book are devoted to measurement. We first consider quantitative measures, and in the chapter after that, qualitative measures.

Summary

This chapter has discussed the research cycle and the importance of clarity about the purposes of the research. We have examined explanations, paradigms, theories, and predictions—the analytical framework of any research undertaking. If you are unclear about what you are trying to prove, you cannot hope that anyone else will be clear about what you have found.

We have also examined eight classic problems of logical organization. Avoiding them will help you launch your research toward findings that will make sense. Yet our job is only half done: we have our hypotheses in hand, but we have yet to measure the key variables in ways that will produce conclusive findings. This is the subject of the next two chapters.

4 Using Quantitative Data

In this chapter we will examine

- the distinction between quantitative and qualitative research;
- different kinds of measurement scales and their value; and
- elementary features of survey sampling and survey-data analysis.

Introduction

All science—perhaps all academic work—is concerned with three main activities:

- naming (identifying or classifying),
- measuring (or counting), and
- linking.

Chapter 2, on research design, and Chapter 3, on asking questions, were concerned with the first of these activities: naming the things that we want to study. This chapter is concerned with the other two activities, especially the second: measuring. We cannot effectively test theories, that is, examine the linkages between named variables, unless we can measure or count them precisely. This leads us to a discussion of how to use quantitative data—data that can be counted or measured using numbers.

Numbers are useful because they are precise and clear. For example, we know that something weighing ten kilos is somewhat heavier than something weighing five kilos. In fact, ten kilos is twice as heavy, not merely "somewhat heavier." Theory-testing requires this degree of precision. The numbers we collect are useful in two quantitative processes. First, using numbers we can measure the strength of a linkage between two variables: how strongly they are associated or correlated. Addressing this is one of the keys to testing a causal theory or explanation. Second, using numbers we can measure the likelihood that our findings occurred by chance. We do this by applying statistical analysis—specifically, laws of probability—to our quantitative findings. Once we are confident that our results were unlikely to have occurred by chance, we can be confident that we have proved (or disproved) our causal theory.

In this chapter, we will see that numbers and quantitative analysis are useful for theory-testing and explanation in all of science, including social science. In research, some social scientists move back and forth between qualitative and quantitative approaches because each has particular strengths and weaknesses. Figure 4.1 compares these approaches.

Qualitative data are most appropriate when the question to be answered is a *how* question: *How does* (or *did*) something come about? Quantitative research, as typified by the survey or experiment, is better at answering *what* and *why* questions. The *what* question asks about stable properties or relationships: *What* kind of people vote for the Conservative Party, buy SUVs, or marry outside their own ethnic group? *What* are the characteristics of societies that enjoy a high level of political participation, high productivity, or freedom of speech? Such research

Qualitative Paradigm	Quantitative Paradigm
Advocates the use of qualitative methods	Advocates the use of methods quantitative
Naturalistic and uncontrolled observation	Obtrusive and controlled measurement
Subjective	Objective
Close to the data: the "insider" perspective	Removed from the data: the "outsider" perspective
Grounded, discovery-oriented, exploratory, expansionist, descriptive, and inductive	Ungrounded, verification-oriented, confirmatory, reductionist, inferential, and deductive
Process-oriented	Outcome-oriented
Valid: "real," "rich," and "deep" data	Reliable: "hard" and replicable data
Ungeneralizable: single case studies	Generalizable: multiple case studies
Holistic	Particularistic
Assumes a dynamic reality	Assumes a stable reality

Figure 4.1 The qualitative and quantitative paradigms compared

Source: Reichardt and Cook (1979). Republished with permission of Sage Publications, from *Qualitative and Quantitative Methods in Evaluation Research*, Charles Reichardt and Thomas D. Cook, 1979; permission conveyed through Copyright Clearance Center, Inc.

cannot easily explain *how* these characteristics came about, but it can accurately generalize about the chances that they will occur.

Quantitative research answers the question *why* (or *when*, or *where*) by specifying the conditions under which events will occur. However, it will not show *how* they occurred in a particular time or place; for this, we depend on qualitative research. For example, quantitative research will show that university-educated women are twice as likely as high school–educated women to marry outside their own ethnic group. However, only qualitative research can help us understand *how* the women made the marriage choices they did, such as why these women were attracted to their spouses and how they overcame their own and their families' prejudices.

Social science research requires an interplay between these different types of data and data analysis. As Mahoney (1999) notes, the choice among different techniques of causal analysis reflects the role of scholarly preferences and skills, as well as the research question. We will focus on quantitative approaches for the rest of this chapter and look at qualitative approaches in Chapter 5. In the end, we will recommend a mixed (quantitative and qualitative) methods approach, which many believe "results in superior research (compared to monomethod research)" (Johnson and Onwuegbuzie, 2004).

Quantitative Data

Uses of quantitative research

Data on amounts of education and earnings are examples of *quantitative data*. They are based on precise measurements in recognizable units. We can say exactly, in dollars and cents, how much a person earns. We can say exactly, in years, grades, or degrees and diplomas, how much education a person has completed. What is more, because we are using common or known units of measurement, we can easily share and discuss our findings. With such quantitative data, we can easily repeat a study another researcher has done—to reproduce it to see if we get the same results. We know exactly what the earlier researcher was measuring and how.

In addition, such precise and clear-cut measures allow us to evaluate results with powerful statistical methods. They allow us to judge whether our findings could have occurred by chance alone. Quantitative measures also let us compare the relative importance of the different independent variables that affect the dependent variable. Finally—and most importantly—they let researchers create mathematical models for their theory. In short, quantitative measures allow social scientists to conduct research that is similar to research in economics and the physical and natural sciences.

Beyond using numerical measures of social variables, quantitative research is associated with a particular way of thinking about social life. Typical quantitative studies are narrowly focused on one part of the social structure. The researcher assumes that reality is stable and knowable, that reality does not change randomly: precise hypotheses, when tested in a rigorous way, will yield reliable and replicable findings. Finally, the researcher assumes that such work will produce conclusions that we can generalize to other people, times, and situations.

Much of quantitative research is obtrusive and controlling: the researcher sets the agenda through the questions being asked and the way he or she designs these questions. Concepts, when measured empirically, become variables in the model, and hypotheses are developed for empirical testing. The researcher then tests the hypotheses by collecting quantifiable data and examining relations between the variables. Statistical tests are used to decide if the hypotheses are valid.

The result is a set of findings that is clear and unarguable (though there may be flaws unaccounted for that must be discussed). Consider, for example, the theory that people become problem gamblers (or gambling addicts) through a combination of childhood traumas (e.g., abuse or neglect), stresses in adulthood, lack of social support, and exposure to gambling opportunities. In principle, each of these variables—trauma, stress, support, exposure— can be operationalized and measured, and we can find out whether the data support our hypothesis. If they do, we will find the childhood histories of problem gamblers contain far more instances of abuse and neglect than do the childhood histories of non-gamblers. If our hypothesis is wrong, the data will reject this hypothesis. Thus, we will find no difference between the childhood experiences of problem gamblers and those of non-gamblers. This means we need to know how to measure the key variables in our theory.

Types of measurement

Quantitative researchers rely on four levels of measurement: nominal, ordinal, interval, and ratio:

> **Nominal level.** Nominal-level measures consist only of named categories, such as "anglophone/francophone/other" or "male/female." These categories cannot be *arrayed* (i.e., displayed or arranged) on a continuum. They are incomparables, like apples and oranges. Categories denote difference.

For example, one is either single, married, separated/divorced, or widowed. Changing the order of these categories does not change the meaning or our understanding of the categories in relation to one another.

Ordinal level. Ordinal-level categories can be arrayed on a scale from most to least, since they are all measured in the same units—ordinal scales denote direction, but not size of difference. For example, "big, bigger, biggest" is a range of sizes whose order we can know and communicate. We have no doubt that "biggest" has more size units (whatever these may be) than "big." What we don't know is whether the difference in size between "biggest" and "bigger" is the same as the difference in size between "bigger" and "big." For some purposes, this information may not be important. Often we cannot get the information. Typically, qualitative research is carried out on variables at the nominal and ordinal levels of measurement.

Interval level. Interval-level measures are most commonly used in quantitative social science research. Their categories are an equal distance, or interval, from one another. An example is the IQ test score. The *average* score for a population is 100. We assume the distance between the score of 100 and 110 has the same meaning as the distance between a score of 110 and 120. One never hears a researcher claiming that someone with an IQ of 140 is twice as smart as a person with an IQ of 70. IQ scores have no absolute zero, meaning a complete lack of intelligence. Only an absolute zero allows such a comparison of two levels.

Stated differently, each score is plotted in relation to an arbitrary "zero" point, denoting both direction and size of difference. The researcher chooses the zero point in an interval scale, to simplify comparison among scores.

Ratio level. Ratio-level scales measure such phenomena as height, weight, and income using "real" numbers. Ratio scales can be understood as an interval scale with a non-arbitrary, or absolute, zero point. Describing someone as twice as tall or rich as someone else is meaningful because we can imagine (and measure) a complete absence of height or money. Researchers often set up attitude measures to contain a zero score, in which case they could claim that one person is twice as satisfied, for example, as someone else (since being "not at all satisfied" is possible).

Most statistical procedures in common use are designed for ratio- or interval-level measures. Especially in research that is aimed at informing social policy, we need to have precise measurements. It would be unreasonable to recommend business or government decisions, risking hundreds of millions of dollars, without precise measures of the problem to be solved and the benefits to be gained by doing so. Simply saying, "Policy *X* will save us a lot of money" or "Policy *Y* will help scads of people" doesn't get you far in the real world.

Operationalization

Operationalization is the part of the research cycle that takes the researcher from ideas to measures. More precisely, it means specifying procedures (i.e., operations) that will measure a concept named in the hypothesis to be tested. Indicators are selected to measure the conceptual variables.

Let's consider the topic of problem, or compulsive, gambling again. We need to have a clear idea what we mean by "problem gambling," and what separates problem gambling from recreational or casual gambling, as well as from real-estate or stock-market speculation. That's why researchers in this area have spent a great amount of time debating and perfecting measures of problem gambling: so they can say with assurance how widespread the problem is, and whether the problem is increasing or decreasing.

Here, any disagreement is not about the value of operationalization, but about whether the chosen operations faithfully capture the meaning of the concepts the researcher has in mind. As a researcher, you must always take care, in doing your own work and in evaluating the work of others, to decide whether the planned operations for collecting data are enough to address the hypothesis as you originally imagined it.

Plan where your data will come from

Once you have decided what your key concepts and intended operations are, you must specify where and how these operations are to be done. Things can get out of hand if more than two or three concepts are involved, with several measurements intended for each. You will find it useful to make a table to keep track of what you are doing. Let's try this now.

In the first column, list all the key concepts in your hypothesis. Consider the following hypothesis as an example: "The chances of migrating are proportional to the job opportunities in the place of destination and inversely proportional to the opportunities in the place of origin." The key concepts are *chance of migrating*, *job opportunities*, *place of destination*, and *place of origin*.

In the second column, list the matching measures or operations to be performed on the data. By *chance of migrating*, do we mean chance based on a projection of migration figures for a given year, or chance based on the stated aim of current residents to migrate in the year ahead, or both, or neither? By *job opportunities*, do we mean *job vacancies* or *expected job vacancies*? In either event, do we mean *all job vacancies* or *job vacancies in the line of work the respondent is used to doing*? When we speak of *place of destination* and *place of origin*, do we mean to compare countries or smaller units—cities or provinces, for example? How we answer these questions will control where we look for our data and how we measure them.

In the third column, specify the data source for each operation. If, for example, you are interested in measuring the chance of migration in terms of the measured migration between two countries (for example, Italy and Canada) during the past year, published or unpublished government statistics will be enough. If, however, you are interested in measuring intended migration in the coming year, you will need a survey, as government statistics will not be sufficient.

After completing the third column, you will know all the data sources that you must tap. You can then reorganize your information, putting the measures from column two into boxes defined by the data sources noted in column three. By doing this, you decide which questions you need to answer using the government statistics; which questions to ask in a survey of current residents; and so on.

Define your categories

Before designing questionnaires or other devices for collecting information, good researchers list the categories of their variables and may even draw up mock tables based on their expected results. These steps direct them to proper measurement, such as the proper wording of questions. With complex, multi-dimensional ideas such as social class, job satisfaction, or quality of life, doing so may even suggest additional questions.

Survey Design

The survey is the most common type of quantitative research in social science. Its purpose is to generalize about the relationships among variables in a population. That population can be an entire nation or city, or some named portion of all people: for example, all voters, car buyers, parents, schoolchildren, and so on.

Survey reasoning begins by showing differences in the likelihood that certain subgroups will behave in certain ways. For example, we expect to see that university-educated women will marry out (of their ethnic/racial group) proportionally more often than will high school–educated women. Or, we might expect that wage workers will be more likely to vote NDP than owners of small businesses.

The data are tabulated as in Table 4.1. Then we introduce control variables, as in Table 4.2, for one of two purposes. If the first bivariate (two-variable) table shows a relationship between the independent and dependent variable, the purpose of introducing a control variable is to make that relationship decrease or disappear. If repeated efforts to make the relationship disappear fail, we assume the first relationship is valid. If introducing a control variable weakens the original relationship, this means either the control variable is intervening in the effect of the independent variable on the dependent variable, or that the control variable is affecting both. This fact will force us to refine our theoretical model to include the new variable. In this case, we see that level of education attained is important only because it affects where someone meets his or her future spouse.

Consider now a second reason for adding control variables, especially where the original table reveals no relationship between the independent and dependent variable: to learn what factors, if any, may be suppressing a relationship we had expected to find in the data. Recall the example (p. 19) of the effect of marriage on suicide-proneness. The data showed that suicide rates are highest

Table 4.1 The likelihood of marrying out, by level of educational attainment

| | LEVEL OF EDUCATIONAL ATTAINMENT | | |
	High School Completed	College Completed	Total
Woman Marries In	160 (80)*	120 (60)	280
Woman Marries Out	40 (20)	80 (40)	120
Total	200 (100)	200 (100)	400

*Percentages are in parentheses.

Table 4.2 The likelihood of marrying out, by level of educational attainment and where woman met spouse

	WHERE WOMAN MET SPOUSE			
	At School		Elsewhere	
	LEVEL OF EDUCATIONAL ATTAINMENT			
	High School	College	High School	College
Woman Marries In	25 (50)*	75 (50)	135 (90)	45 (90)
Woman Marries Out	25 (50)	75 (50)	15 (10)	5 (10)
Total	50	150	150	50

*Percentages are in parentheses.

for married women and unmarried men. Thus, in a survey of equal numbers of men and women, marriage will have no clear effect on suicide. However, if we control for the gender of the respondent, the effect will be strongly positive for women and strongly negative for men.

Finding a third variable, C, that will help to reveal, elaborate, or interpret a first relationship between two variables A and B is an important part of survey-data analysis. This is far from easy because we can combine variables in any data set a great many ways. This problem of finding the right control variable is common to all research, especially research that studies systems of interconnected variables (for an example from industrial engineering, see Gay, Menzies, Davies, and Gundy-Burlet, 2010.)

Types of sampling

No one carries out surveys on entire populations; that would cost too much. Researchers typically sample from the population they are interested in to get a representative picture of certain relationships in it. The science of statistics has refined sampling procedures to a high degree. Arming researchers with the proper knowledge allows them to estimate in advance how large an error they will make in generalizing to total populations from small samples.

Sampling statistics tell us how much confidence to have in our findings from a survey sample and, conversely, how many people would have to be sampled to raise our confidence to an acceptable level. Repeated use of samples in political polls, market surveys, and other purely academic research has shown that we can attach a high degree of credibility to the findings of a well-conducted sample survey.

Central to conducting a good survey is drawing a good sample. A good sample should be large enough to represent the target population and must be selected using unbiased procedures. The least biased surveys are based on random samples, in which respondents are drawn in a way that minimizes the under-representation of certain types of people.

Of the several types of random sampling, some are more suitable (or more practical) for certain types of research than others.

Pure/simple random sampling. The researcher begins with a listing of all the people in the population, assigns each person an identification number, and then uses a table of random numbers (or a computerized random-number generator) to select the specific cases to be studied.

Systematic random sampling. In this equally unbiased procedure, the researcher randomly selects the first case and then every nth case after that. For example, imagine we were randomly sampling the telephone directory, which we knew contained 600,000 entries. If we wanted to sample 500 cases, we would select the first case randomly from the first 100,000 numbers, then take every thousandth case after that one.

Stratified random sampling. Here, the researcher divides the population into subpopulations of interest, such as male and female, and samples randomly within each subpopulation. This procedure ensures the resulting sample will contain a pre-decided number of males and females (which we cannot ensure with simple random sampling), yet will be unbiased in other respects.

Random or probability sampling, where every element in a population has a known or measurable chance (probability) of being selected for inclusion in the sample, is not always possible, however. In such cases, non-random sampling techniques can be used, including the following:

Availability/convenience sampling. This procedure, which is commonly used but far from random, consists of selecting respondents who are available to a researcher standing on a street corner or in a shopping mall. The results gained by this method can only be considered suggestive, since all sorts of potentially important factors will influence who happens to pass by the researcher on a given day. On the other hand, you may be studying people who are normally hard to find through standard sampling and interviewing techniques—for example, young male members of minority groups who live in poor neighbourhoods. If so, you can carry out this sort of sampling in locations where you expect to find these people.

Quota sampling. This is another type of non-random sampling where units are selected to reflect specific proportions of characteristics assumed to be in the population under study. This is similar to stratified random sampling, but the selection process is not random. Consider the following example. You are asked to survey the attitudes of employed and unemployed workers—two subgroups in a population. You know that about 10 per cent of the population under study is unemployed. You want your sample to reflect this, so you decide to survey 90 employed and 10 unemployed workers. In doing this you will face a problem of drawing an unbiased sample of unemployed workers because you have no list of all workers who are unemployed at any given moment. Therefore, the best strategy may be to use availability/convenience sampling, selectively accepting for inclusion the first 90 employed and 10 unemployed workers you encounter, to meet the named quota for your subgroups in the population. This technique, though not random, may be the only way to adequately represent the population of unemployed workers as a proportion of the entire population under study.

Snowball sampling. This technique is also not random and is potentially biased. In this case, a starting sample of respondents gives the researcher the names of others who might take part in the study, and the sample grows like a snowball rolling downhill. This technique is widely used where the behaviour under study is rare or illicit—for example, drug use or criminal activity—although the technique has other uses. Like availability sampling, it provides findings that are suggestive but far from decisive. Snowball sampling is used wherever barriers to accessibility, including cost and time, would otherwise make the research impossible. However, it may be biased because it will only sample people who are members of the networks that contain the first few people sampled. At worst, if you begin the sampling with atypical or unusual people, you will end up with an atypical or unusual sample overall. At best, the sample will be unrepresentative, though interesting.

Social Science Computing Programs

Over the last 30 years, the development and spread of a few easy-to-use computer software packages has revolutionized the way researchers—professionals and students alike—analyze data. These packages, such as SPSS and SAS, make it easy for people with little understanding of computers to define their variables in a data set and carry out necessary data analyses of which they may have no technical understanding. What's more, these analyses are often carried out immediately and at no cost (once we factor in the cost of the computer and a licence to use the software).

The democratization of data analysis through easy-to-use software has improved the speed at which we analyze data and may have increased the quality of good research by good researchers. However, this cut in the cost of data analysis has probably also increased (by a larger fraction) the spread of poor research by poor researchers. Under most circumstances, it costs no more to produce 10,000 correlation coefficients than to produce one. This means we are deluged by more correlation coefficients, as well as more tables, charts, diagrams, and—at the other end—more complex, confusing statistical models and their outputs. Besides, the laws of probability tell us that mere chance will throw up convincing relationships in any body of data if we calculate enough correlations. Thus, not only do we run the risk of wasting our time with too many calculations, but we also risk fooling ourselves about their probative value.

For better or worse, developing SPSS and other data analysis packages has transformed social science within a lifetime. Software designed to help data analysis can be of great help to the professional or student, but only if used to support a well-reasoned argument. Technology can help, but should never replace, the methods used to conduct proper research.

Choosing statistical software

Much research has been done regarding these statistical packages. This research reveals that, because of differing assumptions, different packages will sometimes produce different p (i.e., probability) values from the same set of data (see, for example, Bergmann, Ludbrook, and Spooren, 2000). They vary in general ease of use and flexibility in formatting (Moshiri, 1999), and they differ in their target audiences, capacities, and approaches (Oster, 1998). An entire issue of *The American Statistician* was devoted to assessing the reliability of statistical software packages in such routine operations as random number generation, correlations, and analysis of variance (see McCullough, 1998, 1999). Since then, the Internet has become a powerful tool as well, providing assessments of statistical packages and a variety of free non-commercial software.

The conclusion: the software used to analyze survey data, like other software, is available in a wide assortment of packages that vary in what they will do and how they do it. Packages and features are changing all the time, making them difficult to cover in a book revised every few years. To get the package that best suits your needs, you have to be a wise consumer. Do some research online, or discuss software choices with your instructors to discover the differences among the various packages. Once armed with this information, you can get the software package that suits your needs.

Summary

In this chapter we have explored issues that quantitative researchers must address before, during, and after gathering their data. When well imagined and properly carried out, quantitative research can reveal complex relationships between multiple variables and provide powerful insights into social phenomena. However, such research—even when flawlessly performed—has its limits.

In the next chapter, we will explore qualitative research. Although less rigorously objective than quantitative research, qualitative research—by dealing with people as people, not as statistics—can provide many answers and insights that quantitative research can never reveal.

5 Using Qualitative Data

In this chapter we will examine

- differences between qualitative and quantitative approaches in the social sciences;
- various types of qualitative research, including interviews, focus groups, and ethnographies; and
- approaches in qualitative research committed to social action and change.

Introduction

Qualitative data analysis, or what is often called the "interpretive approach to social science research," has become popular in recent years. Inductivist, naturalistic, holistic, process-oriented, and rooted in the constructionist paradigm, it is an approach that examines the *what* and *how* of social life.

Qualitative research involves non-numeric examination and interpretation of observations for discovering underlying meanings and patterns in social phenomenon. Qualitative researchers hardly ever use numbers to measure variables in their theories; in fact, they rarely talk about *variables* or hypotheses. They are committed to understanding the real world in terms of unique cases to be studied, rather than as a set of variables. Qualitative researchers explore and describe interactions and negotiations between individuals, rather than produce statistical conclusions. They are concerned with how patterns of thinking and acting fit together with the uniqueness and variability of the situation they are studying, and with the interplay between their own consciousness as observers and the consciousness of the people they are studying.

While quantitative data may tell us somewhat more objectively that variables X and Y combine to produce result Z, this objectivity comes at a price— the removal of individual human beings and their rich, real-life experiences.

Statistical research sees numbers, not people; and focuses less on if people do what they do because they are happy or sad, or for any number of other human characteristics that motivate them.

Qualitative research explores relationships intimately, on many levels. This is particularly useful in carrying out case studies, whether the "case" is a family, work organization, community, or nation. Qualitative inquiry is most suitable for answering *how* questions. For example, *how* do recent refugees adapt to city life in Canada? *How* have small organizations been affected by the widespread use of social media? *How* do gay men living in a rural area deal with living in a community dominated by heteronormative standards and expectations? We can answer none of these questions without understanding the consciousness of the subjects, their subtle social relationships, and the changes these people make at various stages of the process under study.

Types of Qualitative Research

There are various methods of collecting and analyzing qualitative data. We'll outline a few below.

Interviews

Interviews are used to collect both quantitative and qualitative data. While quantitative researchers use a structured interview (surveys) to collect the data they need, qualitative researchers use a less structured, more conversational and non-directive interview to explore a broader range of factors, including the thoughts and feelings of study participants. Put simply, quantitative approaches are closer to multiple-choice questions on a test, while qualitative interviews are similar to short answer or essay questions, which let you answer in your own words.

While semi-structured, less formal interviews tend to include a smaller sample of individuals compared to more structured surveys, they can reveal much that larger, structured, survey-type interviews cannot. Consider a survey designed to explore the reasons some abused women remain in relationships with their abusive partners. It is hard to design a survey that can illuminate the complexities of such experiences. Nevertheless, with an experienced interviewer in the right setting, it is possible for a woman to feel comfortable enough to open up and discuss her motives for staying, as well as her fears, hopes, and plans to change her situation.

Such interviewing is difficult: the interviewer must establish a rapport with the participant before she or he will open up. Developing rapport is essential, yet difficult to teach from a textbook. Researchers often use their intuition to effectively and ethically persuade the interviewee to speak openly. Still, some interviewees will have an easier time relating to some researchers than to others. In the case of abused women, a female interviewer may have an easier time establishing rapport with an abused woman than a male interviewer would.

Focus groups

In a focus group, researchers interview a group of participants at the same time about their feelings on a certain topic, event, person, or program. For example, focus groups have been used extensively to collect people's opinions about a political candidate or a product.

The interaction between the individuals creates dynamic results, with each member expanding on, or offering counter-examples to, the comments of others. One downfall is that participants may feel pressure to express opinions that conform to the prevailing attitudes in the group, when in fact they may disagree; however, an experienced researcher can provide direction to ensure that he or she hears various opinions, but not so much direction that natural exchanges are stifled.

Focus groups have gained popularity across a range of academic and applied research areas, including sociology and political science. Their popularity has resulted in focus group research being conducted by video conferencing or online, via "virtual focus groups" (see Galloway, 2011; Williams, 2007). A comparison of different types of focus groups found that certain types are better suited for different kinds of research questions (Gothberg et al., 2013).

Focus group research can strengthen the validity of other data-collection methods—such as questionnaires—by highlighting concerns of real people that might otherwise be neglected. Questionnaires are limiting in the way they ask questions and in the response options available to the study participants (Raby, 2010). Focus groups allow people to raise concerns on their own and respond in their own words.

The following are some examples of focus group research:

- Researchers studying gender have used focus groups to examine how immigrant and Aboriginal girls in Canada struggle for social inclusion and identify themselves vis-à-vis the dominant culture (de Finney, 2010).

- Researchers studying sexuality have examined the barriers faced by young men in sex-education classes in schools (Limmer, 2010) or the decision-making associated with help-seeking for sexual-health concerns among adult men in Zimbabwe (Pearson and Makadzange, 2008).
- Researchers studying health have examined the growing awareness of the health impacts of environmental contaminants on children by interviewing new mothers and conducting focus groups with public health key informants in two public health units in Ontario (Crighton et al., 2013).

There are disadvantages to focus group research. For instance, few standards have been developed so far for evaluating focus group research findings (Acocella, 2012). Of particular concern is the fact that shared information prevails over information that is not agreed upon by all members of the group (Acocella, 2012), and that the findings of focus groups can be manipulated by altering the composition of the groups (Unger, 1999). For example, imagine how different the focus group dynamics may be if you are studying sexuality in a group of heterosexual men and women, together, compared to one made up of gay men only, or a group made up of younger Canadians compared to one made up of seniors.

Ethnography

Ethnographic research consists of trying to understand a culture from the insider's perspective. It is a means of learning about social situations, the way they develop and change, and how they are understood and experienced by insiders (Brunt, 1999). Classical ethnography has been rooted in the study of people interacting with one another in their natural settings (what is called *naturalistic study*).

Unlike participant observation, to which it is related, ethnography is sometimes concerned with setting up new research ethics and inventing new moral discourses (Gans, 1999). Often, ethnographers—especially critical ethnographers—are immersed in the injustice and oppressions of their time, and challenge the reader to reconsider his or her moral outlook (Denzin, 1999; Dennis, 2009; Barron, 2013). The researcher abandons strict objectivity and gets inside the study environment. Done this way, ethnography accomplishes the twin goals of scholarship and engagement.

If the researcher is not a member of the subculture being studied, informants must be used to gain entrance to the community and to learn its rules of conduct. Long-term intensive fieldwork is the main method of ethnography, which is interactional, interdependent, and collaborative. It is often combined with interviews to gain a deeper understanding of the norms of the subculture and the behaviours of its members. The ethnographic researcher is, in anthropologist Lévi-Strauss's sense of the term, a *bricoleur*—someone who uses whatever is at hand to solve problems (Hammersley, 1999).

Ethnographic research gives us, for example, insights into how articles of clothing or jewellery can show gang affiliation or sexual orientation. Ethnographic research gives us a bottom-up understanding of social phenomena using case studies, interviews, and naturalistic observation. For example, critical ethnography afforded researchers the opportunity to validate the testimony of immigrant and refugee women's experiences with postpartum depression (O'Mahony, Donnelly, Este, and Bouchal, 2012).

Ethnographic research can be used to show that a theory is reasonable, but it can never prove a theory because the research is too specific and does not lend itself to generalization. There are also possible ethical challenges associated with it. For example, what do you do when you learn through your research on gangs that someone is going to be robbed or injured? You must also consider that through observations, you are often doing research without the consent of those being studied (as they would likely alter their behaviour if they knew they were being studied), and that you may cause harm to the group or its members by doing so.

The best ethnographies respect the complexity and ambiguity of social life while giving voice to the experiences of people who might not otherwise be heard.

Field observation

All ethnography requires *field observation*—in-place, naturalistic, and unobtrusive observation—as opposed to experimental, manipulated observation. One kind of field observation is *participant observation*, which is useful for studying small populations that exist outside the mainstream. It involves the collection and recording of a wide range of observed data.

Ethnographers using field observation aim to provide detailed accounts of the situations they are viewing: in particular, accounts of the ways in which participants understand their worlds—the processes and principles by which people make sense of reality. However, in the end, the researcher is still an outsider.

When in the field, record your data carefully and keep track of the chronology of data collection. Often the unfolding of a social process or the timing and stages of the process will be as important as the character of the changes. Field notes, related documents, and collected artifacts (like art and photographs) record the experiences and observations of the researcher. Conversations conducted or overheard should be noted in enough detail to capture the meaning and importance of events, and illustrate them for a reader. Several obstacles must be overcome in such research. You must get close enough to the situation to understand it, yet stay distant enough to see it objectively. You must be familiar and friendly with the participants to win their trust, yet detached enough to avoid being drawn into their intrigues and conflicts. Taking a stance with one section of a community over another will inevitably have political and social consequences.

Gaining entry into a group is challenging. A researcher should let the group know that he or she is a researcher. Secrecy about identity and general purpose is unethical; however, it is inadvisable to provide a detailed description of his or her purpose, theories, and expectations.

Avoid intruding on the way the group normally functions. Be quick to listen and slow to talk; be present, but not noticed; and be slow to form and express judgments about the group and its members. Do you best to not interfere with the group's way of thinking and doing things. Social scientists have long known that their presence may influence group functioning. This is known as the *Hawthorne effect*: the production of changes (especially improvements) in group behaviour by the mere awareness of being observed. Researchers should study social processes as unobtrusively as possible.

Document analysis

Document analysis, or documentary research, is common in history and political science. It aims to examine and interpret original records as data about the activities and beliefs of a person or group not otherwise available to the researcher. Such documents may include speeches, books, and essays by eminent figures; parliamentary debates; pamphlets, magazines, online communication and other popular writing; and even folk tales, and art.

The first concern in documentary analysis is to confirm the authenticity of the document. Did person *X* really give this speech at this time and place? The second concern is to discover the meaning of the document, which, at times, may be obscure. Perhaps the document originally appeared in a foreign language. Is reading a translation enough, or must you read it in the original language? Another concern relates to references to contemporary events, persons, and writings. You should read other sources to get the background and context.

You need to understand the nuances, unstated assumptions, and local meanings hidden in the document. What is meant if the document refers to an eminent figure—the king, for example—as *dashing* but not *wise* or *good*, or to parliament as *overcautious* or *foolhardy*, or to a piece of legislation as *radical*? What is *good, overcautious, foolhardy*, or *radical* in one context may not be considered so in another. Therefore you must understand the shades of meaning in the document, and only then place them in relation to contemporary debates.

Two main approaches are available. One is to examine prevailing interpretations of the document: how other researchers have interpreted the document and the reasons for their interpretations. The other approach is to examine supporting documents: other written materials by the same person or group, originating at the same time and place. The concept of *construct validity*—the tendency of measures of the same underlying phenomenon to point in the same direction—is no less important in documentary research than in survey research. If you understand one document to say that a certain figure was disloyal, radical, or ambitious, you should support your interpretation with other contemporary materials expressing similar concerns.

You must learn the language and unspoken assumptions in which the document is grounded; make and test theoretical interpretations about what you are observing; and test these interpretations for coherence against other information: other documents, other information about the society, and other scholarly interpretations of the same document, group, and society.

Historical analysis

Developing explanations of social life by using historical data has become more popular in recent years. To a degree, because most historical research relies on historical documents, we covered the aspects of historical analysis in the previous section on document analysis. However, historical analysis, like all social analysis, is enmeshed in prevailing ideologies and beliefs. The field of historiography is concerned with the problem of separating historical "facts" from mere belief.

Webb (1998) compares the writing of history to the writing of an accident report. In accident reports, as in historical accounts, we know in advance what we have to explain, and we organize our understanding of past events so they converge in the present. Such analyses are subject to the purposes and expertise of the observer. The true causes of accidents (or historical events) may be infinite in number. The framework of our search depends on how we define the events, and the framework we use may contain gaps. The methods for causal selection are poorly developed, and the methods of proof lack objectivity.

Selectivity and subjectivity pervade the writing of historical accounts, from how key facts are chosen to how facts are combined into a story. Archives are partial, limited, and subjective. Archives are selective testimonies to past relations between individuals and events, or between individuals. Archival research is a dialectical and dynamic process, itself subject to politics and change. As a result, archivists and historians are moving beyond attempts to look at the past in terms of neutral reconstructions of lives and events (Dodge, 2006).

Writing history has its own methodology and methodological debates. Historians recognize that the knowledge systems that we encounter in everyday life, including historical analyses and classifications of past events, contribute to domination of the socially vulnerable, and to supremacy of the West (Lal, 1997). Historical works have ideological as well as research interest. There are strong links between the writing of history and political ideology. A historical account—like any story or account—is creative work that endeavours to capture and conform to the agreed-upon "facts" about the past. It provides people with a way of thinking about their lives. Because it has political implications and consequences, the writing and interpretation of historical "fact" is always a contested terrain.

Content analysis

One type of data analysis that bridges the gap between qualitative and quantitative data is *content analysis*. Its goal is to quantify large amounts of qualitative data for generalization.

Imagine that you have read 30 magazine stories about the late musician Prince. How should you analyze these data? You can give a general impression of what the articles said. Or you can analyze their content by looking for systematic patterns and counting the occurrence of specific words, messages, or images. You can also map change over time.

Each story is coded to produce numerical data. For example, if the story presents a positive account of the entertainer, you assign the value 1 in the category labelled *overall message*. If the story presents him in a negative light, you assign the value 2. Researchers have used content analysis to study diverse kinds of texts, from looking at leaflets in order to understand the rhetoric of environmental sustainability (Myers and Macnaghten, 1998) to examining family sociology textbooks to investigate shifts in content and theoretical perspectives since the 1960s (Eichler, 2014). There have also been content analyses of television advertising (Warren, Wicks, Wicks, Fosu, and Chung, 2007), gender and racial representations in children's television programming (Al-Shehab, 2008), and the types of comments written by YouTube users (Edgerly et al., 2013; Madden et al., 2013).

Such data can be analyzed statistically. Their value rests mainly on the quality of the coding scheme and the objectivity of the person (coder) reading and interpreting the stories. If the researcher uses an inadequate scheme for coding the textual materials or observed behaviours, the resulting data will be worthless. If the researcher employs coders to apply a good coding scheme but makes no effort to train the coders and ensure their uniform, unbiased application of the scheme, the resulting data will be worthless. In the end, the most important job in content analysis is good coding—something that is hard to achieve.

To establish coder reliability, it is important to have two or more people code the same content independently. A high degree of agreement will show that the interpretations are not flawed by the biases of particular coders. Assessing inter-rater reliability—whereby data are coded by independent researchers and compared for agreement—is important. Some qualitative researchers argue that assessing inter-rater reliability is an important method for ensuring rigour, while others argue that it is unimportant. Some argue that a single rater may not extract all the important information contained in the transcripts, but that a second set of eyes may identify different but equally important trends.

Some challenges will be minimized by the spread of new computer-assisted qualitative data analysis software (CAQDAS). However, the resulting computerized data analysis will be only as good as the coding scheme devised by the investigator.

Feminist Research: Qualitative Research for Social Action

Feminist research is distinct from mainstream research in its aim to create social change that will improve the lives of women, and in the value it puts on subjectivity and the lived experiences of those studied.

A wide range of topics are explored within a feminist research framework, including issues of difference, social power, and commitment to political activism and social justice. Feminist research has made notable contributions to our understanding of health and education, social movement formation, and policy analysis (see Tolhurst et al., 2012).

It is important to distinguish between the terms *method* and *methodology* as they are used by feminist researchers. A research *method* is merely a way of collecting data; methods are not gender-specific (Hesse-Biber et al., 2004: 15). Feminist *methodology* exists in opposition to mainstream and conventional ways of data collection and analysis, which often reflect androcentric values. Some have argued that feminist methodology is a theory in itself, connected to the struggle of empowering women and other oppressed people (Sprague and Zimmerman, 1993: 266; Smith, 2008). It represents feminist values and world views, highlights the inclusion of women from diverse social and ethnic backgrounds, and values the relationship between the researcher and the subject (see Gouin, Cocq, and McGavin, 2011; Enloe, 2007; Ackerly, Stern, and True, 2006).

Feminist researchers use a wide range of qualitative and quantitative research methods to collect data, sometimes combining methods to obtain data from different perspectives and in different forms. Oral history interviewing is a preferred method of research because the questions in this method, being less predetermined, are better at capturing the meanings women attach to their lived experiences (see Sugiman, 2009). Feminists often favour in-depth interviews, which allow the researcher to develop a connection with the participant, lessening the status difference between researcher and interviewee. This methodological approach provides more insight into the lives of individuals and produces a more varied set of responses. Some feminist research involves study participants in the generation of research questions, making them partners in the data collection. This is often referred to as *participatory action research* (see Gouin et al., 2011; Cahill, 2007). In this case, the researcher does much more than share results with the participants. The researcher typically asks participants for their unique insight on identifying key issues that need to be researched.

Community-Based Research: Qualitative Research for Social Action

Community-based research is a model used to examine a broad range of issues, including community health, environmental problems, and education. In community-based research, the unit of identity is not the individual, but the community. A community can be a geographic area, or an actual or virtual group that shares ethnic, racial, sexual, or other identities or their combination. Research takes place in a community setting and involves its members at different stages of the design and implementation of the research project. This makes community-based research fundamentally participatory, with outcomes that should benefit the community.

A key feature of community-based research that sets it apart from other methods is its involvement of community members in the design of the project. For example, Tobias, Richmond, and Luginaah (2013) used a collaborative, community-based approach to health research with Anishinabe communities in northern Ontario as a means of advocating for change, to address the health disparities between Indigenous and non-Indigenous peoples in Canada. Community members typically remain throughout the research and can influence the direction of the project. By exercising their power over the research, community members can make sure it is carried out according to its original goals. Because of its emphasis on the non-hierarchical relationship between the researcher and participants, researchers and community members learn from each other. A main purpose behind carrying out community-based research is to incite action and solve problems. This was the case in Tobias et al.'s (2013) research with Anishinabe communities.

Systematic Literature Reviews and Meta-analyses

A systematic literature review (SLR) and meta-analysis is the methodical review of research literature that attempts to answer a particular research question. It combines the results of many studies to get a "big picture" of the answer to the original research question.

In the health sciences, for example, this involves a meticulous, step-by-step process where researchers identify, retrieve, review, and summarize the research questions asked in each study, the methods used, and the relevant outcomes. In the social sciences, however, analytical goals are sometimes less focused and so the proper methods are harder to identify. Roelfs, Shor, Falzon, Davidson, and Schwartz (2013: 75) explain:

> Conventional approaches to meta-analysis often prioritize "concept-driven" literature searches. However, in disciplines with high theoretical diversity, such as sociology, this search approach might constrain the researcher's ability to fully exploit the entire body of relevant work.

Most attempts at meta-analysis are quantitative, but there are qualitative studies as well. The choice of quantitative versus qualitative seems to come down to a question of subject matter: subject areas that are not as readily quantifiable (for example, those dealing with sentiments or subjective experiences) are more likely to use qualitative measures of investigation such as interviews. These tend to summarize the current state of the field in question, rather than attempt to confront and overcome the statistical limitations of individual studies.

A meta-analysis first involves finding articles based on a set of search criteria (such as being peer reviewed, being in English, and so on). Once found, the studies of interest are further narrowed down based on such criteria as sample size and the methods used by the study. The studies included in the final review can vary from as few as five to as many as dozens and even hundreds.

By aggregating the results in a systemic fashion, we begin to see the flaws and limitations of the ways a topic has been studied up to the present. The typical approach is to compare the mean of the experimental group and the mean of the control group. By combining the results into an aggregate summary statistic, the data are then used to answer the question: What is the effect of a particular kind of intervention? The most basic way of doing this is to average these results and then infer the size of an effect. One problem with this method is that different studies employ different methodologies and measure key variables in different ways (Shaw, 2010).

One solution is to restrict the number or type of studies that are included in the review, to homogenize the studies included. However, doing this would limit the number of studies that could be used. Another solution is to use what is known as the *random effects approach*, which uses studies, rather than individual participants, as the unit of analysis (Maas, Hox, and Lensvelt-Mulders, 2004). This contrasts with the *fixed effects approach*, which uses individual participants as the unit of analysis. Using the fixed effect approach, the researcher treats the studies as being different from each other—as having distinct characteristics that actually affect the results of the studies.

Taking study characteristics into account allows for a closer approximation and allows the researcher to control for factors that would otherwise bias the results. However, it is very difficult to take every difference into account, so bias resulting from omitted variables remains a serious concern (Maas et al., 2004).

Other problems that occur with SLRs, and that you should keep in mind, include the following:

- Many studies that are relevant to the research question may fail to report the necessary statistics needed to calculate the effect size (for instance, the standard deviation).
- Studies that report non-significant findings are less likely to be published at all—the "file drawer" effect (Roelfs et al., 2013). This failure may result in an overestimation of the results of the meta-analysis.
- Many of the studies limit their search to English-language articles only, restricting the sample size of studies included in the meta-analysis. This is a thorny issue for meta-analyses with culturally sensitive results, where results may vary for social or cultural reasons.

Summary

In this chapter, we have examined some of the methods used by qualitative researchers and how they differ from quantitative analysis. Qualitative research is concerned with exploring individual cases and events, rather than with quantifying things to produce statistical conclusions. However, qualitative research should not be seen as antithetical to quantitative research; as we shall see in the next chapter, the two approaches can be combined to produce a more detailed picture of the subject under study. In the next chapter, we will take a closer look at some ethical problems social scientists face and some of the ways to avoid them.

6 Exercising Judgment and Good Ethics

In this chapter we will examine

- two kinds of tests your research must pass: scientific and ethical;
- ways to assess validity and reliability in your data; and
- ways to ensure the data are gathered and handled in ethical ways.

Introduction

Now that we have discussed how to start collecting data, measuring concepts, and exploring your research question, we can discuss how to analyze your data. First, in order to produce trustworthy conclusions, the measures used to get the data must be both valid and reliable. So it's essential that you know how the research findings—your own or those of another researcher—were collected.

In the first part of this chapter, we will examine the various ways of judging validity and reliability. We will then look at the unavoidable problem of flawed data and suggest ways of dealing with it. Then we will explore some of the kinds of situations that pose ethical problems for social science researchers, and we will suggest ways of collecting and using data properly. In the final part of the chapter, we will discuss the importance of being aware of cultural and gender sensitivities, and will look at ways of handling these sensitivities in your writing. Our overall goal is to carry out research that meets rigorous scientific standards and rigorous ethical standards.

Judging Your Data

Measures should have face validity

In general, validity means that a measurement reflects or represents what we intended it to measure. To start, the way a concept or variable is measured should make sense to an objective observer, given their understanding of that concept. This is what researchers mean by the *face validity* of a measure. Consider the problem of measuring whether a person has a gambling addiction or compulsion, as we discussed in Chapter 4. We cannot measure this with a single question, because the problem is complex and has many aspects. Here, for example, are the items included in the Canadian Problem Gambling Index, developed by gambling researchers Ferris and Wynne (2001) and widely used by researchers today:

- How often have you bet more than you could really afford to lose?
- How often have you needed to gamble with larger amounts of money than before to get the same feeling of excitement?
- How often have you gone back another day to try to win back the money you lost?
- How often have you borrowed money or sold anything to get money to gamble?
- How often have you felt that you might have a problem with gambling?
- How often have people criticized your betting or told you that you had a gambling problem?
- How often have you felt guilty about the way you gamble or what happens when you gamble?
- How often has your gambling caused any financial problems for you or your household?
- How often has your gambling caused you any health problems, including stress or anxiety?

All of these questions have face validity in that they adequately address the issue of addictive gambling—gambling that has negative consequences for the gambler who, seemingly, cannot give up the habit. Though these items ask relevant, related questions, they do so in different ways. Some of them look at the element of compulsion: people feeling unable to keep themselves from gambling. Others look at the element of adverse consequences: people knowing that they are involved in an activity that is harmful and dangerous.

Measures should have construct validity

Measures of the same variable or concept should be correlated with one another in *scales*. A scale is a spectrum of responses to a series of related questions that are believed to measure the same underlying concept. *Construct validity* is the degree to which all the items on a scale are correlated with one another and the scale, as a whole, is distinct from other scales. This also means that we can expect a particular measure to change in a logical way when other conditions change.

Imagine, then, that you had asked all the questions about gambling addiction mentioned above. The answers should be correlated with one another: a person who answers "yes" to one question should be answering "yes" to most of the others, too. Researchers have statistical methods to measure how strong that correlation between items is and to help construct a gambling addiction score from many related items. Such a score can then be used with confidence as the dependent or independent variable in empirical research.

However, common-sense expectations do not always prove correct. There may be many reasons why certain items do not group, the most likely being that one or more items have been poorly measured. For example, the categories used may have been inappropriate, or the respondent may not have understood the questions. A second reason is technical. The statistical methods used to construct scales often have strict requirements about the form of the data, especially the distribution of answers. (More detail on this can be found in statistics courses and textbooks.)

A third reason items may not group together is that the concept being measured is *multi-dimensional*. In other words, the concept has many parts, so the items group into two or more distinct, uncorrelated scales, each one having its own construct validity. Such multi-dimensionality can be seen, for example, in people's attitudes toward computers in the workplace. One might expect a series of questions about satisfaction with the effects of computerization to reveal a single satisfaction measure—people either love computers or hate them—but they do not. In one study at least, two major dimensions, or scales, appeared. One of these measured the workers' approval of the increase in efficiency brought about by computerization. The other measured workers' concern about the increase in managerial control that computerization made possible. A worker could be favourable toward the computer as an instrument of increased efficiency, but unfavourable toward it as an instrument of increased control. So there may be no single overall measure of satisfaction, but multiple measures instead.

Measures should be reliable

Measures should be reliable, or stable (consistent), over time—each respondent's answer should be the same at various points in time. If we find marked or frequent changes in response, we should try to explain these changes.

As well, you should ensure a high degree of reliability or agreement in the responses produced by different interviewers (or coders). These two types of agreement—agreement of the respondent with himself or herself over time and agreement of one coder with another reacting to the same stimulus—constitute what researchers mean by reliability in social science research.

The need for such reliability is obvious. We cannot reasonably explain something with attitudes or behaviours that are constantly changing. Yet people's attitudes *do* change over time. If they change in a random, unpredictable way, with great frequency, a researcher should not use them in an explanation. If they change in predictable ways, however, the explanation should include variables that predict these changes. So, for example, if people's willingness to save or invest money changes with their job security or their view of political and economic stability, we should include measures of these experiences and views in our explanation of saving.

One common way of being certain about your measures is to adopt the ones that other researchers have already tested and used. Widely used measures of intelligence, anxiety, socio-economic status (SES), work satisfaction, and family cohesion, to name just a few, thrive. They all have known properties: thoroughly considered face validity, statistically tested construct validity, and measured reliability. A scale with high reliability and validity is easily justified in any research. One without these features is used at the researcher's peril, for it may yield inconsistent or unreliable results.

Make sure the variables can vary

In Chapter 3, we noted that constants should never be used in an explanation because they never vary, and explanations need variables. Measured variables should be able to vary as widely as reality does. In general, researchers should allow respondents to give various answers wide enough to capture their true range of feeling. The wider the range of variation the questions make possible, the more widely the answers will vary. The more widely answers vary, the greater the possibility for a good explanation. Thus, questions allowing wide variation offer the best chance for a good explanation.

Variables with only two data points—yes/no, agree/disagree, and so on—are weak. Such limited variables should not be used if others offering a greater range of possible answers can be substituted: yes/no/maybe, strongly agree/agree/no opinion/disagree/strongly disagree, and so on. At the point of dwindling returns, however, adding more categories adds nothing to the ability of the respondent to answer truthfully. For example, asking respondents to judge their satisfaction with an undergraduate course on a 17-point scale ranging from "hugely satisfied" to "hugely dissatisfied" will probably not produce better results than asking them to judge their satisfaction on a 7-point scale ranging from "very satisfied" to "very dissatisfied." The human ability for gradation is limited, at least in this form.

If researchers need a finer gradation, they should use many *yes/no* questions. The answers can then be summed together, or scaled (summing weighted values), to give a score that ranges widely from very high to very low. For example, if you want to measure how satisfied people are with their lives, you might ask each respondent to rate his or her satisfaction from 0 to 10, where 10 shows extreme satisfaction. Or you might ask each to answer 10 questions—"Are you satisfied with your work?", "Are you satisfied with your friendships?", "Are you satisfied with your sex life?", "Are you satisfied with your standard of living?", and so on—where each *yes* answer is worth 1 point and each *no* answer is worth 0. (Different weights can be attached to questions according to their theoretical contribution to the overall result, so a *yes* answer to the question "Are you satisfied with your marital situation?" might be worth more than a *yes* answer to the question "Are you satisfied with your job?".) The latter approach, which is preferable, will produce a total score ranging from 0 for some respondents to 10 for others.

If an independent variable does not vary much, it cannot "explain much variance" in the dependent variable: it will not appear, statistically, to have a strong causal effect. If the dependent variable does not vary much, the explanatory model as a whole cannot "explain much variance": it will appear that the independent variables, taken singly or together, fail to provide an acceptable explanation. Failures of these kinds account for many of the non-findings in social science.

If the problem lies with faulty measurement, the researcher should make sure that revised measures adequately reflect the range of variety in the real world, by refining his or her categories to tap the available variance. However, the problem may lie with the real scarcity of extreme or unusual cases in the world (for example, morons and geniuses versus people with ordinary intelligence, or saints and villains versus people with ordinary morality). If so, this should be dealt with at the design or sampling stage. One method is to oversample unusual cases—to select a greater number of extreme cases for study than would normally turn up in a random sample. Such oversampling is justified if the purpose of the research is to examine cases within this entire range of possible variation.

For example, suppose we are interested in studying the reasons people hold the views they do on smoking marijuana. A random sample might show that 10 per cent of the Canadian population is opposed to marijuana use under any circumstances and 10 per cent is in favour of its decriminalization. The remaining 80 per cent is sympathetic to both views and undecided, or tolerant of marijuana use under only certain specific circumstances (such as when used for medicinal purposes). With so many people holding down the middle position, our dependent variable (attitude toward marijuana use) varies little. Therefore, it may not matter how many good independent variables we measure—how many questions we ask, or how refined our categories are. We will still find a weak statistical correlation between the dependent and independent variables: a weak model of explanation.

If, on the other hand, we compose our sample to include one-third opposing marijuana use under all circumstances, one-third favouring decriminalization, and one-third in the middle, we increase the range of measured variation in the dependent variable. Doing this shows our explanation—the entire collection of independent variables—to work much better than it did before.

Pretest your own measures

Respondents may not always understand the questions asked on a survey. That is why researchers pretest their questions on a small sample before using them in a larger study. Such pretesting often involves asking the respondents why they answered what they did in cases where their answers did not seem consistent with their answers to other questions. Some researchers give the respondents a chance to comment on the survey as a whole and to offer any suggestions on how to make it clearer or more accurate.

In large surveys where, because of the cost, the results of mistakes are greater, researchers often pretest questions many times on different groups. This practice has the value of showing whether questions are worded well. If the researcher finds unexpected differences among groups, further study may be needed to clarify the reason for these differences.

This strategy was used in the classic study of the authoritarian personality by Adorno, Frenkel-Brunswik, Levinson, and Sanford (1969). Researchers in that study not only pretested their questions and scales on dozens of different groups in various versions, but also checked the responses against other kinds of data through interviews and projective tests. Only items that repeatedly satisfied the criteria of both face and construct validity across many groups and types of data were used in the final measures of authoritarianism.

Use a native expert or key informant

Studies designed to examine the views of people from different nations are more common in some social sciences than in others. Comparing nations is unavoidable if the unit of analysis is society as a whole, or some institutional feature of society, such as an economy, a polity, or a workforce. Comparing societies is also unavoidable if the goal is to show that a certain theory holds universally.

Such comparisons are also useful for cross-sectional correlational studies designed to test developmental and evolutionary theories. The effect of literacy on voting behaviour, for example, can be tested within a single society. However, complete illiterates are few—indeed, deviant—in our own society. Therefore, researchers should compare the effects of literacy on voting in societies with different literacy and voting patterns. This will typically mean comparing modern with modernizing or pre-modern societies.

One of the difficulties in doing cross-national studies is developing comparable measures of the key concepts. Standards of literacy may be higher in one society than in another. Similar problems of measurement attend most social concepts, including urbanization, poverty, satisfaction, freedom, and inequality. One cannot impose the same definition on many different societies. The social meaning of a phenomenon (for example, what it means to earn $25,000 a year, to be poor) may greatly vary from one society to another. People act on the basis of this cultural meaning, so we need to understand the cultural meanings of the people we are studying.

Suppose that poverty for a family of four is defined in India as annual income less than $500 and in Canada as annual income less than $20,000. These different measures give an identical social meaning, but they violate our common sense. After all, certain material differences in lifestyle are associated with these different levels of poverty, including differences in nutrition and life expectancy.

Solving this problem of the two realities, cultural and material, is never easy. As a researcher, you must at least be aware of the forms the problem takes. Doing so means familiarizing yourself with the societies and cultures you are studying. A good way to do this, if possible, is through discussion with an indigenous expert or key informant. We should try to find someone who has lived all of his or her life in the community and is well informed about community activities and sentiments. Such an informant can tell you the ways your key variables are seen in the foreign country and whether your theory is likely to hold there. Most importantly, this informant will be able to tell you whether the measures you plan to use on data from the foreign country will likely have your intended meaning and produce your intended result.

Living with Flawed Data

Prepare for flawed measures

Most social science measures are flawed in some respect. No matter how careful researchers may have been, their measures are likely to be imperfect in potentially harmful ways.

First, measures may suffer from respondent reactivity. As we discussed in Chapter 5, respondents may react to what they think the researcher is looking for and give answers that are more strongly positive or negative than their true feelings. This problem is greatest in research on intimate or deviant behaviour (for example, premarital sex or drug use), attitudes about controversial subjects (for example, capital punishment), or attitudes toward a group that exercises control over the respondents' lives (for example, a workplace manager, the police, or the government).

Some groups are more likely than others to react strongly to certain kinds of questions. For example, immigrants from countries where power is exercised in an authoritarian manner often hesitate to answer survey questions about the police or the government, despite assurances their answers will be treated confidentially. (Sometimes researchers are pleasantly surprised to find that respondents enjoy the opportunity to safely air their grievances, but we can never rely on this reaction.)

Bias on the part of the researcher and especially biases built into the data collection will produce flawed results. This problem includes questions not asked, or asked in pointed ways that discourage certain kinds of answers (for example, "Don't you think the government ought to limit the number of Chinese refugees it accepts?"). However, such biases also include certain types of under-enumeration—specifically, the systematic failure to count, observe, or survey certain kinds of people or behaviours.

Under-enumeration is common in even the best surveys. The national censuses of modern countries always under-enumerate by a large proportion—perhaps 5 to 10 per cent of the total population in North American censuses. People most likely to be missed are the poor, the transient, and the young. Most surveys are likely either to miss these same kinds of people or to find non-random—therefore, potentially biased—pockets of them. Telephone surveys will miss people who do not have their own telephones—again, the poor, the transient, and the young. Door-to-door surveys will tend to select for people who are at home a lot—homemakers, the ill, the unemployed, or the retired. They miss people who are at work, have no fixed address, or are hiding from the authorities (for example, illegal immigrants).

Studies relying on volunteer respondents are also biased. For example, volunteers are known to differ in their characteristics and attitudes, at least toward surveys and experiments, from respondents selected by more random means. Other kinds of biases infect institutionally collected data: for example, police and court statistics on arrests and convictions. These data are well known to over-represent the poor, the young, and the transient and to under-enumerate offences by the well off, the middle-aged, and the socially and economically stable. This is because the rule enforcers, including the police, decide whom to leave alone and whom to process. As a result, certain crimes go unreported and certain charges are dropped. For these reasons, homicide rates are often the most reliable crime statistic, as discretion and bias play little (if any) role in generating the published rates.

Another government statistic that is often widely doubted and debated is the unemployment rate. This statistic fails to consider people who would be counted as unemployed had they not temporarily dropped out of the workforce (i.e., into school or household duties) or accepted part-time or inappropriate work (the so-called underemployed).

Questions asked of the people processed by institutions will also reflect institutional theories about what causes a particular behaviour (for example, mental illness, criminality, delinquency, or drunkenness). For example, questions asked at intake of mental patients into hospitals reflect theories about causes of mental illness. This bias may cause us to neglect variables that may be needed to test a theory.

When social scientists are unable to experiment with ordinary people in natural settings, their ability to devise ideal measures, to control the data collection, and to select a representative sample of respondents will be hampered. They are often stuck with analyzing measures that other people have devised, data collected under unsatisfactory or unrepeatable conditions, and unrepresentative respondents that have been treated as though they were representative.

Know the social processes producing your data

Data can be biased by the ways they are collected. Therefore, the researcher needs to know how data collection has affected the data: what respondents were expecting in a survey, how interviewers were behaving, and how institutions carried out their data collection.

You may be able to correct biases you know about. For example, some sampling procedures are unlikely to capture many poor, transient, or young people. If so, you can get a fairer measure of some attitudes for *all* members of society by giving extra weight to the under-enumerated social types.

However, biases in the data cannot always be corrected after the fact. The best cure is prevention.

Combine qualitative and quantitative measures

Understanding why people do or think what they do is difficult. Qualitative data allow us to understand best because they invite the respondent to speak, answer, or behave in less constrained ways. By contrast, quantitative measures force respondents to answer in certain fixed categories that may not accurately reflect how they feel.

Because of their limited choices, quantifiable answers are easy to analyze with powerful statistical techniques. In this limited sense, quantitative data, because they are more precise, are better measured than qualitative data. What is gained in precision, however, may be lost in accuracy—in the "true-to-life-ness" of the findings. To solve this problem, where possible, researchers try to combine qualitative and quantitative measures of the same thing.

Qualitative measures gained by field observation, semi-structured interviewing, or analysis of written materials (for example, documents, letters, or diaries) can be effectively combined with quantitative measures in various ways. For example, in the study of authoritarian personalities by Adorno et al. (1969) previously mentioned, quantitative data were used to make up scales. Based on these scales, respondents were sorted into high- and low-authoritarianism categories. Then samples of high- and low-scorers were interviewed in a semi-structured, informal way. The respondents also completed projective Rorschach and Thematic Apperception tests, which needed them to make up stories about largely neutral stimuli—in the first case, inkblots; in the second, sparse line drawings of people.

Then the researchers determined whether, in a general sense, the qualitative data agreed with the quantitative data: whether people who scored high on the quantitative authoritarian scales also appeared authoritarian in the qualitative data. The two types of data proved to sort people the same way and, when combined, gave a rich picture of the personality type under study.

Research findings from a single project are rarely decisive. However, our confidence increases if we find the same result independently, using different approaches. Corroboration from different phases of an interview is one example; corroboration of survey findings through equality-tested census data is another. Therefore, whenever possible we should include items in a survey that allow such corroboration.

Develop a summary measure or scale

To test a theory, the researcher should use many less-than-perfect measures than one alone. This allows you to see if alternative measures, taken separately, show the same pattern of findings, or to create a summary measure or scale by combining many imperfect measures. This approach takes advantage of the virtues of each measure while minimizing the effects of its weaknesses. Combining flawed measures in scales makes the final measure of key variables more valid and reliable, and this is as true in the scaling of many quantitative items as in the scaling of quantitative and qualitative items together.

For example, recall the study of family adjustment to chronic illness discussed in Chapter 3. *Family adjustment* is a complex notion that is difficult to assess with a single measure. The direct question "How well adjusted is your family?" will not produce a valid or trustworthy response because respondents may not understand what the question means or may react against it and give false answers. The researcher should ask many subtler, less-direct questions about the attitudes and behaviours considered characteristic of a well-adjusted family.

Respondents should also be encouraged to speak freely, in whatever way they like, about the way their family works. From this you can infer whether the family is "well adjusted" in the sense you intended. Finally, you might want to watch the family interact. Watching it will allow you to assess the quality of communication and emotional interplay.

All three types of data should be used to cross-validate one another. Some families will score well or poorly on *adjustment* regardless of which method is used. In this particular instance, choosing a single summary measure is difficult, but possible. An ideal summary measure will have used many different data sources, each with its own strengths and weaknesses.

The summary measure you select may be a single measure, the one that best correlates with all the others, or it may be the arithmetic sum of scores by a family on various measures. Combining interval- and nominal-level measures arithmetically may prove more trouble than it's worth, but it can be carried out by statistical scaling techniques too complex to go into here.

Exercising Good Ethics

Now that we have considered issues associated with exercising good judgment where your data are concerned, we turn to another problem of judgment: that of exercising good ethics. Any research you do as an undergraduate will be guided and supervised. However, you still need to understand the ethical implications of your work and your responsibilities as a researcher.

Codes of professional ethics arise from the need to protect vulnerable or subordinate populations from harm incurred, knowingly or unknowingly, by researchers interfering in their lives and cultures. As a social scientist, you have a responsibility to respect the rights, and be concerned with the welfare, of all populations affected by your work. In the pages that follow, we will discuss some common ethical problems carefully. These issues are important and we take them seriously. So must you, as a student researcher.

In doing research, as a student, employee, or scholar, you must recognize the debt you incur to the communities in which you work. Equally important, you must not exploit individuals or groups for personal gain. You should be sensitive to the possible exploitation of people in the research, and you should try to minimize the chance of such exploitation in the conduct of research. You must also be sensitive to cultural, individual, and role differences in studying groups of people with distinctive characteristics.

Above all, be sure that you conduct research only within the boundaries of your ability, based on your education, training, supervised experience, or professional experience.

Problems that may arise

Consider some of the ethical problems that arise when people are doing important social research. Below are a few examples that will help you understand why associations of professional social scientists, and national funding bodies and research councils, create rules of ethical conduct.

For access to a major Canadian initiative to promote ethical conduct in research involving human subjects, see the Tri-Council Policy Statement (http://www.pre.ethics.gc.ca/pdf/eng/tcps2/TCPS_2_FINAL_Web.pdf).

Ethnographic studies

Imagine that you are an ethnographer conducting a study of the socialization of children. During your research, you witness one child beating up another. Should you intervene?

Typically, ethnographers prefer to avoid interfering in the situations they are studying. In ethnographic research with children, adult researchers must seek to avoid intrusive adult roles of authority—that is, they must avoid intervening in the processes they are watching. So, if one child is fighting with another child, the ethnographer should not intervene. Keeping clear of such conflicts allows the ethnographer to avoid shifting the power imbalance between themselves and children. On the other hand, it also decreases children's views of adults as advocates on their behalf (Eder and Corsaro, 1999).

Consider a more dire situation: what if ethnographers watch and record the folkways of drug addicts who may be risking contamination from HIV by using infected needles. Ethnographers consider it inappropriate to alter the culture they are watching; yet some consider it harmful to view potentially fatal acts that may be easily prevented (Novick, 1996). Should ethnographers intervene? What is the proper ethical stance?

Studies of vulnerable people

Researchers must consider the ethical concerns that arise when conducting ethnographic research on populations that are vulnerable or submissive to authority. These may include children, disabled people, or people living in "total institutions," such as prisons or nursing homes. Even studies of problem gamblers and other addicted people raise ethical issues because data collection sometimes reveals information about criminal behaviour (for example, embezzlement) or domestic violence. Equally problematic, respondents may come to interviews with the (inappropriate) hope they will receive sympathy and advice, when the purpose of the meeting is only to collect data.

Alternatively, think about the problems associated with studying a prisoner population. How should a researcher solve the ethical challenges presented by issues of informed consent, accountability, and the need to balance the needs and goals of inmates with those of correctional officials when studying prison inmates? Prison inmates in general are characterized by their official lack of power, personal autonomy, and freedom. Anthropological research, if done ethically, helps to empower the subject by promoting the cause of a vulnerable group—in this case, prison inmates. Thus, the researcher may find himself or herself in the middle of a conflict that pits the interests of prison inmates against those of correctional officials (Waldram, 1998). For a review of other ethical considerations in prison research, see Brewer-Smyth (2008).

Some researchers engage in so-called emancipatory or empowering research, which is often used to document and publicize the plight of a disadvantaged population. In doing so, they may recognize a conflict between their activities and conventional research. Core principles of emancipatory research include surrendering claims to objectivity and voicing both the political and the personal. These principles create problems in balancing the twin needs of political action and academic rigour (Stone and Priestley, 1996). In Canada and the United States, social science researchers—and especially ethnographers—have little legal protection against being forced to testify in court or having their data seized. Researchers should be aware of this, both for their own good and for that of their subjects. Researchers must be prepared to face jail if they carry out research that involves certain kinds of information from sources they wish to protect. One researcher, Rik Scarce, was jailed for 159 days for refusing to reveal the content of confidential research interviews in a federal grand jury investigation into vandalism by an animal rights group (Scarce, 2005, 1994).

This risk can be reduced, if not avoided, with a randomized response technique (RRT), which provides anonymity to subjects and *legal immunity* to the researcher. Not only does this RRT protocol afford some protection to both researchers and their subjects, but, in a study of business ethics, use of this RRT protocol has led to far higher admissions of illicit behaviour than did the conventional protocol. Subjects were far more likely to admit deviant or illegal behaviour than they would have been under traditional data collection techniques (Dalton, Wimbush, and Daily, 1996). To see how RRT is used to reduce social desirability bias (giving inaccurate answers to sensitive questions) in research on male date rape, see Himmelfarb (2008). This study shows that using RRT resulted in higher reports of rape-supportive attitudes, beliefs, and sexual aggression among male college students.

Randomized clinical trials

Ethical standards dictate that patients and clinicians should not consent to randomized treatment for the study of clinical therapeutics except under the condition of *equipoise*—an equal or balanced uncertainty about the superiority of any treatment choices compared to others. However, true equipoise is rarely present. Most randomized trials, therefore, present challenging ethical problems. Should some subjects—those making up a control group—be deprived of treatment that may improve their health, merely to satisfy the needs of experimental design? Or, as Avins (1998) asks, should more subjects be assigned to treatment conditions the experimenter believes are likely the most effective? The latter choice is ethically better, but produces more questionable research results.

Reporting unethical research behaviour

What should you do if you discover that another researcher is behaving in unethical ways—for example, misusing research funds or reporting fraudulent results? Should you report this to his or her research team, or tell an administrator, dean, journal editor, funding agency, professional society, or reporter (Wenger, Korenman, and Berk, 1999)? Researchers hold differing views on this question, according to their research experience and administrative responsibility.

However, "grey areas" persist, and many ethical rules are broken or ignored. Professional research communities state many principles and pass rules that cannot be enforced for practical reasons, or because large numbers of community members reject them. The community has to satisfy itself that, for symbolic reasons, it has stated a principle or enacted a rule, though it cannot or will not oversee enforcement. Gradually, ethical rules and principles that enjoy the support of a majority pass into ordinary practice, while rules and principles with little support fall into disuse and are forgotten. Note, however, that these rule-breaking processes of communities are cyclical: ethical concerns return repeatedly, with new solutions being suggested and old solutions revived. Ethical problems never go away, and no final resolutions are to be found.

Protecting people in the research environment

As a researcher, you have a responsibility to ensure the physical, social, and psychological well-being of research participants is not harmed by your work. You should always strive to protect the rights of those you are studying, as well as their interests, sensitivities, and privacy.

You must tell research participants of their right to refuse participation whenever and for whatever reason they wish, regardless of compensation. You should also discuss the potential uses of the data you collect, especially when the data may be shared with other researchers.

Be aware of the possible effects of your work. Wherever possible, you should try to expect and guard against harmful effects for those who have agreed to take part in your research study. Gaining consent from your research participants does not relieve you of responsibility for their well-being.

Informed consent

As far as possible, social research should be based on the freely given, informed consent of those studied. You are responsible to explain as fully and clearly as possible what the research is about, who is undertaking it, why research is being done, and how the research will be promoted. You should take special care when research participants are vulnerable because of factors such as age or social status. You should also recognize the possibility of undue influence or subtle pressures on subjects that may arise from researchers' expertise or authority and consider this in designing informed consent procedures.

You must not expose respondents to risk of harm. Be sure to obtain informed consent when the risks of research are greater than the risks of everyday life. Increased risk may occur in a wide variety of situations, especially when the research threatens to reveal social practices that are illegal. You should not ask people to risk their lives by telling you, for example, about drug dealers in their community, or the members of their immediate family who practise incest or violence. Nor should you endanger them by needlessly seeking information about their contacts in a spy network, or terrorist acquaintances planning to bomb an airport. They have a right to know how you plan to use the information they are giving you and what assurances you can provide that they will not be identifiable as sources. This is especially important for people who live in total institutions—prisons, mental hospitals, military bases, residential schools, monasteries, and (for children) families and schools. Here, they are continuously at risk of observation and retribution if they are viewed as "snitches."

You must tell research subjects that they have the right not to answer particular questions and the right to withdraw without penalty at any point in the research. (This does not apply to cases where informants have a duty to provide information, such as public servants.)

Getting a signed consent form will often serve to verify informed consent. However, in the study of cross-cultural contexts, illegal activities, or politically sensitive settings, it may be difficult or culturally inappropriate to get voluntary (let alone written) consent from everyone in the field setting. Sometimes, getting signed consent forms from everyone studied may violate anonymity and create risks for some groups of subjects. Therefore, the signed consent form may be inadequate or inadvisable in certain circumstances, in which case you should employ culturally suitable methods to allow subjects to make continuing decisions to engage in or to withdraw from the research.

Imagine a situation in which we are studying people who commit fraudulent acts or other kinds of white-collar crimes for which they have not yet been caught. We have found these people through snowball sampling, and they have informally agreed to take part in our study. However, they may be unwilling to sign a document agreeing to take part because, in effect, doing so admits to having committed a criminal act. This could, in principle, be used as evidence against them in a criminal trial later.

When informed consent is needed, you should give research participants or their legal representatives the opportunity to ask questions about any aspect of the research, during or after their participation in the research.

You must explain that a refusal to participate in the research or a decision to withdraw from the research involves no penalty, as well as any foreseeable results of declining or withdrawing. You must clearly discuss confidentiality. When your research needs informed consent, keep records of this consent confidential.

Gaining consent is critically important. However, you may seek waivers of this requirement when (1) the research involves no more than slight risk for research participants, and (2) the research could not practicably be carried out if informed consent were required.

Confidentiality

You have a duty to ensure that confidential information is protected. When gathering confidential information, you should consider the long-term uses of the information, including its potential placement in public archives and the examination of the information by other researchers or practitioners.

You must take reasonable steps to ensure that records, data, and other pieces of information are preserved safely, recognizing that law or institutional principles may also govern people and the ownership of records, data, and information. When transferring confidential records, data, or information to other people or organizations, you should get assurances that the recipients of the records, data, or information will employ measures to protect confidentiality at least equal to those you originally pledged.

The duty to preserve confidentiality extends to members of research or training teams and collaborating organizations that have access to the information. To ensure that access to confidential information is restricted, researchers, administrators, and principal investigators must instruct staff to take the steps necessary to protect confidentiality.

Sometimes confidential information about research participants or clients is entered into databases or other records available to people without the prior consent of the relevant parties. Under these conditions, you should take care to protect confidentiality and anonymity, either by not including personal identifiers or by employing other techniques that mask or control disclosure of individual identities. When using private information about individuals collected by other researchers or institutions, you should protect the confidentiality of details that might identify the people that it concerns. Information is private when an individual can reasonably expect the information will not be made public with personal identifiers (for example, medical or employment records).

Limits of confidentiality

When performing research, you must find out about all laws and rules that may limit or compromise guarantees of confidentiality and limit your ability to guarantee confidentiality. You should tell research participants or others about any limits to this guarantee at the start of the research.

During your work, you may confront unanticipated circumstances where you become aware of information that threatens the lives or health of research participants and others. In these cases, you must balance the importance of guarantees of confidentiality with other principles, standards of conduct, and applicable law.

As a researcher, you should discuss confidential information or evaluative data about research participants only for proper scientific or professional purposes and only with people concerned with such matters.

Confidentiality is not needed for observations of people or activities in public places or other settings where no rules of privacy are provided by law or custom. Similarly, confidentiality is not needed with information available from public records.

Use of deception in research

Do not use deceptive techniques unless the following conditions apply:

1. the use of deceptive research techniques will not be harmful to research participants and is justified by the study's prospective scientific, educational, or applied value;
2. no equally effective alternative procedures that do not use deception are feasible; and
3. you have gained the necessary approvals from your academic institution.

Never deceive research participants about important aspects of the research that would affect their willingness to take part, such as physical risks or unpleasant emotional experiences. When deception is an integral feature of the design and conduct of research, you must try to correct any misconception that research participants may have before finishing the research. This is often referred to as *debriefing*.

On rare occasions, you may need to hide your identity to undertake research that could not practicably be carried out if subjects knew that you were a researcher. Under such circumstances, undertake the research if it involves no more than slight risk for the research participants, and only if you have gained approval to continue in this manner.

Use of recording technology

Gain informed consent from research participants or others before filming or recording them in any form. You may only bend this rule if these activities involve naturalistic observations in public places and you do not expect the recording to be used in a way that could lead to identification or personal harm.

Offering inducements for research participants

Be careful to avoid offering excessive or inappropriate financial or other inducements to secure the involvement of research participants, especially when it might force their participation. Researchers differ widely in their views on when financial inducements are excessive or inappropriate. A higher inducement is needed if the research participant is required to spend more time away from home or if the researcher intends to engage the research subject in activities that are unpleasant. Few interviews or questionnaires fall into this category, so inducements for such research are typically uncommon.

Providing an incentive, whether monetary or not, increases response rates; it also increases response completeness early in the interview (Willmack, Schuman, and Pennell, 1995). For example, a symbolic incentive of $1 raised the response rate in a study of nurse practitioners from 66 to 81 per cent (Oden and Price, 1999). This symbolic $1 incentive has also proved effective in other studies, for example, with exercise professionals (Hare, Price, and Flynn, 1998). It's true that other strategies, such as a letter of introduction or an intensive follow-up, can also increase the response rate (Summers and Price, 1997). However, the modest $1 incentive sometimes proves more effective than a non-monetary incentive (Easton, Price, and Telljohann, 1997).

Where substantial (non-symbolic) incentives are given, increasing them—for example, from $10 to $25—may also increase compliance with interview arrangements. Under these conditions, respondents will keep their appointments and may even agree to be physically evaluated in a clinic (Pavlik, Hyman, and Vallbona, 1996). It also seems that people prefer cash inducements to lottery tickets and charitable donations (Warriner, Goyder, and Gjertsen, 1996). However, under some conditions, respondents prefer non-cash incentives over cash incentives (Shaffer and Arkes, 2009).

In doing research, are material incentives harmful, harmless, or neither? In a classic study of the topic, Grant and Sugarman (2004: 717) conclude the following:

> Incentives become problematic when conjoined with the following factors, singly or in combination with one another: where the subject is in a dependency relationship with the researcher, where the risks are particularly high, where the research is degrading, where the participant will only consent if the incentive is relatively large because the participant's aversion to the study is strong, and where the aversion is a principled one.

The prevailing norms are clear in grant programs governed by the Social Sciences and Humanities Research Council of Canada (SSHRC), or the National Institute of Mental Health (NIMH) in the United States. Here, paid inducements are acceptable, but they must be justified. The researcher is expected to find the "right level" of payment and then to justify it to the funder. Often researchers choose to provide a small gift or honorarium rather than a dollar amount, which might be interpreted, by the funder or the participant, as signalling a pro-rated fee for time worked. This gift is meant only to show gratitude for help provided. Sometimes, gift cards or certificates (for example, to bookstores or restaurants) may be provided, rather than cash. Note, too, that respondents are sensitive to issues of fairness in giving out incentives.

Researchers must be aware of the power and influence they wield when using inducements to conduct their research. A small financial incentive may be innocuous when used to secure the participation of research subjects whose only reason for not taking part in a study is the lack of suitable motivation. In other situations, however, inducements can be coercive and even destructive. Such inducements as money offered to poor people, connections offered to isolated people, or a means of expression (or "a voice") offered to ignored people may be impossible to turn down. At best, these people will be over-studied, and their participation will make for an unrepresentative sample. At worst, their dignity will be compromised, their thoughts distorted, and their lives disrupted. Participants may also fear losing their inducement if they choose to drop out of the study and will, thereby, be coerced into continuing. The social scientist must be aware of this.

Reporting findings

As a social scientist, you have a duty to report results openly, unless they are likely to endanger research participants or violate their anonymity or confidentiality. Social scientists have a responsibility to report their findings accurately and truthfully. You should also make clear the methodological and theoretical bases of the study and state the limits of the data.

Research reports must disclose all sources of financial support for the research and any other sponsorship or special relationship with investigators. However, you must consider carefully the social and political implications of the information you give out. Always strive to ensure that such information is well understood, properly contextualized, and responsibly used.

Recognizing the contribution of others

Thank everyone who has contributed to your research and publications. Attribution—ordering and recognizing contributions—should accurately reflect the contributions of all main participants in both research and writing.

Confronting ethical issues

Finally, if you have any doubts about any ethical problems with your work, talk to a professor or an institutional ethics review committee. They will be able to help you resolve the issue.

Watch your language

Many people today are aware of the language they use when referring to particular groups of the population, including those defined by gender, race, religion, cultural origin, sexual orientation, and physical and mental ability. As a social scientist, you should be aware of the meanings and implications of the language you are using—and exercise good judgment in this area of your work, as in all others.

Gender

Man has been used to refer to people in general for a long time, and academia (long dominated by men) has been as guilty as any other institution of perpetuating this use of the word. You may have seen textbooks that refer to "man's impact on the environment" or taken courses with titles like "Man and Society." However, such use of the term is no longer considered suitable. In fact, using *man* in this way now appears ignorant: women have played as important a role in everything *man* has done—leaving them out makes it appear as though you are not aware of this obvious fact. Using *humankind* or *people* is better, and *women and men* or *men and women* are acceptable substitutes as well.

In addition, *man* is still used in many English compound words that refer to women as well. Such terms are easy to avoid by substituting, for example, *police officer* for *policeman*, *fire fighter* for *fireman*, *synthetic* for *man-made*, and so on. Note, however, that excessive dedication to gender-inclusive language can lead to silly terms such as *horsepersonship* (here it might be better to use something like *equestrian skill*). Also, some words that contain the prefix *man-* are derived from the Latin word *manu*, meaning *hand*. Thus, we have no need to find alternatives for words like *manufacture, manipulate,* or *manuscript.*

Race

You should be able to identify and avoid common racist terms that are more often found in street language than academic writing, even if the term is accepted in common vernacular. However, you must be aware of subtleties in using terms to identify people by their "race," to avoid giving offence.

For example, you must be careful to avoid overgeneralizing based on the geographic origin of racial groups. To refer to someone as, for example, *African* shows that you have little appreciation for the variations among the many different peoples that populate the African continent. It also shows that you have not taken the time to find out where your subject's national origins lie.

Acceptable words also change with time and place. Many writers used the term *Negro* just a few decades ago, but today it has been superseded by terms like *African-Canadian* or, less specifically, *people of colour*. *Black* is also widely used now, but is by no means universally accepted.

Acceptance of the term *Indian*, to refer to the original inhabitants of Canada, has also decreased over the last few decades. The term is still used in some official capacities to refer to people indigenous to North America. For instance, the US government still has a Bureau of Indian Affairs, and some Canadian government legislation still recognizes *status Indians* and *non-status Indians*. (Respectively, these are people who are and are not members of bands that have signed treaties with the government.) In Canadian government, the term *Indian* is still used when distinguishing among the three groups of Aboriginal peoples: Indians, Inuit, and Métis. However, even in this capacity the term *Indian* is becoming less and less common, and many of the people themselves prefer alternative terms such as *First Nations citizen*. When in doubt, be sure to find out the term preferred by the people you are discussing and use that term.

Culture

While someone is born with certain racial characteristics, *culture* is a general term that refers to how people live their lives. No one is born with a culture: a person develops a culture as he or she grows up, based on family and surroundings. When defining a group by its culture, you must consider its language, religion, traditions, clothing, art—even the foods that members of the group eat. These distinctions, in many ways, define who a person is, while their race does not. This is why cultural distinctions are important; your language should reflect your appreciation of this fact.

Catholics and Protestants would not approve of being mislabelled; similarly, a Sunni Muslim wouldn't want to be confused with a Shia Muslim, or vice versa. And while some North Americans may not see the differences between, for example, people of Chinese, Japanese, or Korean origin, members of these cultural groups will not appreciate being confused.

Even within nations, we may find sharp divisions between cultures. Canada is a perfect example of this. To refer, for example, to French Canadians as a particular race is incorrect because they are not racially distinct from most Canadians (the largest percentage of whom are Caucasians), although they do have some cultural differences. Further, some within Quebec object to the use of the term *French Canadian*. In turn, many French Canadians refer mistakenly to most others in Canadian society as *English*, irrespective of their national origins. Be precise: use *race* when that term is suitable, and use *culture* likewise. Always respect cultural sensitivities in your work. As a social scientist, you should promote the understanding of differences between people, not ignorance of these differences.

Summary

With good design, good judgment, and good ethics in hand, you are ready to argue the merits of your theory. Largely, the argument will make itself. If you have thought enough about theory and design in advance, data that agree with the theory will persuade the fair-minded reader without any need for rhetoric.

But research results are rarely clear-cut, and inconsistent findings are commonplace. Despite our best efforts, flawed data are the norm, not the exception. To make a persuasive case—to make sense in social science—you must show not only that your explanation is reasonable, but also that your explanation is better than other candidates. Furthermore, this should be done with style. How to do this is the subject of the next chapter.

7 Arguing and Writing with Style

In this chapter we will examine

- how to develop an argument by putting theory and data together in a coherent way;
- a series of steps and reminders aimed at helping you tell a sound and convincing story;
- the value of making clear and thoughtful points, but also of giving the opposition its due; and
- how to develop your own distinctive voice and writing style.

Introduction

Being able to argue and write with style does not come naturally. It takes time and practice—and learning a few tips doesn't hurt. Following steps and advice may seem constraining at first, but with practice you will become a more creative, critical, and effective writer. Let us begin by tracing some of the origins of clear and convincing academic arguments and writing.

The Classical Ideal: Clear and Simple

The philosopher René Descartes, who published his famous *Discourse on Method* in 1637, believed that anyone is smart enough to learn the truth, so long as he or she breaks down the problem into solvable parts, goes from the easiest to the hardest parts, reviews his or her reasoning, omits nothing, and does not accept anything as true unless evidence shows it to be so. This sounds simple and obvious, but let us consider what this assumes.

Descartes' approach reveals a belief in human powers of reasoning over what faith tells us to be true. The idea that anyone is able to find some truth through logic and scientific evidence is a modern, liberal view. Descartes' belief in reason and science exemplify what historians call *Enlightenment thinking*.

Enlightenment thinkers believed that we can attain rational knowledge of society that is superior to religion, ideology, common sense, superstition, or prejudice. This knowledge will be universal and objective, cumulative and progressive, and the basis for liberation and human betterment. From this comes the *classic stance on writing*.

In their book *Clear and Simple as the Truth*, Thomas and Turner (2011) describe the classic stance on writing style as including the following assumptions:

- Anyone can know and express truth; it is pure, disinterested and universal.
- Expression of the truth is frank and open. The reader is competent and interested, so the writer should be competent and genuine.
- Good prose is a window on the truth. It should be seamless, clear, and exact. Good prose is efficient but not rushed, energetic but not anxious. Every word counts.

These aspects of good writing are not only important in themselves, as means of conveying what you want to say most effectively, but they also show that you have accepted conventions of thinking associated with the Enlightenment, which are central to modern post-secondary education.

Facts do not speak for themselves

The meaning of any fact is not self-evident. It has been sarcastically observed, by the statesman Benjamin Disraeli and by the author Mark Twain, that "there are three kinds of lies: lies, damned lies, and statistics." They meant that even facts can be twisted to suit a desired interpretation. Facts make sense only within a given paradigm, or interpretation. Is the glass half empty or half full? No facts can answer this question. Facts say only how much is in the glass. The rest is interpretation. Do Canadians accept income equality for men and women doing similar jobs? No simple fact or set of facts can answer this question either. To answer it, we must first enter the realm of personal values and conceptual definitions. A complex process of inference from observed facts to conclusions and theories lies between the observed and the observer. As John Stuart Mill (1859: Chap. 2) wrote, "Very few facts are able to tell their own story, without comments to bring out their meaning." Facts always need interpreting. Statistics provide forms and standards for examining data so that the reader can have some confidence in the conclusions drawn.

What statistics show

Francis Bacon (1620: Aphorism xxxvi) established that facts—however difficult to interpret—are needed to understand the world. The discipline of statistics has provided science with an array of tools to analyze facts.

Statistical methods fall into two main types: descriptive and inferential. *Descriptive statistics* are ways of using numbers to describe or convey information about some population or social process. *Inferential statistics* are ways of using numbers, and statistical principles, to determine the strength of relationships between variables and their degree of significance (or non-randomness). Hypothesis testing relies on inferential statistics.

Descriptive statistics help to summarize data in precise ways. For example, a description of how poor and rich families differ in their spending patterns is more informative than the statement that rich families lead a more luxurious life than poor people. For this reason, the study of budgets is informative—whether dollar budgets (how people spend their money) or time budgets (how people spend their time).

Inferential statistics allow us to decide whether findings occurred for the reasons we think—because an explanation is correct—or by chance. The testing of "statistical significance" falls into this second category; however, significance tests do not measure the substantive importance of a finding—they only show whether it likely occurred by chance. Inferential statistical procedures help us to judge the relative importance of explanatory variables. Such procedures (including analysis of variance and regression) are far more valuable for understanding the data than significance tests are. We recommend that you take a course on statistics or consult a textbook in your discipline. We encourage you to explore your data thoroughly, think creatively about it, and seek out the best explanations that unlock the story behind your facts.

Telling the Story

The importance of a literature review

Whatever your own ideas or findings, never undervalue the ideas prevailing in your discipline. If most professionals would agree with your explanation, you are on solid ground. To make sure, do a second review of the literature on your topic. You will already have done an initial review at the beginning of your research. A second review will help you bolster your opinion and refine your argument by making sure the discipline supports you.

Your instructor will not expect the impossible, but you invite disaster if you ignore the discipline's thinking entirely. Make a good attempt to learn what others have said and incorporate their thinking into your own. Your argument will be stronger and more persuasive if you show your reader that there is a body of thinking behind it.

Remember there are at least two sides to every story

In Chapter 3 we noted that in every social science you will find at least two paradigms, or ways of thinking about the same question. This means that to explain your data, you need to take more than one interpretation into account.

Even within a single paradigm, more than one interpretation is possible. To be persuasive you must either argue *in favour* of the interpretation you prefer and *against* the best alternative explanations, or better still, attempt to assimilate both into a single explanation.

For example, Canada's lack of a revolutionary past, and Canadians' deference to tradition and authority, or its "conservatism," can be explained in several ways. One is cultural: Canada has preserved a way of thinking, promoted by eighteenth-century Loyalist settlers and early British immigrants, that was anti-revolutionary and anti-republican (because it was anti-American). An alternative explanation is economic: Canada, economically dependent, first on Britain and then on the United States, has a ruling class that has encouraged subservience. Ordinary Canadians have been taught to accept a subordinate status within their own country and in the world as a whole. This produces the illusion of conservatism.

Any study of Canadian political behaviour, whether a historical study of government institutions or a contemporary study of voting, will need to examine these alternative interpretations of Canada's perceived conservatism. Each interpretation points to a different explanation and to different predictions about the future.

Some scholars prefer to argue in a way that sharpens the distinctions between alternative interpretations. Other scholars prefer to blur the differences, taking elements from different approaches as they seem useful. The philosopher Isaiah Berlin (1953: 1, 2) calls the latter thinkers *foxes* and the former *hedgehogs*, following the Greek poet Archilochus: "The fox knows many things, but the hedgehog knows one big thing." Berlin describes hedgehogs as those who "relate everything to a single central vision." The foxes, on the other hand, are those "who pursue many ends, often unrelated and even contradictory, . . . seizing upon the essence of a vast variety of experiences [without] seeking to fit them into . . . any one unchanging, all-embracing . . . unitary inner vision."

As Berlin shows, both camps have included great, innovative thinkers. Both approaches are useful and defensible, subject to two warnings. First, write for your reader. If the professor wants you to be a hedgehog rather than a fox (or vice versa), do what is desired, no matter your personal inclination. Second, if you are convinced that fox-work—using a variety of paradigms and approaches—is the best way to go, be sure to demonstrate to the reader that you are capable of understanding the distinctions you are blurring. Don't let the reader think you are a fox because you are not clever enough to be a hedgehog.

A good argument will compare at least two interpretations of the same facts: yours and the best alternatives you can find. Be assertive when you present your interpretation, even if the results you obtain do not fit easily within a dominant paradigm, for this may signal an important discovery.

Good alternatives are usually complementary

No theory is ever conclusively right or wrong. It is only better or worse than alternative theories. In fact, some good arguments are complementary: they will fit together, even when they seem to argue opposing sides.

Researchers have two related goals in making an argument: to test a theory and show it to be better than another; and to understand thoroughly the phenomenon under study. In order to better understand a phenomenon, you may have to assimilate the best parts of an alternative theory into your own—recognizing, for example, that *both* cultural *and* economic forces help to shape Canadian political behaviour. Try to create a better theory than the one you started with.

Researchers start with a question narrowly defined within a given paradigm and try to prove their hypothesis right (or wrong) and their interpretations better than others. Observations that don't fit the theory are signs that a more comprehensive way of thinking is needed. Paradigms fall apart when anomalies become too numerous to ignore and too contradictory to accepted thinking. In time, more complete paradigms are created; and understanding progresses.

Come down hard

Do not argue half-heartedly. You may be right and the rest of the discipline wrong; if you are of two minds about an issue, be of two minds assertively. State clearly why a single resolution is not possible. Ambivalence is justified if competing interpretations are equally suitable and a single explanation is not adequate. Like disconfirmatory results, ambivalence points to the need for new thinking, and a broader paradigm.

Dealing with Disappointment

Acknowledge shortcomings

Ignoring weaknesses in your argument will not make them go away. You should always assume that your readers will challenge you on weak points that you fail to address.

Readers who share your view may make allowances and simply judge your work as sloppy. Others, however, may dismiss your whole argument as weak, in which case your work will have been wasted.

Bite the bullet

Your findings may prove your argument wrong. If so, admit it. Do not try to deny what will be obvious to any reader.

Suppose, for example, that you studied the effects of industrialization on people's behaviour. You theorized that the more people interact with machinery at work, the more likely they are to adopt modern attitudes in other parts of their lives, such as toward politics, social relations, and family life. Accordingly, you collected data in developing countries from farmers, small artisans living in cities, and factory workers. You predicted that factory workers would appear the most modern of your respondents, and you measured a great many attitudes and behaviours to test this.

A statistical analysis found that experiences with modern machinery had a statistically significant (i.e., non-random) effect on modernity, but one that was much less important than the effect of education. What *most* appears to modernize people is education, not working with machinery. You were right, but not to the degree you had hoped. The best thing to do is admit it.

Never let a little data spoil a good theory

You may wrap up your writing by admitting that you were wrong, or you might look for the source of the problem in your measurement. But if the problem does not lie in the measurement, you're back to biting the bullet or adopting another strategy of data analysis.

You could move into a relational-study design and look at deviant cases. You might compare highly modern workers with less modern ones to find conditions under which modern machinery does and does not modern-ize attitudes. You might find that modern machinery has no modernizing effect within a traditional factory organization, where traditional forms of authority prevail. Such effects may be *facilitated* by a work organization that rewards expertise, productivity, and excellence, and undermines those old loyalties. In other words, the effect of machinery is suppressed or magnified by the form of work organization. In this case, you will have improved on the original theory and salvaged the argument that machinery modernizes people.

Suppose that no conditions can be found under which the theory holds true. The most honest thing to do is admit that the theory is wrong. Perhaps the error traces back to fundamental assumptions about human nature or social organization. If so, other research based on the same assumptions needs reinterpreting and may be proved wrong.

Admitting that you were wrong may yield more understanding in the long run.

Admit the strengths of opposing arguments

Deal thoroughly with opposing points of view. Assume that your reader will challenge you if you do not. Failure to acknowledge your opponents will weaken the credibility of even your best findings.

It is hard to admit the merits of an opposing argument, let alone think creatively within its framework. Yet this is exactly what you should be learning to do as an undergraduate. Ideally, once your education is complete, you will be able to take any problem within your field and ask, "What would _____ (Marx, Weber, Durkheim, Malinowski, Freud, Skinner, Milton Friedman, Mill, Adam Smith, Rousseau, de Beauvoir, Foucault, bell hooks, etc.) have said about this?" And you will be able to give a reasonable answer. Your education in social science should train you to play a wide variety of intellectual roles. You must learn the strengths and weaknesses of the main theoretical positions in your discipline and be prepared to address them when they run counter to your argument.

Things to Remember
Do not be intimidated by other people's ideas

Admitting that other people's ideas have merit does not mean giving up your own ideas. It can, however, be especially difficult to defend your argument against other points of view if your ideas are unpopular. You must make your points clearly, and give the opposition its due. If you hold distinctly unpopular views and can defend them, do so.

There is no shortage of unpopular ideas that may or may not be true. In particular, ideas about inequality generate angry responses—for example, the ideas that members of certain racial groups are less intelligent than people from other racial backgrounds; that unemployed people show less initiative (are more apathetic) than employed people; or that well-paid people work harder than poorly paid people. Each of these ideas is controversial, not only because each points to inequality but because there are people who might try to use these inequalities to justify broader social inequality: higher pay, higher status, or greater social acceptability for some over others.

Yet empirical studies have found support for these unpopular ideas. Some equate intelligence with the score on an IQ test, and certain racial groups have tested lower than others in some studies. Similarly, some unemployed people *are* apathetic, and well-paid people *do* in some cases work harder. Do not deny such data. Instead, draw appropriate conclusions from them.

If some racial groups have lower-than-average IQs, this may result from poorer access to education or from cultural biases in the IQ tests. The appropriate conclusion is not that members of these groups deserve less pay or respect than others, but that they should be given better education or less biased tests.

If unemployed people are more apathetic, this may tell us less about the *causes* of unemployment than about its disheartening *effects*. Far from deserving less help, unemployed people may need more help in feeling worthy, in mobilizing politically, and in finding jobs.

Finally, if well-paid people work harder than poorly paid people, this may direct our attention to the reasons why people work hard. If hard work is something we want to stimulate, we may need to pay average workers more and give them more satisfaction in their work than they presently enjoy.

By addressing unpopular ideas creatively rather than avoiding them, you may contribute something socially as well as theoretically valuable. Do not be put off by people's aggressive reactions against what you are saying. They may think they know where you are headed, but you have every right to demand a hearing.

Deal fairly with the data

Just as you should not be intimidated by other people's ideas, neither should you argue in an obnoxious fashion. Emotional appeals to decency or common sense count for nothing in a logical argument. In fact, they undermine your credibility by supplying unnecessary rhetoric instead of calm reason.

Our goal is objectivity and value neutrality. At the same time, we should invest ourselves fully in the things we study. Because we argue for things that matter to us, we cannot easily be unemotional. However, once you have chosen a problem that is personally significant, you must deal with it fairly, remaining unbiased and unemotional in your data collection, analysis, and argument. Valid results established in this way can then be used confidently in the emotional, political world of action.

Don't fake it

Be accurate in reporting the literature. If the literature goes against your argument, say so. Do not let disappointment, haste, sloppiness, or an unwillingness to accept your own findings lead you to make assertions that can easily be shown to be false. If your reader takes the time to check your references and finds them incorrect, your entire work will be called into question. Make sure that you always cite your sources thoroughly and scrupulously.

Another form of fakery is the use of tainted authorities to bolster your argument. Examples include published works that lack scholarly acceptance, are taken out of context, or are misinterpreted to your benefit; published data you know to be untrustworthy or irrelevant; and earlier theories that are so general or vague as to be open to almost any interpretation. Published social science research is so diffuse that you can find studies or theories to support nearly any position. At best, authorities can make your good theory and good data look better. They cannot turn a bad argument into a good one.

A second point to remember is that individual authorities have often said a great many things. Many great thinkers have changed their thinking over time, modifying and even rejecting earlier ideas. How to deal with the early ideas and what status to give them is something you should consider.

A third point is that authorities should not be used indiscriminately. Using Marx to support one part of your argument, Freud to support another, and Adam Smith to support a third will not result in a convincing argument. In fact, your three authorities are so different, their concerns, assumptions, and conclusions so at odds with one another, that unless you are exceptionally brilliant you cannot bring them together in a single argument. This is a good reason for working with one familiar paradigm, rather than across several. Try to do justice to one way of thinking.

Lastly, it may be permissible (ask your professor!) to defend your argument with references to scholars from other disciplines—to cite sociologists in an anthropology paper, or economists in a political science paper. But the majority of your references should be to scholars within the discipline for which you are writing. Doing otherwise may suggest that you are submitting the same work for two different courses.

Let other people judge your argument

Once researchers feel they understand the people they have studied, they sometimes tell them what they have concluded. This helps to refine their argument by confronting additional, unnoticed facts or facts that do not fit into their argument. It is dangerous because it tests the researcher in the hardest possible way, but if the argument passes *this* test, it has a good chance of passing every other. Thus, if at all possible, you should try to perform it.

Confronting the people studied is common in applied research. It is not foolproof, however, because the subjects may not understand themselves in the same way that the researcher does. Still, one is likely to learn something useful in this process. Consider a study of Canada's declining fertility. Annual birth records show that fewer children are being born to Canadian women compared to past decades, and that the women bearing them are, on average, older than mothers were in the past. How do we explain this?

We might begin by analyzing existing survey data on fertility decisions to develop and test a theory about the timing and number of children that women are bearing. But the researchers would do well to also conduct intensive interviews with selected samples of women: for example, women who have followed the new pattern (women giving birth in their 30s and having few children) and women who have violated the pattern (women who have borne many children early in life, or had no children at all). These interviews may be useful in checking the theory, illustrating child-bearing decisions with quotations and anecdotes, and most importantly, getting a reaction to the researcher's theory. Such a procedure has the dual advantage of confronting a theory with the people theorized about, and corroborating a finding with various types of data.

Try the "laugh test"

In Chapter 1, we recommended using the "laugh test" to see how persuasive your argument is. Tell your explanation to a disinterested person. If doing so makes you feel ridiculous or provokes laughter in your audience, your argument may be deficient.

The laugh test is not a sure thing. It may prove only that you feel uncomfortable presenting your ideas to others or that your listener is not taking the exercise seriously. If so, find another listener, and try again. You may find that another listener might be able to point out where your argument is not persuasive or where your reasoning seems flawed. Chances are that problems detected by your disinterested listener will not go unnoticed by the person grading your work.

Writing with Style

Writing with style does not mean packing your work with fancy words. Writers known for their style are those who have infused a distinctive voice in what they write. It takes time to develop a unique style. To begin, decide what general effect you want to create.

Taste in style reflects the times. In earlier centuries, many respected writers wrote in an elaborate style that we would now consider too wordy. Today, journalists have led the trend toward short, easy-to-grasp sentences and paragraphs. The most effective style is one that is clear, concise, and forceful.

Be clear

Because sentence structure is dealt with in Chapter 12, this section will focus on clear wording and paragraphing.

Choose clear words

The key to good writing is using clear words. Two tools that will prove indispensable are a dictionary and a thesaurus, easily accessible in electronic form.

A good dictionary will help you understand unfamiliar words and offer sample sentences that show how certain words are used. If you are uncertain whether or not a particular word is too informal for your academic writing, or if you have concerns that a word might be offensive, a dictionary will give you this information. Be aware that Canadian usage and spelling may follow either British or American practices, but usually combines aspects of both.

A thesaurus lists words that are related in meaning. Use it when you want to avoid repeating yourself or when you are fumbling for a word that is on the tip of your tongue. But make sure you remember the difference between *denotative* and *connotative* meanings. A word's denotation is its primary or "dictionary" meaning. Its connotations are any associations it may suggest; they may not be as exact as the denotations, but they are part of the impression the word conveys. If you examine a list of synonyms in a thesaurus, you will see that words with similar meanings can have different connotations. For example, alongside the word *indifferent*, your thesaurus may give the following: *uncaring, apathetic, unconcerned, careless, unambitious,* and *half-hearted.* Imagine the different impressions you would create if you chose one or the other of those words to complete this sentence: "Questioned about the experiment's chance of success, he was _____ in his response." In order to write clearly, you must remember that a reader may react to the suggestive meaning of a word as much as to its "dictionary" meaning.

Use plain English

Plain words are often more forceful than fancy ones. Many of our most common words—the ones that sound most natural and direct—are short. By contrast, some longer words, even if used for centuries, can sound artificial. To start, beware of words loaded with prefixes (*pre-, post-, anti-, pro-, sub-, maxi-*, etc.) and suffixes (*-ate, -ize, -tion*, etc.). These Latinate attachments can make individual words more precise and efficient, but putting a lot of them together will make your writing seem dense and difficult to understand. In many cases you can effectively substitute a plain word for a fancy one:

Fancy	Plain
accomplish	do
cognizant	aware
commence	begin, start
determinant	cause
finalize	finish, complete
firstly	first
modification	change
numerous	many
obviate	prevent
prioritize	rank
remuneration	pay
requisite	needed
subsequently	later
terminate	end
utilize, utilization	use

Suggesting that you write in plain English does not mean that you should never use unfamiliar, long, or foreign words. Sometimes such words are the only ones that convey what you mean. Inserting an unusual expression into a passage of plain writing can also be an effective way of catching the reader's attention—as long as you don't do it often. And writing clearly does not mean that you should avoid all words that have specific scientific meanings. In many circumstances, such words are invaluable for conveying precise and appropriate meanings, and using them correctly will indicate your understanding. Your instructors will not be impressed by the presence of technical language if the terminology is not used correctly.

Be precise

Always be as precise as you can. Avoid all-purpose adjectives like *major, significant*, and *important*, and vague verbs such as *involve, entail*, and *exist*, when you can be more specific:

> **orig.**   The interview involved ten questions.

> **rev.**   The interview asked study participants ten questions.

Here's another example:

> **orig.** Introducing the Universal Child Care Benefit of $100 per month per child under the age of six was a significant legacy of Stephen Harper's years as prime minister.

> **rev.** Introducing the Universal Child Care Benefit of $100 per month per child under the age of six was a costly legacy of Stephen Harper's years as prime minister.

> (or)

> **rev.** Introducing the Universal Child Care Benefit of $100 per month per child under the age of six was a beneficial legacy of Stephen Harper's years as prime minister.

Avoid unnecessary qualifiers

Qualifiers such as *very*, *rather*, and *extremely* are overused. Experienced writers know that saying something is *very poor* may have less impact than saying that it is *poor*. For example, compare these sentences:

> Haiti is a <u>poor</u> country.

> Haiti is a <u>very poor</u> country.

Which has more punch?

When you think that an adjective needs qualifying—and sometimes it will—first see if it is possible to change either the adjective or the phrasing. Instead of writing:

> The company made a <u>very big</u> profit last year.

write:

> The company made an <u>unprecedented</u> profit last year.

or (if you aren't sure whether or not the profit actually set a record):

> The company's profits <u>rose 40 per cent</u> last year.

In some cases qualifiers not only weaken your writing, but are redundant because the adjectives themselves are absolutes. To say that something is *very unique* makes as little sense as saying that someone is *rather pregnant* or *very dead*.

Avoid fancy jargon

All disciplines have their own terminology, or jargon. It may be unfamiliar to outsiders, but it helps specialists to explain things to each other. Precise disciplinary jargon is appropriate for certain audiences, such as your instructor. But sometimes people use technical language unnecessarily, thinking it will make them sound knowledgeable. Too often the result is not clarity but complication. Use specialized terminology only when it helps you explain something precisely and efficiently to a knowledgeable audience; otherwise stick to plain prose.

Create clear paragraphs

Paragraphs come in many sizes and patterns, so no single formula could possibly cover them all, but two basic principles to remember are these:

1. a paragraph is a means of developing and framing an idea; and
2. the divisions between paragraphs are not random—they indicate a shift in focus.

With these principles in mind, you should include three elements in each paragraph:

1. the topic sentence, to indicate the subject of the paragraph;
2. a supporting sentence or sentences, to convey evidence or to develop the argument; and
3. a conclusion, to indicate to the reader that the paragraph is complete, and when possible, to form a bridge or transition into your next topic or paragraph.

While none of these are rules, they may be helpful in improving your writing. Below is some additional advice.

Develop your ideas

You are not likely to sit and ask yourself, "What pattern shall I use to develop this paragraph?" What comes first is the idea you intend to develop.

The shape that follows flows from the idea itself and the way you want to expand it.

It may take more than one paragraph to develop an idea completely. Even for a definition, you could write 1 paragraph or 10, depending on the complexity of the subject and the nature of the assignment. Just remember that ideas need development and that each new paragraph signals a change in idea.

Consider the topic sentence

Skilled skim-readers know that they can get the gist of a book by reading the first sentence of each paragraph. This is because most paragraphs begin by telling the reader what the paragraph is about, or the point to be made.

Like the thesis statement for the essay as a whole, the topic sentence in a paragraph is not obligatory. In some paragraphs the main idea is not stated until the middle or even the end, and in others it is merely implied. Nevertheless, it's a good idea to think about a topic sentence for every paragraph. That way you'll be sure that each paragraph has a definite point and is connected to what comes before and after. When revising your draft, see that each paragraph is held together by a topic sentence, in which the central idea of the paragraph is either stated or implied. If you find that you can't formulate one, it could be that you're uncertain about the point you are trying to make; in this case, rework the paragraph.

Maintain focus

A clear paragraph should contain only details that are related to the central idea. The details need to be easily *seen* to be related. One way of showing these relations is to keep the same grammatical subject in most of the sentences in the paragraph. When the grammatical subject is shifting all the time, a paragraph loses focus, as in the following example (based on Cluett and Ahlborn, 1965: 51)

> ***orig.*** Students at our school play a variety of sports these days. In the fall, football still attracts the most, although an increasing number now play soccer. For some, basketball is the favourite when the fall season is over, but you will find that swimming or gymnastics are also popular. Cold winter temperatures may allow the school to have an outdoor rink, and then hockey becomes a source of enjoyment for many. In spring, though, the rinks begin melting, and so there is less opportunity to play. Then some students take up soccer again, while track and field also attracts many participants.

Here the grammatical subject (underlined) changes from sentence to sentence. Notice how much stronger the focus becomes when all the sentences have the same grammatical subject—either the same noun, a synonym, or a related pronoun:

> **rev.** <u>Students</u> at our school play a variety of sports these days. In the fall, <u>most</u> still choose football, although an increasing <u>number</u> now play soccer. When the fall season is over, <u>some</u> turn to basketball; <u>others</u> prefer swimming or gymnastics. If cold winter temperatures permit an outdoor rink, many <u>students</u> enjoy hockey. Once the ice begins to melt in spring, though, <u>they</u> can play less often. Then <u>some</u> take up soccer again, while <u>others</u> choose track and field.

It's not always possible to retain the same grammatical subject throughout a paragraph. If you were comparing the athletic pursuits of boys and girls, for example, you would have to switch back and forth between boys and girls as your grammatical subject.

Avoid monotony

If most of your paragraph's sentences have the same grammatical subject, you should be careful not to bore your reader. Here are two easy ways to do this:

- **Use stand-in words.** Pronouns, either personal (*I, we, you, he, she, it, they*) or demonstrative (*this, that, those*), can stand in for the subject, as can synonyms (words or phrases that mean the same thing). The revised paragraph on school sports, for example, uses the pronouns *some, most, others,* and *they* as substitutes for *students*. Most well-written paragraphs have a liberal sprinkling of stand-in words.
- **"Bury" the subject by putting something in front of it.** When the subject is placed in the middle of a sentence rather than at the beginning, it is less obvious—and less boring—to the reader. Looking at the revised paragraph, you'll see that in several sentences there is a word or phrase in front of the subject, giving the paragraph a feeling of variety. Even a word such as *first, then, lately,* or *moreover* will do the trick. (This is useful to remember when you are writing an application letter and want to avoid starting every sentence with *I*.)

Link your ideas

To create coherent paragraphs, you need to link your ideas clearly. Linking words are connectors—conjunctions and conjunctive adverbs—that show the *relations* between one sentence, or part of a sentence, and another. They are also known as transition words because they bridge one thought to another. Make a habit of using linking words when you shift from one grammatical subject or idea to another, whether the shift occurs within a single paragraph or as you move from one paragraph to the next. Here are some common connectors and the logical relations they indicate:

Linking Word(s)	Logical Relation
and	
also	
again	
furthermore	
in addition	addition to previous idea
likewise	
moreover	
similarly	
although	
but	
by contrast	
despite	
even so	
however	change from previous idea
in spite of	
nevertheless	
on the other hand	
rather	
yet	
accordingly	
as a result	
consequently	
hence	
for this reason	summary or conclusion
so	
therefore	
thus	

Numerical terms such as *first, second,* and *third* also work well as links (but avoid *firstly, secondly,* and *thirdly*).

Vary the length, but avoid extremes

Ideally, academic writing will have a balance of long and short paragraphs. Avoid the extremes—especially the one-sentence paragraph, which can only state an idea without explaining or developing it. A series of short paragraphs is sometimes a sign that you have not developed your ideas in detail, or that you have started new paragraphs unnecessarily. A succession of long paragraphs can be difficult to read. In deciding when to start a new paragraph, consider what is clearest for the reader.

Be concise

At times you will be tempted to pad your writing. Whatever the reason—because you need to write 2,000 words but have only enough to say for 1,000, or because you think length is strength and hope to get a better mark for the extra words—padding is a mistake. Most professors will not be impressed with unnecessary verbiage.

Strong writing is concise. It leaves out anything that does not serve a communicative or stylistic purpose. Concise writing will result in better essays and exams.

Use adverbs and adjectives sparingly

Avoid the scattergun approach to adverbs and adjectives. Don't use combinations of modifiers unless you are sure they clarify your meaning. One well-chosen word is better than a series of synonyms.

> **orig.**   As well as being <u>costly</u> and <u>financially extravagant</u>, the venture
> is <u>reckless</u> and <u>foolhardy</u>.
> **rev.**   The venture is <u>foolhardy</u> and <u>costly</u>.

Avoid noun clusters

A recent trend in some writing is to use nouns as adjectives, as in the phrase *noun cluster*. This device can be effective occasionally, but frequent use can produce a pile-up of nouns. Breaking up noun clusters may not result in fewer words, but it will make your writing easier to read.

orig.	smartphone utilization manual
rev.	manual for using your smartphone

orig.	pollution investigation committee
rev.	committee to investigate pollution

Avoid chains of relative clauses

Sentences full of clauses beginning with *which*, *that*, or *who* are wordier than necessary. Reduce some clauses to phrases or single words:

orig.	The solutions <u>which</u> were discussed last night have a practical benefit <u>which</u> is easily grasped by people <u>who</u> have no technical training.
rev.	The solutions discussed last night have a practical benefit, easily grasped by non-technical people.

Reducing clauses to phrases or words

Independent clauses can often be reduced by subordination. Here are a few examples:

orig.	The report was written in a clear and concise manner, and it was widely read.
rev.	The report, written in a clear and concise manner, was widely read.

(or)

rev.	Clear and concise, the report was widely read.
orig.	His plan was of a radical nature and was a source of embarrassment to his employer.
rev.	His radical plan embarrassed his employer.

Strike out hackneyed expressions and circumlocutions

Trite or roundabout phrases may flow from your pen without a thought, but they make for stale prose. Unnecessary words are deadwood; chop ruthlessly to keep your writing alive:

Wordy	*Revised*
due to the fact that	because
at this point in time	now
consensus of opinion	consensus
in the near future	soon
when all is said and done	[omit]
in the eventuality that	if
in all likelihood	likely

Avoid it is *and* there is *beginnings*

Try to avoid *it is* or *there is (are)* beginnings. Your sentences will be crisper and more concise:

> **orig.** There is little time remaining for the employees and management to reach a settlement before a strike is called.
>
> **rev.** Little time remains for the employees and management to reach a settlement before a strike is called.

> **orig.** It is certain that crime will increase.
>
> **rev.** Crime will certainly increase.

Be forceful

Developing a forceful, vigorous style means learning common tricks of the trade and practising them until they become habit.

Choose active over passive verbs

An active verb creates more energy than a passive one does:

> **Passive:** The ball <u>was thrown</u> by her.
>
> **Active:** She <u>threw</u> the ball.

Passive constructions tend to produce convoluted phrasing. Writers of bureaucratic documents are among the worst offenders:

> **orig.** <u>It has been decided</u> that the utilization of small rivers in the province for purposes of generating hydroelectric power <u>should be studied</u> by our department, and that a report to the deputy <u>should be made</u> by our director as soon as possible.

The passive verbs make it hard to tell who is doing what. The passage is clearer without passive verbs:

> **rev.** The minister of natural resources <u>has decided</u> that our department <u>should study</u> the use of small rivers in the province to generate hydroelectric power, and that our director <u>should make</u> a report to the deputy as soon as possible.

Passive verbs are appropriate in four specific instances:

1. When the subject is the passive recipient of some action:

   The politician <u>was heckled</u> by the angry crowd.

2. When you want to emphasize the object rather than the person acting:

   The anti-pollution devices in all three plants <u>will be improved</u>.

3. When you want to avoid an awkward shift from the subject of a sentence or paragraph. Using the passive will sometimes help maintain focus:

   The contractor began to convert the single-family homes to apartments but <u>was stopped</u> by the police because a permit had not been issued.

4. When you want to avoid placing responsibility or blame:

   The plans <u>were delayed</u> when the proposer became ill.

When these exceptions don't apply, make an effort to use active verbs for a livelier style.

Use personal subjects

Wherever possible, make the subjects of your sentences personal. Sentences become livelier with active verbs and a personal subject:

orig. The <u>outcome</u> of the union members' vote <u>was</u> a <u>decision</u> to resume work on Monday.

rev. The <u>union members voted</u> to return to work on Monday.

Here's another example:

orig. It can be assumed that an agreement was reached because there were smiles on both management and union sides when the meeting was finished.

rev. We can assume that management and the union reached an agreement because both bargainers were smiling when they finished the meeting.

(or)

> ***rev.*** Apparently <u>management and union reached</u> an agreement
> because, when <u>they finished</u> the meeting, both <u>bargainers</u>
> <u>were</u> smiling.

Use concrete details

Concrete details are easier to understand—and remember—than abstract notions. When discussing abstract concepts, try to provide specific examples; if you have a choice between a concrete word and an abstract one, choose the concrete. Consider this sentence:

> The French explored the northern territory and traded with the Indigenous inhabitants.

Now see how a few specific details can bring the facts to life:

> The French voyageurs paddled their way along the river systems of the north, trading their blankets and copper kettles for furs.

Adding concreteness doesn't mean getting rid of all abstractions; it's simply a reminder to balance them with accurate details. The additional information, if it is concrete and correct, can improve your writing.

Make important ideas stand out

Experienced writers manipulate sentences in order to emphasize certain points. Here are some of their techniques.

Place key words in strategic positions

The positions of emphasis in a sentence are the beginning and the end. To add force, don't put key words in the middle of the sentence. Save them for the end:

> ***orig.*** People are less afraid of losing wealth than of losing face in this image-conscious society.

> ***rev.*** In this image-conscious society, people are less afraid of losing wealth than of losing face.

Subordinate minor ideas

Children connect incidents with a string of *and*s, as if everything were of equal importance:

> Our bus was delayed, *and* we were late for school, *and* we missed our class.

As they grow older they learn to make one part of a sentence less important in order to emphasize another:

> Because the bus was delayed, we missed our class.

Major ideas stand out and connections become clearer when minor ideas are subordinated:

> **orig.** The revolution started and average citizens took to the streets.
>
> **rev.** When the revolution started, average citizens took to the streets.

Make your most important idea the subject of the main clause, and try to put it at the end, where it will be most emphatic:

> **orig.** I was relieved when I saw my marks.
>
> **rev.** When I saw my marks, I was relieved.

Vary sentence structure

One way of adding variety to writing, and making an important idea stand out, is to use a periodic rather than a simple sentence structure.

Most sentences follow the simple pattern of subject–verb–object (plus modifiers):

> The dog bit the man on the ankle.
>   S   V   O

A *simple sentence* such as this gives the main idea at the beginning and therefore creates little tension. A *periodic sentence* does not give the main clause until the end, following one or more subordinate clauses:

> Since he had failed to keep his promises or to inspire the voters, in the next election he was defeated.
>   S   V

The longer the periodic sentence, the greater the suspense and more emphatic the final part. Because this high-tension structure is more difficult to read than a simple sentence, don't use it often. Save it for those times when you want to create a special effect or play on emotions.

Vary sentence length

A short sentence can add punch, especially when it comes as a surprise. This technique can be effective in conclusions, but don't overdo it. A string of long sentences may be monotonous, but a string of short ones can make your writing choppy.

Use contrast

Just as a jeweller highlights a diamond by displaying it against dark velvet, so too can you highlight an idea by placing it against a contrasting background:

> **orig.** Most employees in industry do not have indexed pensions.
>
> **rev.** Unlike civil servants, most employees in industry do not have indexed pensions.

Using parallel phrasing will increase the effect of the contrast:

> Although she often spoke to university audiences, she seldom spoke to business groups.

Use a well-placed adverb or correlative construction

Adding an adverb or two can help to dramatize a concept (but don't overdo it):

> **orig.** After finishing the experiment, he realized he had made a mistake.
>
> **rev.** After hastily finishing the experiment, he quickly realized he had made a mistake.

Correlatives such as *both . . . and* or *not only . . . but also* can be used to emphasize combinations as well:

> **orig.** Professor Miceli was a good lecturer and a good friend.
>
> **rev.** Professor Miceli was both a good lecturer and a good friend.
>
> (or)
>
> **rev.** Professor Miceli was not only a good lecturer but also a good friend.

Use repetition

Repetition can add emphasis and help stir emotions:

> He fought injustice and corruption. He fought complacent politicians and inept policies. He fought hard, but he always fought fairly.

Only use such a dramatic technique on rare occasions.

Use your ears

Your ears are your best critics. Make use of them. Before producing a final copy of your writing, read it *out loud*, in a clear voice. The cumbersome passages will be obvious as you read.

Summary

It is difficult to put all this advice into practice as you start to write. It would be hard to get anything down on paper. Concentrate on these techniques during the editing process, when you are looking critically at what you have already written. Some experienced writers can combine the creative and critical functions, but most of us find it easier to write a rough draft first, before starting the detailed task of revising.

8 Planning and Organizing an Essay or Report

In this chapter we will

- Learn how to choose and analyze a topic or thesis;
- Understand the best ways to research your topic and avoid pitfalls;
- Discuss the standard format of a research report; and
- Show how to make the most of your computer, using popular programs.

Introduction

Writing an essay can be easy if you follow three important steps to guide you in the process. First, find the nugget—the most interesting and valuable point you want to make. Second, set that nugget at the centre of a logical data arrangement, so it makes sense and seems true. Finally, use elegant language and rhetoric to beautify the argument—to show it off to its best advantage.

In other words, writing an essay is like creating and displaying a beautiful piece of jewellery. (I bet you never suspected that!) Yet creating and displaying a beautiful piece of jewellery isn't easy, and neither is writing a perfect essay. Writing a good essay is manageable though; thousands of students manage to do so every day, and we will discuss how to approach that task.

Most experienced writers say the planning stage is the most important part of the whole process. The design, plan, or structure of the essay *is* the story. Just like a household budget tells a lot—almost everything, sometimes, about how people live—an essay plan tells a lot, indeed almost everything, about the essay to come. All the rest, some would say, is ornamentation. The evidence shows that poor planning leads to disorganized writing. In the majority of essays written by students, the single greatest improvement would not be better research or better grammar, but better organization.

Here is an example of an essay outline. It shows evidence of clear thinking and careful planning. As you read through this chapter, ask yourself whether it also meets the other criteria for good essay writing we discuss here.

Sample Essay Outline

Essay Question: Compare and contrast the Chinese and Japanese attitudes and policies regarding modernization starting at the time of sustained European contact but concentrating on the period between 1840 and 1910. How did their status change in the eyes of the Europeans?

I. Introduction
  a. <u>Background</u>: Europe dominated most of the world by 1840; looking to Asia now.
  b. <u>Main Point #1</u>: Both China and Japan resisted Western influence at first
  c. <u>Main Point #2</u>: After opening to West, Japan later begins massive modernization program
  d. <u>Main Point #3</u>: China does not modernize; actively resists Westernization
  e. **<u>Thesis</u>**: Even though both countries were reluctant to modernize at first, Japan's modernization caused it to go from a third-world country to a major world player; whereas China, who refused to modernize, went from being one of the greatest empires in the world to being a resource to be divided among the more powerful nations.

II. Body Paragraph #1
  a. **<u>Topic Sentence</u>**: Both China and Japan had long considered the Europeans to be barbarians and were not interested in goods or ideas from Europe.
  b. <u>Evidence</u>: China—Portuguese traders = "Ocean Devils" = No Trade
  c. <u>Evidence</u>: Japan—Europeans = "Gijin," "hairy, (smelly) barbarians"
  d. <u>Evidence</u>: George III sends trade mission to China; seen as "tribute" by Chinese Emperor
  e. <u>Evidence</u>: Japanese want guns but distrust Jesuits
  f. <u>Evidence</u>: Jesuits (most Europeans) expelled from China over issue of ancestor veneration
  g. <u>Evidence</u>: Japanese Policy of Seclusion (1636–1844)
  h. <u>Transition</u>: Unfortunately, as Western power grew so did their desire to use Japan as a resource and market.

III. Body Paragraph #2

a. **Topic Sentence**: After Japan was forcibly reopened to the West in the 1840s, the Japanese government decided that in order to protect their country they would have to modernize.

b. Evidence: Japanese government sends people abroad; learn everything, come back and teach

c. Evidence: Development of modern constitution

d. Evidence: Lack of resources = development of zaibatsus

e. Evidence: University system—US; Army—Germany; Navy—England

f. Evidence: Japan defeats China (1894) and Russia (1905) = Rising power

g. Transition: Despite their successes, Japan's mainland neighbour continued to refuse to modernize.

IV. Body Paragraph #3

a. **Topic Sentence**: Despite the advances made in Europe and Japan, the Chinese continued to believe in their inherent superiority and saw no need or reason to adopt modern ways, with disastrous consequences for their country.

b. Evidence: Government/Civil Service based on Confucian ideas, not modern

c. Evidence: First Opium War: Open 6 ports to West, lose Hong Kong, British extraterritoriality

d. Evidence: Second Opium War: Open 11 more ports, missionaries allowed, trade on Yangtze, embassies in Beijing

e. Evidence: "Hundred Days of Reform" smashed

f. Evidence: Boxer Rebellion leads to humiliating Boxer Protocols

g. Transition: It was obvious that China was now simply viewed as a carcass to be carved up by the Europeans and Japanese.

V. Conclusion

a. Review of Essay: Japan modernizes and becomes powerful, China does not and gets chopped up

b. Short—term importance: Japan seen as #3 naval power in world (Washington Naval Conference, 1924); Chinese throw out Q'ing dynasty in 1912, form republic

c. Long—term importance: Japan's growth=conflict=WWII; China has civil war=Communist government

Source: Accessed at http://stnk.hicam.net/outline-sample-for-essay.html. Republished with permission of Palomar Community College District.

Keep in mind that an insistence on planning doesn't rule out exploratory writing. Many people find the act of writing itself is the best way to produce ideas or overcome writer's block. The hard decisions about organization come after they've put something down on paper. Whether you organize before or after you begin to write, at some point you need to plan.

Reading primary material

It may be helpful to read some primary material to get a better idea of your subject before you choose a thesis for your essay or report. Primary material is the direct evidence—the books, articles, or research studies or reports—on which you will base your essay. As surprising as it may seem, the best way to begin working with this material is to give it a fast initial skim. Don't start reading from cover to cover; instead, first look at the table of contents, scan the index, and read the preface or introduction to get a sense of the author's purpose and plan. Getting an overview will allow you to focus your questions for a more purposeful and analytic second reading. Make no mistake: a superficial reading is not all you need. You still have to work through the material carefully a second time, but an initial skim followed by a focused second reading will give you a much more thorough understanding than one slow plod ever will.

Choosing a Topic or Thesis

After you have read some primary sources on your subject, you will have enough background information to narrow your scope and plan a tentative thesis. Plan your thesis before you turn to secondary sources—you'll save time and produce a more original essay.

Analyze your subject: Ask questions

Whether the subject you start with has been assigned or suggested by your instructor or one that you have chosen yourself, it is probably too broad for an essay topic. You will have to analyze your subject to find a way of limiting it. The best way of analyzing is to ask questions that will lead to useful answers.

How do you form that kind of question? Journalists approach their stories through a six-question formula: *who? what? where? when? why?* and *how?* Answers to these questions will lead you to other questions. Most early questions and their answers to them tend to be general, but they will stimulate more specific questions that will help you refine your topic and frame *the* central question. The most important question can be posed within your statement of purpose or transformed into a thesis statement, perhaps as a hypothesis. Remember to make your statement limited, unified, and exact.

Try the three-C approach

A more systematic scheme for analyzing a subject is the three-C approach. It forces you to look at your topic from three different perspectives, asking basic questions about *components*, *change*, and *context*:

Components:
- What parts or categories can you use to break down the subject?
- Can the main points be subdivided?

Change:
- What features have changed?
- What temporal and spatial patterns can be observed?
- Is there a trend?
- What caused the change?
- What are the results of the change?

Context:
- What is the larger issue surrounding the subject?
- In what tradition or school of thought does the subject belong?
- How is the subject similar to, and different from, related subjects?

What are the components of the subject?

Begin by thinking about how the subject might be broken down into smaller elements. This question forces you to take a close look at the subject and helps you avoid oversimplification. Suppose that your assignment is to discuss the policies of Justin Trudeau. After thinking about possible components, you might decide to split the subject into (1) domestic policies and (2) foreign policies. Alternatively, you might divide it into (1) economic policies, (2) social policies, and (3) political policies. If these components are too broad, you might break them down further, splitting economic policies into (a) fiscal and (b) monetary policies, or splitting political policies into (a) relations with the provinces and (b) relations with other countries.

What features of the subject reflect change?

Ask yourself, did Trudeau alter his policies in a certain area over a period of years? Did he express contradictory views in different documents? What caused changes in policy? What were the effects of these changes?

What is the context of this subject?

Into what particular school of thought or tradition does this subject fit? What are the similarities and differences between this subject and related ones? For example, how do Justin Trudeau's policies compare with those of other Liberal prime ministers? With Conservative or NDP policies?

As general as most of these questions are, you will find that they stimulate more specific questions—and thoughts—about the material, from which you can choose your topic and formulate a thesis. The ability to ask intelligent questions is one of the most important, though often underrated, skills that you can develop for any work, in university and outside.

Analyzing a prescribed topic

Even if the topic of your essay is supplied by your instructor, you still need to analyze it carefully. Underline key words to make sure that you don't neglect anything. Distinguish the main focus from subordinate concerns. A common error in dealing with prescribed topics is to stress one part while overlooking or minimizing another. Give each part its proper due, and make sure that you do what the instructions tell you to do. To *discuss* is not the same as to *evaluate* or to *trace*; to *compare* means to show differences as well as similarities. These verbs tell you how to approach the topic and shouldn't be confused. The following definitions will help you decide how to approach your assignment:

outline   state simply, without much development of each point (unless asked).

trace   review by looking back—on stages or steps in a process, or on causes of an occurrence.

explain	show how or why something happens.
discuss	examine or analyze in an orderly way. This instruction allows you considerable freedom, as long as you take into account contrary evidence or ideas.
compare	examine differences as well as similarities.
evaluate	analyze strengths and weaknesses to arrive at an overall assessment of worth.

Develop a hypothesis

As we have seen in Chapter 3, the hypothesis plays an essential role in the research cycle, but a hypothesis can also be useful when you are writing an essay that does not require a specific thesis. In fact, most students find it helpful to think of an academic essay as a way of demonstrating or proving a point because the argumentative form is the easiest to organize and the most likely to produce forceful writing. In such cases, your hypothesis can be nothing more than a working thesis—an intended line of argument, which you are free to change at any stage in your planning.

At some point in the writing process, you will probably want to make your hypothesis into an explicit thesis statement that can appear in your introduction. Even if you do not, you should take the time to develop your working thesis carefully. Use a complete sentence to express it, and make sure that the sentence is limited, unified, and exact.

Make it limited

A limited thesis is one that is narrow enough to be examined thoroughly in the space you have available. Suppose, for example, that your general subject is the former and short-lived Canadian Alliance party. Such a subject is much too broad to be handled properly in an essay of a few thousand words: you must limit it in some way and create a line of argument for which you can supply adequate supporting evidence. Following the analytic questioning process, you might find that you want to restrict it by time: "The New Democratic Party in the 2010s is indistinguishable in its social welfare policies from the CCF Party in the 1940s." Or you might prefer to limit it by geography: "The rise of the Parti Québécois had less to do with its politics than with political opportunities emerging in Quebec at the time."

To take an example from anthropology, suppose that your general subject for a 2,000-word essay is the role of religion in daily life. You might want to limit it by discussing a prominent religious ritual in one or two societies. So, for example, you might discuss how ritual dancing in one society directly expresses a prayer for divine intervention in a hunt or battle, whereas in another society dancing has no obvious goal but to promote a sense of ecstasy and social communion. Make sure that your topic is narrow enough that you can explore it in depth.

Make it unified

For your essay to be unified, your thesis must have one controlling idea. Beware of the double-headed thesis: "Prime Minister Brian Mulroney introduced some of the boldest economic policies in Canadian history, but his failure to bring Quebec into the Constitution led to his downfall." What is the controlling idea here: the boldness of Mulroney's economic policies or the reason for his downfall? The essay should focus on one or the other. You may have two or more related ideas in a thesis, but be sure one is in control, with all the other ideas subordinated to it: "Although Mulroney was widely applauded for his efforts to bring Quebec into the Constitution, his eventual failure in this endeavour was the cause of his downfall."

Make it exact

You should avoid vague terms such as *interesting* and *important*, as in "Osama bin Laden was the interesting leader of al-Qaeda." Does *interesting* mean effective or daring in his policies, personally charming, or violent and unpredictable? This is especially true of thesis statements. Don't simply say that "Freud's analysis of dreams is an important feature of his writing" when you can be more precise about the work you are discussing. In this case, you can focus on the kind of dreams Freud analyzed, and what he inferred from them: "In his study of the 'Wolf Man,' Freud uncovered crucial clues about the ways people repress and reinterpret childhood experiences, which come to light in dreams and bizarre behaviour."

Be as specific as possible when creating a thesis in order to focus your essay. Don't just make an assertion—give the main reasons for it. Instead of merely stating, "Many Westerners are resentful of central Canada," add an explanation: ". . . because of historic grievances, such as tariffs and freight rates." If these details make your thesis sound awkward, don't worry: a thesis is only a planning device, something to guide the organization of your ideas. You can change the wording of it in your final draft. Finally, avoid vague and wishy-washy language—often the offenders are adverbs and adjectives—that give you wiggle room but confuse the reader. Check your prose to make sure you haven't abused or overused the following words: *actually, almost, apparently, basically, certainly, completely, fairly, generally, merely, nearly, quite, really, relatively, roughly, simply, slightly, somewhat,* and *very.* Along similar lines, avoid overusing *appear to, seem to,* and *tend to.*

Research Your Topic

Once you have chosen your topic, you may require more facts or evidence, or you may want to know other people's opinions on the subject. In this case, you will need to do some additional research.

Secondary sources

When researching, be sure you have a firm grasp of the primary material before you turn to secondary sources (commentaries on or analyses of the primary sources). If you turn to commentaries as a way around the difficulty of understanding the primary source, or if you base your argument solely on the interpretations of others, your essay will be trite and second-hand. Your interpretation could be downright wrong because at this stage you may not know enough about a subject to be able to evaluate the commentary. Secondary sources are an important part of research, but they can never substitute for your own active reading of the primary material.

Peer-reviewed sources

You may have noticed that some sources such as journals or books are often seen as higher calibre than other "official" sources of information like government or institutional websites, newspaper reports, blogs, and other postings by non-academics. In large part, the defining feature of high-calibre material is peer review. Peer review is an important tool for quality control in the social sciences. It evaluates the quality of research and can help determine what research receives funding and publication (Bornmann and Hans-Dieter, 2006).

Remember that research grants are not primarily awarded on the basis a scholar's fame or history of publication. Far more important, in reviewers' minds, is the significance of the problem studied, the quality of the data collected, the rigour of the data analysis, and the credibility of the research findings. So, a paper that uses unfamiliar or unbelievable sources in its literature review will be distrusted; in fact, the expertise of the author will be doubted. To avoid this problem in your own work, use peer-reviewed sources in your essays: that means articles published in respected, peer-reviewed academic journals, and books written by well-known and well-respected academic authors.

Note, however, that in some circumstances, non–peer-reviewed sources might be useful. For example, it may help your argument if you quote a verified tweet from a political figure on Twitter or cite a television show as an example of popular depictions of disability.

Web sources

As mentioned above, academic articles may not supply all of the information you're looking for, especially if you want the depth that qualitative data can provide best. By contrast, the Internet is vast and is continuously being updated; so one might expect to find everything one needs there. But how should we judge whether what we find is admissible in academic work?

Imagine, for example, that you are conducting research on the prevention of AIDS. You want to find out what information is available, what types of organizations are disseminating it, and who is accessing it. Web-based content is changing all the time, and any academic journal articles that exist on the subject may already be out of date. In this case, you may do better to conduct your research online.

Be aware that unlike academic journals, which are peer reviewed and tend to be reliable sources of information, many websites do not have editorial boards and publish material that has not undergone a review process. Anyone can publish online, as the proliferation of blogs will attest. You need to be sure the author or publisher of any material you use has the necessary authority to lend credibility to the site.

Checking the reliability of material you find online is never easy; however, various strategies may satisfy you that the material is worth using. First, look for signs of credibility or believability. Ask yourself whether the website author provides contact information and any educational credentials you can trust. Is the author or site part of an organization you can trust? If the author, the organization, and therefore the site seem doubtful, the information may lack credibility. You should continue with caution and look for corroborating sources.

Keyword searching

Keyword searching is the most common form of text search on the Web. Most search engines, such as Google, do their text query and retrieval using keywords. A keyword is any word on a Web page. Precisely because you can search by any word in the English language—in fact, any word you can imagine in any language—you need a strategy to ensure you search with the "best" words and the best search engines in order to find the best websites with the most useful material.

To start, brainstorm some keywords that are most likely to capture the ideas or issues you want to research. You may find a thesaurus useful for suggesting relevant synonyms. Finding which ones work best is largely—in the beginning stages, entirely—a matter of experimentation, or hit-and-miss.

Most search engines allow you to do either a basic or an advanced, or refined, search. In a basic search, you just enter a keyword without limiting or modifying it in any way. This is likely to pull up a vast number of responses, many without any obvious connection with your desired outcome. As well, increasingly, you are likely to pull up a lot of advertisements, also without much direct relevance to your research undertaking. You should also note that some search engines give priority to certain "featured" websites based on their own agendas; thus, even if the link is at the top of the page it is not necessarily relevant to your search.

Many search engines also let you refine your search with Boolean operators: these include the terms AND, OR, NOT, NEAR, and FOLLOWED BY. The meanings of these operators should be clear, but here are some examples. Suppose you want to find information on Canada's relations with some foreign countries and not others; you could either define all the countries you want to include (using OR) or define all the countries you want to exclude (using NOT). The term AND means that you wish to see only websites that provide information about both or all of the specified terms: for example, information about relations with both Russia AND China (not Russia OR China).

You can also input phrases or sentences that you think capture the essence of your topic or problem. Suppose you wanted to study 1960s counterculture.

To search this, you might try entering a phrase like *sex, drugs, and rock and roll 1960s*. This may pull up fewer but more usable results than, say, *1960s counterculture*.

If your keyword is a common one, or if it has multiple other meanings, you could end up with a lot of irrelevant hits. Consider any of the common terms in social science writing to see the problem: *class, power, authority, race,* or *sexuality*. Try searching Google on any of these terms and see what you pull up. Most search results will be unrelated to social science research. That's why, when you research, you have to be specific and often use complex search phrases and precise language to get exactly what you want.

The credibility of *Wikipedia*

The Internet is a huge, rapidly expanding, remarkably diverse, and, at times, frustrating resource. It can be an extremely useful research tool if used correctly, but it can be overwhelming for research novices and full of potential pitfalls. You can quickly find huge amounts of material using a search engine such as Google. Type in *arranged marriage*, for example, and you will find thousands of links to websites of varying value. Some will be academic, others will be commercial, and others—blogs, for instance—will be personal. Surprisingly, many in each category are likely to contain useful ideas and references, but each should be used with caution and care. Google has a separate "Google Scholar" search engine to search only scholarly sources, which can be of great use to finding potential sources. One of the most popular sources, which requires your particular attention when you use it, is *Wikipedia*, the world's largest publicly edited online encyclopedia.

Wikipedia's popularity and accessibility attracts both regular, active users—reliable Wikipedians—and vandals. The latter are out to intentionally write nonsense or insert malignant content (suspect edits). Acts of deceit carried out by people with specific agendas and frequent vandalism (mass deletions, for example) and inaccuracy have called some content into question and should act as a reminder to users to handle the source with caution.

Correct or incorrect, suspect or not, the English-language *Wikipedia* receives about 16 edits per minute, with 22 per cent of these coming from anonymous users (Black, 2008). "Wikipedia Statistics" itself says that Wikipedia and its "sister projects develop at a rate of over 10 edits per section." The most recent peer-reviewed studies of its content have, for the most part, found it reliable and valid (Hu, Lim, Sun, Lauw, and Vuong, 2007; Anthony, Smith, and Williamson, 2005). Furthermore, members of the *Wikipedia* community take issues of quality seriously and act quickly to repair and restore content (Black, 2008).

Wohner and Peters (2009) assure us that we can be fairly confident of an article's quality—that is, its accuracy and validity—if it has been frequently edited over an extended period of time and most of the edits have been retained. They base this finding on a systematic comparison of articles nominated by users for deletion, compared with articles deemed "good" or nominated to be a featured article. The worst are articles with the smallest number of persistent (or surviving) edits.

Wikipedia contains a great deal of good material—as good as you would find in any textbook or encyclopedia; and the same is true of Internet materials more generally. But a lot of the material there is poor, invalid, outdated, or biased. Unless you already know a lot about the topic you are researching, you may be unable to tell the good stuff from the bad. That's why you need to be careful when evaluating material in the public domain, like the material found in *Wikipedia*. So, *Wikipedia* and other Internet-based materials may be used as a quick reference when trying to identify key concepts, dates, and figures, but not without verification. Using verified information as a reference or starting point, you should then turn the bulk of your efforts to finding research materials in peer-reviewed sources.

Problems with online databases

Searching online databases like *Wikipedia* is easy, but some databases have important limitations. The greatest of these limitations is the fact that online databases are not always current—even less current than academic journals. In some cases, only after an article has been written, submitted to a journal, reviewed, and printed will it be archived to a database. In other cases, the display of research reports may be delayed or suppressed for political reasons. This is true of government organizations like Statistics Canada (or comparable organizations in other countries) when they are subject to political meddling; and may also be true of non-governmental organizations (e.g., UNESCO, the World Bank, or the World Health Organization) that are subject to other types of political influence.

Second, most databases contain only the article abstracts, and these may not be the abstracts the authors originally provided. The abstracts may have been edited for content, length, consistency, or any one of many other factors. This can make it more difficult to determine if the articles returned from your search are relevant to your topic.

Finally, you will need to have some idea of what you're looking for. Many databases contain hundreds of thousands of abstracts. Trying to browse until you find something of interest to you may make your search far longer and less productive than it should be.

Incorporating unusual sources

The Internet provides an outstanding venue for the inspection of personal postings in chat rooms, blogs, bulletin boards, and listservs, especially when it comes to social science. Always remember that consent may be required if you decide to use these unusual data, especially if the findings are to be made public and the names of speakers (or bloggers) identified. Robinson (2001: 714) notes that "If the researcher adheres to the principles of scientific rigor and the ethical protection of human subjects, these powerful narratives can be appropriately used in qualitative inquiry."

Explore the library

Even with the abundance of research material available online, it's always a good idea to get to know your way around the library. You don't want to be so overwhelmed by its size and complexity that you waste time and energy trying to find information in the wrong places. Most academic libraries have orientation seminars or tours specifically designed to show you where and how to find what you need. Take advantage of these services. Librarians will be glad to show you how to find and access bibliographies, indexes, online databases, and other reference tools for your field of study. Once you are familiar with these resources you will be able to check systematically for available material.

Library materials are often also accessible through your college or university website. Typically, your college or university library will have subscribed to hundreds of electronic databases, portals, and e-journals. So, for example, you will likely be able to access such databases as Sociological Abstracts, PsycINFO, or MEDLINE electronically, even from the comfort of your own home. This enables you to carry out a thorough, lengthy literature review at any time of day or night, in your pyjamas or underwear, if you like. If you are unfamiliar with how to access and navigate these sorts of databases, ask your reference librarian or sign up for a tutorial at your school's library.

Take good notes

Finding your research material is one thing; taking notes that are dependable and easy to use is another. More and more, students are using computers for note-taking. Students should be wary of the disadvantages of solely using computers, such as the ever-looming possibility of system crashes, and should always keep backup files and hard copies. However, most students have computer access most of the time, and the advantages of taking notes on a computer far outweigh their disadvantages.

For one thing, using a computer enables you to revise and reorganize your material endlessly in little time, with little trouble. What's more, you can easily access your computerized notes using keywords, so you can rapidly find everything you collected on a given topic. Existing software programs are designed to do exactly that with large bodies of research data collected by professionals. You can keep your notes in individual files the same way you would write them out on an index card. If you're taking notes from an online source, remember to include the full URL and the date you accessed the site. Get used to using your computer creatively. It will make your research process faster and easier.

With time, you will develop your own method. Some students prefer the index-card system. Each new idea or piece of evidence is recorded on a separate card. The number you will need depends on the range and type of your research. When you've finished note-taking, you can easily arrange the cards in the order in which you will use them.

Whatever method you use, remember that exact records are essential for proper footnotes. For every entry, check the bibliographic details are complete, including the name of the author, title of the source, place and date of publication, and page number, as well as the library call number. For online sources, record the URL in full and the date you accessed the site. Nothing is more frustrating than using a piece of information in an essay only to find that you aren't sure where it came from. If you take several ideas from one source, you can put the main bibliographic details about the author and work on one card or type it into one document, and then use a separate card or document for each particular idea or theory.

Also remember to check that quotations are copied precisely and include page numbers for every reference. Even if you paraphrase or summarize the idea rather than copy it word for word, a page number should be referenced.

McRoberts, Kenneth. 2001. <u>Catalonia: Nation Building Without a State.</u> Toronto: Oxford.

- Compares the "Catalan Law" to Quebec's <u>Charte de la langue francaise</u>:

    "The Charte requires that <u>all</u> outdoor advertising be exclusively in French; the <u>Llei de Politica Linguistica</u> applies to advertising only in public institutions." (pg. 157)

    [DP302.C68 M32]

The previously unheard-of convenience of modern research is not to be taken for granted: it has revolutionized scholarship over the last 20 years. More importantly, it has raised the expectations of your graders and instructors. You will now be expected to provide appropriate, up-to-date references on any topic you are writing about. And remember, your grader can easily find references online; you can't get away with using mouldy references from 1972, 1985, or even 1998 anymore, just because your older sister (or mother) used them. If you are using a reference from an earlier millennium, be sure you can justify the article referenced as "a classic" or "the most recent," or at least, "the most appropriate" reference.

Research Reports

Research reports in the social sciences follow certain conventional patterns. They differ in many respects from essays and book reports and are similar to scientific or technical writing in the "hard sciences." A typical report consists of four sections—*Objectives, Background, Methods,* and *Results*—that mirror the stages of the research project itself as we have outlined them in this book: design, theory, measurement, and argument. We will discuss each of these in turn as they relate to the writing of a research report.

Objectives (Design)

The first section of a research report is typically called *Objectives* or *Goals* or *The Research Problem*. It corresponds to the part of the research project we have called *design* in that it provides a general overview of the structure of the research task. This section states the topic to be discussed or the question to be answered. It also indicates whether the goal of the report is an unstructured description and exploration or one of the more highly structured approaches we have discussed at length: explanation, prediction, examination of conditional relationships, or study of a system of relationships.

An author may also use this section to indicate the anticipated practical or theoretical value of the research he or she has done. Where the research is justified on the grounds of its social utility, the author may want to provide some facts about the magnitude of the problem to be solved and the ways in which the research may help to solve it. Where the value of the research lies in its contribution to a scholarly debate, the author can lead directly into the next section of the paper, the "literature review," which is a close discussion of these debates.

So, for example, you might begin a research paper on teenage suicide by stating that your purpose is to gather and analyze comparative cross-national data on recent trends. You might suggest practical benefits that may flow from such knowledge—for example, steps that governments or schools might take to reverse the trend in countries with the fastest growing suicide rates. You might also suggest theoretical benefits that may follow—such as a better understanding of the ways certain social or cultural factors (e.g., excessive competitiveness in school performance) may contribute to the problem.

Background (Theory)

The next section of a research report, typically called *Background* or *Previous Research* or *Literature Review*, reflects the *theory* behind research. Its purpose is to review, in a brief but systematic manner, the current state of knowledge about the problem under consideration.

To write this section you must first review the literature. In many areas, the existing literature is voluminous, running to hundreds or even thousands of books and articles. Worse, these materials may be spread through dozens of different sources. For example, you could look for literature on teenage suicide in journals and books in the fields of sociology, psychiatry, psychology, social work, family studies, epidemiology, and family medicine, to name only a few! You can't carry out a credible literature review using the hit-and-miss method of rummaging through a few textbooks in a single field of social science.

Literature reviews

As we discussed in Chapter 3, a literature review will inform you of the current state of knowledge in your chosen area. All good primary research begins with a literature review to ensure that a study being contemplated has not already been done elsewhere.

Literature reviews may also reveal far more than the results of previous research. They may indicate trends in research and show what questions are being asked and why. They may also illustrate gaps in the existing research, which may give you some ideas for a research topic. Many outstanding scholars have been inspired by questions that have not yet been asked. Others have worked to expand upon research done by their intellectual predecessors.

Literature reviews, until recently, required considerable time and effort. Today, however, with the availability of so much information on the Internet and in various electronic databases, comprehensive searches can be done quickly and easily. As secondary research becomes increasingly easy, more professors will expect you to demonstrate that you've done a thorough review of the literature.

Accuracy of data

Having judged your research material credible, you want to assess its accuracy or correctness. Is the information provided up to date and comprehensive? Are the quotes or statistics from last year (even better, last week) or from 1972? Older data are fine if they are unlikely to have changed: it doesn't matter much whether you take the 1971 population of Canada from a source dated 1975 or a source dated 2005. However, it matters a great deal if you want current estimates of drug use in Canada, acceptance of homosexuality, support for the Conservative Party, or percentage of couples living common-law. That's because all of these things change from decade to decade, sometimes even from year to year. In these cases, older data are unsatisfactory, and a website that provides older data is not credible, let alone accurate.

As well, to judge if the source is suitable for your needs, ask yourself why the website was created. For example, a website that contains only research showing the negative aspects of divorce, homosexuality, or premarital sex may have an alternative agenda or target audience and is, therefore, no place to find sociological evidence about the state of modern families. The source is biased, not objective and even-handed. Ask yourself whether the information provided is reasonable, fair, and objective. Unless you want to document the existence, types, and extent of bias, stay away from sources that are obviously biased. "Listen" to the website's tone. Is the tone calm and reasoned, or is it passionate and dogmatic? A good academic or informational website should at least sound unbiased and neutral. If not, it probably cannot be trusted to deliver the facts you need.

Sometimes, a website's URL will contain elements that suggest the source of the content. For example, the domain name *.gov* often indicates a government source, while *.com* may indicate a commercial site, and *.org* may reveal that a particular organization is behind the site. Yet the Internet is always changing, and the naming of websites and their domain names may not always correctly indicate the reliability of your source. In June 2008, the Internet Corporation for Assigned Names and Numbers (ICANN) made sweeping changes to the way top-level domains (TLDs) are assigned. The next several years should see a less structured approach, with virtually any TLD allowed. However, until the new system is widely adopted, domain names will provide you with some means of assessing the nature of a site and how reliable it might be.

In short, here is some general advice:

- Determine the currency of the site. There should be a clear indication of the date when the material was written, the date when it was published, and the date when it was last updated.
- Evaluate the accuracy of the information by checking facts and figures with other sources. Data published on the site should be documented in citations or a bibliography, and research methods should be explained.
- Be wary of blogs. Some companies have official blogs that can offer good advice about subjects such as the stock market or real estate, but many blogs are simply online diaries published by a rapidly increasing number of people who are expressing personal opinion and nothing

more. Using such unverified material can seriously undermine your essay, as many students have discovered.

- Assess the overall quality of the site as indicated by its level of correctness and writing standard.

Methods (Measures)

The next section of the research report, typically called *Methods*, may include subsections called *Indicators* (or *Measures*), *Sampling*, and *Data Collection*. This is the section in which you state the hypotheses you wish to test.

Returning to our example of teenage suicide, the literature may show that suicides by teenagers are most common around exam time; that suicide notes reflect teens' concerns with academic and other kinds of personal failure; and that suicide is more common among career-conscious middle-class teens than among job-conscious working-class teens. These findings would suggest the following hypotheses:

A. Teenage suicide will rise in periods when adults are expressing the greatest concern about the job market and their children's career prospects, and it will decline in periods of economic prosperity; and

B. Teenage suicide will be greatest in countries where educational *streaming* is most severe—that is, where a child's life chances will be largely determined by a set of exams taken in adolescence.

Hypothesis *A* predicts that North American suicide rates for teenagers will be highest in the periods 1975–85 and 1929–39 (i.e., periods of high unemployment), while hypothesis *B* predicts that suicide rates for teenagers will be higher in Japan, France, and England (where educational streaming prevails) than in Canada and the United States (where it does not). Your research goal is now to test these hypotheses.

Your goal will be to collect thorough and reliable data on teenage suicide in different times and places. To do this, you will have to access published, official statistics. You will have to make sure that these statistics are comparable: for example, that they define death by suicide in the same ways and provide statistics for the same age groupings. Where the data are not strictly comparable, this should be clearly stated and they must be adjusted to be as comparable as possible. This section of the paper is often long and complex, especially if you have had to create a special data-collection instrument or procedure for coding published statistical data.

Results (Argument)

The final section of a research paper is typically called *Results* or *Findings*, with subsections often headed *Data Analysis*, *Discussion*, and *Conclusions*. Taken together, these make up the portion of the report that we have called the *argument*. Its purpose is to present and interpret the data collected; to judge whether they supported the hypotheses; and, based on that judgment, to draw conclusions about the theory that gave rise to the hypotheses. This section—and the report itself—may end with a modified version of the original theory, some shortcomings of your study, and suggestions for further research that will test the revised theory.

For the example of teenage suicide, we may find that our hypotheses are partly valid and partly invalid. The data may show that although teenage suicide rates were higher during the recession of 1975–85 than during the boom of 1955–65, both rates were higher than during the Depression of 1929–39. Likewise, they may show that although teenage suicide rates are consistently higher in Japan and France than in Canada and the United States, they are not higher in England than in Canada; and further, they may show the difference in rates between Canada and the United States is as great as that between the United States and Japan. These findings, while partly supporting our theory, contain too many anomalies for comfort.

The next task would be to try to account for these anomalies. Was the original theory wrong? Or do some other factors, yet unexamined, also enter into the explanation? If the latter, what might these factors be, and how might we conduct a project to determine whether they are contributing to teenage suicide?

A good research project reaches backward and forward: backward, by situating itself in the existing literature of competing findings and theories; forward, by contributing new findings, revised theories, and suggestions for further research that will refine our understanding of the topic. It may be too much to expect that a student research paper will provide a breakthrough in knowledge, or even a significant reinterpretation of the problem. However, it should at least demonstrate a grasp of the purposes, conventions, and techniques of social science research, however miniaturized.

Sometimes it helps to review samples of research reports before starting on your own. Many examples are available online, including reports issued by Statistics Canada. You can access some of the most recent health reports by visiting http://www.statcan.gc.ca/pub/82-003-x/4060784-eng.htm. From there you can access health research reports, available as PDF files, on a wide range of topics. In fact, you may do well to browse the Statistics Canada website (http://www.statcan.gc.ca/) when working on any number of research topics.

Abstracts and proposals

You will note that most articles in a scholarly journal begin with a brief *abstract*, which provides a summarized version of the entire report. About one double-spaced page in length, this section is extremely useful for the reader, as you will understand once you have conducted a literature review. Abstracts are not always required for student work, but writing an abstract may also help you to see what you have accomplished. In an applied-research report written for government or business, such an abstract is expanded to several pages and is called an *Executive Summary*. Because most readers only read this part closely, it assumes a great deal of importance for the researcher. Learning how to write a proper abstract may come in handy later on in your report-writing career.

At the moment you may be thinking: "I'll *never* have a report-writing career!" You may be surprised to find that once you're in the workforce, a wide range of employers will expect you to write reports. For example, an American study found that two-thirds of salaried employees in large American companies and more than two-thirds of professional state employees have some writing responsibility (Flink, 2007). Employers may also ask you to write *research proposals*, when applying for funding from various sources. Research proposals are typically detailed and formal responses to various agencies' calls for the development of new research often aimed at generating new knowledge in an area of need.

The key thing about writing a good research proposal is to address all of the questions or concerns expressed in a Request for Proposals. So, for example, if a Request for Proposals calls for research that will measure and explain the extent of child poverty among five different subgroups of a city's population, be sure that your proposal does just that: namely, specifies the five different subgroups in the specified city, says how it will measure child poverty in each of those groups, and says how (and with what variables) it hopes to explain poverty.

If you are doing student research that has asked you to specify both the research problem and the research design, be sure to match up what you say you are going study with specifically how you are going to study it: why the problem is important, how you will obtain the data, how you will analyze those data, and last but not least, why you are convinced you have the resources (time, money, experience, contacts, etc.) to carry out this research plan.

That is because proposals are judged based on many factors, including (but not limited to) fit to the call; importance; quality and novelty of the scientific case; track record of applicant(s) and/or their potential within the field; value for the money granted; ethical considerations; general research approach; partnerships with other research councils, industry, and charities; and predicted long-term outcomes arising from the proposed studies (Davey, 2007). Many suggestions and examples of successful research proposals may be found online (also see Davey, 2007; Vivar, McQueen, Whyte, and Armayor, 2007; Molfese, Karp, and Siegel, 2002).

We should finish this brief discussion by reminding you that doing a good job on a small problem (or a small portion of a big problem) is better than doing a poor job on too big a problem. Remember too that every research project will get bigger than you had anticipated as you carry it out. So start small and let the project grow. If you do this with a problem worth researching, you cannot fail to produce something of value.

Making the Most of Your Computer

Computers are invaluable at all stages of the research process, from the literature review, through data collation and analysis, to the final production of your report. Computers cannot make you a better writer, but they can be extremely useful by letting you revise your work quickly and easily. They will also help you produce clear and attractive tables, charts, and graphs to present your results. In this section, we discuss the features of some common programs that will be of use to social science researchers. We encourage you to explore these tools and learn to use them to help make your data as professional in its appearance as it has been in its collection.

Back up your files!

Murphy's Law says that what can go wrong, will. What seems more common to professors is that what can go wrong the night before a paper is due, will. The trick is not keeping all of your eggs in one basket. Save your work regularly in case of a power outage or system crash and make backup copies at the same time. You can also email yourself a copy of the file, thereby storing it on your email server. Some websites let you store files on them. On Dropbox.com, for example, accounts are free. It can be handy to be able to access your files from any computer with Internet access, so that no matter where you are, you can get to your work if you have to.

Using word processors to edit your work

Most word processors will let you track changes to your documents. This feature is handy when you are co-authoring a report, revising successive drafts of a document, or even letting a friend or colleague proofread your work. It enables you to see exactly what someone thought should be added or cut, and then you can decide to keep—or delete—the proposed changes.

Your word processor will have a built-in spell-checker and grammar checker, but be warned: computers find only the obvious mistakes. Computers can't catch the *wring* word, only *works* that aren't in its dictionary—see what we *bean*? Always proofread your work thoroughly, and have someone else proofread your work as well. Your work (we hope) makes sense to you, and knowing what you wrote makes it difficult to see your own mistakes; another reader will help you find places where you have not been clear.

Using spreadsheets

A spreadsheet program lets you input data into a table and perform calculations on it. You can enter a column of numbers and have the spreadsheet determine sums and averages, among hundreds of other functions. Most usefully, the table updates all of its calculations as you work with the data, so you'll immediately be able to observe the effects of manipulating the data across all of your work.

Spreadsheets also come with features that let you produce charts and graphs of your data in seconds. You select which data you would like to represent graphically and in what form you would like to present them (pie chart, bar graph, etc.), and the computer does the rest. Your graphics will also be updated automatically as you work with the source data in the tables.

Spreadsheet software is indispensable in social science research. Not only does it allow you to sort and update your data; it gives you a tool to enhance your assignments with graphs and charts.

Using graphic presentation software

Graphic presentation software, such as PowerPoint, enables you to place text and graphics in slides that can be either projected onto a screen or displayed on a computer monitor, and shown in sequence to an audience. Throughout your academic career and beyond, you will need to present information to different audiences. Spending some time to learn how to do it effectively using the latest technology is a worthwhile investment.

The following are things to keep in mind when using presentation software:

- Be consistent in the styles you use for lettering and formatting.
- Use colour wisely. Certain colours—yellow and orange, for instance—are hard to read unless you're using a plain, dark background. Don't overuse colours by using different colours for each slide. A consistent use of colour makes a stronger impression.
- Choose a simple, clean, readable font. Sans serif fonts such as Tahoma or Arial are among the better ones to use. Times New Roman is also very popular.
- Use a size of type that can be read with ease from the back of a room. You may wish to try several sizes before identifying the best size for your purpose.
- Don't overload any slide with too many words. Use point form to create succinct statements, and avoid embellishments. Don't include anything that is not essential to the information being conveyed.
- Finally, don't be seduced into using only the ready-made templates available with your software. Think differently. Spend some time considering exactly what you want to show and how you want it to appear. Formatting the slides yourself guarantees that you will get the look you want.

Don't let the system rule your thinking

Your computer can make your work look great, but don't be fooled into thinking that fancy graphics and a slick presentation replace intelligent thinking. Your paper must be well organized and your data clearly presented; laying it out neatly and adding graphics are just finishing touches. The computer is an extremely useful tool, but most of all, your professor will want to see that you've been using your head!

Summary

As we have repeatedly stressed throughout this book, good writing in the social sciences is not magic or the result of good luck. Instead, it is the result of careful thinking, planning, and execution. This chapter has discussed the problems you face in planning an essay, then finding and evaluating the data you need to write your planned essay. While the Internet has made finding evidence much easier than ever before, it has significantly complicated the problem of evaluating your evidence, for the Internet contains every kind of information from hidden jewels to flagrant rubbish. We can offer no simple formula for separating jewels from rubbish, because rubbish is often dressed up in fancy language to persuade the unwary searcher. So, searching, like planning, is a skill that takes time and effort to develop. In this chapter, we have made a start in that direction.

9 Writing an Essay, Proposal, or Exam

In this chapter we will examine

- strategies for organizing your research, thinking, and writing into clear and coherent essays and exams; and
- plagiarism and how to avoid it.

Introduction

Success in your courses will be determined by your ability to write clear and convincing essays, present your work persuasively to others, and show that you have understood and are able to integrate course material in exams. These skills take time to perfect, so essays and exams are often sources of stress for students. They don't have to be. Careful preparation, thoughtful organization, a few simple rules, and a great deal of practice will help you.

Writing an Essay

Whichever method you use to collect data for an essay, you will end up with a collection of research findings on your topic. You now need to put these into meaningful order. To start, you should be looking for

- findings that are repeated so often as to seem undisputable;
- findings that are disputed or opposed (anomalies); and
- theories that seek to explain these findings.

Reflect upon some of the interesting patterns and anomalies in your findings, and then think about how they link back to your original theory or hypotheses. It is often easiest to start the writing process with an outline.

Creating an outline

Writers differ in their need for a formal plan. Some never use an outline, while others maintain they can't write without one; most fall somewhere in between. Because organization is a common problem in student papers, it's a good idea to start with a plan. The exact form it takes will depend on whether you are defining, classifying, or comparing. We will discuss these terms in more detail later in the chapter.

If you have problems with organizing material, your outline should be detailed, formal, and written in complete sentences. On the other hand, you may find it's enough just to jot down a few words on a scrap of paper. For most students, an informal, well-organized outline in point form is most useful:

I. Introduction
   THESIS: When Prime Minister Pierre Elliott Trudeau first came to power in Canada, his personal style was seen as an asset; however, by the '80s the same style was increasingly seen as a liability.

II. Trudeau's early style perceived in a positive light
   A. Charismatic
      1. Public adulation; "Trudeaumania"
      2. Media awe
   B. Intellectual
   C. Tough
      1. Handling of journalists
      2. Handling of Quebec
   D. Anti-establishment
      1. Swinging lifestyle
      2. Disregard for government traditions

III. Later reversal: Trudeau's image becomes a liability
   A. Irritating
      1. Public opinion polls
      2. Media disenchantment
   B. Out of touch with economic reality
   C. Confrontational
      1. With individual dissenters

      2. With premiers

      3. With Opposition leaders

   D. Arrogant

      1. Extravagant lifestyle in time of recession

      2. Autocratic approach to governing

  IV. Conclusion

The guidelines for this kind of outline are simple:

- **Code your categories.** Use different sets of markings to establish the relative importance of your entries.
- **Categorize according to importance.** Make sure that only items of equal value are put in equivalent categories. Give major points more weight than minor ones.
- **Check lines of connection.** Make sure that each of the main categories is linked to the central thesis. Then see that each subcategory is linked to the larger category that contains it. Establishing these connections is the best way of making your paper convincing and cogent. It keeps you on topic and focused.
- **Be consistent.** In arranging your points, be consistent. You may choose to move from the most important point to the least important, or vice versa, as long as you follow the same order every time.
- **Use parallel wording.** Phrasing each entry in a similar way will make it easier to be consistent in your presentation.
- **Be logical.** While checking for connection and organizational consistency, ensure that the overall development of your work is logical. Does each heading, idea, or set of data flow into the next, leading the reader through your material in a logical manner?

A final word

It is likely that your outline will change throughout the writing process. Your outline is not meant to restrict your thinking but instead to provide you with a roadmap for where you are heading. Like a good map, a clear outline prevents frustration and dead ends. At the same time, the act of writing will usually generate new ideas, so be ready to modify your original plan. Just remember that any revisions must maintain the consistency and clear connections required for a unified essay.

The Writing Stage

Writing the first draft

Rather than strive for perfection from the beginning, most writers find it easier to compose a first draft relatively quickly and do extensive revisions later. Never treat your first draft as the final copy. Skilled writers know that revising is one of the most important parts of the writing process, and that care taken with revisions makes the difference between a mediocre essay and a good one.

You don't need to write all parts of the essay in the order in which they are to appear in the final copy. In fact, many students find the introduction the hardest to write. If facing the first blank page frightens you, leave the introduction until later and start with the first idea in your outline. If you haven't been able to draw up an outline, just charge ahead. Try starting with a simple "My initial thoughts on this topic are . . .". Don't worry about grammar or wording. The object is to get your writing juices flowing.

You will probably need to do a great deal of reorganizing, but at least you will see words on a page. Many experienced writers—and not only those with writer's block—find this the most productive way to proceed.

Developing your ideas: Some common patterns

The way you develop your ideas will depend on your essay topic, and essay topics can vary enormously. Even so, most essays follow one or another of a handful of basic organizational patterns. Here are some common patterns and ways to use them effectively:

Defining

Sometimes a whole essay is an extended definition, explaining the meaning of a term or concept that is complicated, controversial, or important to your field of study: for example, *nationalism* in political science, *monetarism* in economics, or *culture* in anthropology. You may want to begin a discussion of a topic by defining a key term, and then shift to a different organizational pattern. In either case, make your definition exact. A good definition builds a kind of verbal fence around a word, herding together related elements and cutting off outsiders.

For a discussion of a term that goes beyond a bare definition, you should give concrete illustrations or examples. You can also identify various uses of the term within your discipline. Depending on the nature of your essay, these could vary from one or two sentences to several paragraphs or even pages. If you are defining *monetarism*, for instance, you would probably want to discuss at some length theories of leading monetarists.

It's useful to point out the differences between the term in question and others that are connected or often confused with it. For instance, if you are defining *deviance* you might want to distinguish it from *crime* or *criminality*; if you are defining *religiosity* you might want to distinguish it from *spirituality* or *fundamentalism*.

Classifying

Classifying means dividing something into its separate parts according to a given principle of selection. The principle or criterion may vary. You could classify kinship, for example, according to whether it is traced through the mother's line or the father's, or both; whether it is by blood or marriage; and whether it includes only immediate parent–child (nuclear) relationships or more distant (extended) relations. Members of a given population might be classified according to age group (or cohort), occupation, income, and so on. If you are organizing your essay by a system of classification, remember the following:

- All members of a class must be accounted for. If any are left over, you need to alter some categories or add more.
- Categories can be divided into subcategories. You should consider using subcategories if there are significant differences within a category. If, for instance, you are classifying the workforce according to occupation, you might want to create subcategories according to income level.
- Any subcategory should contain at least two items.

Explaining a process

Explaining a process refers to showing how something works or has worked, whether it is the process of urbanization, industrialization, or the stages in a political or military campaign. Take a systematic approach. Break down the process into a series of steps or stages. Although it may vary, most often your order will be chronological, in which case you should see that the sequence is accurate and easy to follow. You can make the process easier to follow if you start a new paragraph for each stage.

Tracing causes or effects

Showing how certain events have led to or resulted from other events is a complex process, and one that is not always obvious. You must be careful not to oversimplify a relationship between cause and effect. You should also recall that these relationships can take a number of forms, each with distinct purposes or goals. For a detailed discussion of causal analysis, see Chapter 2.

Comparing

Students sometimes forget that comparing things means showing differences as well as similarities—even if the instructions do not say "compare and contrast." The "contrast" is implied. The easiest way of comparing two things—though not always the best—is to discuss the first subject in the comparison thoroughly and then move on to the second:

Subject X: Point 1
Point 2
Point 3

Subject Y: Point 1
Point 2
Point 3

The problem with this kind of comparison is that it often reads like two essays slapped together.

You can alleviate this problem if you integrate the two subjects, first in your introduction (by putting them both in a single context) and again in your conclusion, where you should bring together the important points you have made about each. When discussing the second subject, try to refer repeatedly to your findings about the first subject (e.g., "Unlike X, Y does such and such . . ."). This method may be the wisest choice if the subjects you are comparing seem so unalike that it is hard to create similar categories or themes by which to discuss them—when the points you are making about X are of a different type than the points you are making about Y.

If you can, find similar criteria or categories or themes for discussing both subjects. The comparison will be more effective if you organize it like this:

Category/theme 1:   Subject *X*
                     Subject *Y*

Category/theme 2:   Subject *X*
                     Subject *Y*

Category/theme 3:   Subject *X*
                     Subject *Y*

This kind of comparison is more tightly integrated, making it easier for the reader to see the similarities and differences between the subjects. As a result, the essay is likely to be more forceful.

Introductions

The beginning of an essay has a dual purpose: to indicate your topic and the way you intend to approach it, and to grab your reader's interest. One effective way of introducing a topic is to place it in a context—to supply a backdrop that will put it in perspective. The idea is to step back a pace and discuss the area into which your topic fits, and then gradually lead into your specific field of discussion. Sheridan Baker and Lawrence Gamache (1998: 65) call this the *funnel approach*, where a broad statement at the beginning of your essay narrows to the argument that you explain and develop in the body of your essay. For example, suppose that your topic is the industrialization of a nation in the global south. You might begin with a more general discussion of industrialization and then move on to industrialization in select advanced countries in your general region of interest before focusing on your specific topic. A funnel opening is applicable to almost any kind of essay. Just a word of warning: do not begin very far off from your topic. You'll leave your reader wandering, wondering, and confused.

Try to grab your reader's interest from the start. You know from experience how a dull beginning can put you off a book or film. If a reader has to get through 30 or 40 similar essays, it's all the more important for yours to stand out with an interesting introduction. A funnel opening isn't the only way to catch the reader's attention. Here are three common leads:

- **The quotation.** This approach works well when the quotation is taken from the person or work that you will be discussing. You can use a quotation from an unrelated source, as long as it is relevant to your topic and not so well known that it will appear trite. A dictionary of quotations or a comparable Web-based resource can be helpful by letting you search quotes by author, keywords, or topic.
- **The question.** A rhetorical question will annoy the reader if the answer is obvious, but a thought-provoking question can make a strong opening. Just be sure that your essay answers the question.
- **The anecdote or telling fact.** Journalists often use this kind of concrete lead to grab their readers' attention. Save it for your less formal essays—and remember that the incident must highlight the ideas you are going to discuss.

Whatever your lead, it must relate to your topic: never sacrifice relevance for originality. Finally, make sure that by the end of your introduction, the reader knows exactly what the purpose of your essay is and how you intend to accomplish it.

Conclusions

Endings can be painful. Too often, the feeling that one ought to say something profound and memorable produces the kind of prose that suggests a melodramatic fanfare in the background. You know the sort of thing:

> Clearly, Milton Friedman's insight into the operation of Western economies is both intellectually and emotionally stimulating. He has opened broad vistas and forced us to reassess the moral and political underpinnings of economic decision-making in the modern world.

This is over-the-top and ineffective. It's nothing more than a collection of clichés.

Experienced editors often say that many essays would be better without their final paragraphs: in other words, when you have finished saying what you have to say, it is best to just stop. This may work for short essays, where the central point is in the foreground and you don't need to remind the reader of it at the end. However, for longer pieces, where you have developed a number of ideas or a complex line of argument, you should provide a sense of synthesis and closure—a wrap-up. Readers welcome an ending that helps tie the ideas together. Don't leave them dangling. Remember, the final impression is often the most lasting, so finish strong. Simply restating your thesis or summarizing what you have already said may not be forceful enough. What are some other options?

- **The inverse funnel.** The simplest conclusion is one that restates the thesis in different words and then discusses its implications. Baker and Gamache (1998) refer to this as the *inverse funnel approach*, as opposed to the funnel approach of the introduction. In this type of conclusion, the specific arguments made in the body of the essay widen to a more inclusive final statement. Using this approach, you would move from the very specific—a rewording of your thesis—to a more general discussion connected to your topic. One danger in moving to a wider perspective is that you may try to include too much. When a conclusion expands too far it tends to lose focus and turn into an empty cliché, like the conclusion in the preceding example. It's always better to discuss specific implications than to end with vague generalities.
- **The new angle.** A variation of the basic inverse funnel approach is to reintroduce your argument with a new twist. Suggesting a fresh angle can add excitement to your ending. Think about new questions, directions, or issues your essay uncovered, but could not address. But beware of introducing an entirely new idea, or one that's only loosely connected to your original argument: the result could be jarring or off-topic.
- **The full circle.** If your introduction is based on an anecdote, a question, or a startling fact, you can complete the circle by referring to it again in relation to some of the insights revealed in the main body of your essay.
- **The stylistic flourish.** Some of the most successful conclusions end on a strong stylistic note. Try varying the sentence structure: if most of your sentences are long and complex, make the last one short and punchy, or vice versa. Sometimes you can dramatize your idea with a striking phrase or vivid image. Keep your eyes open for fresh ways of putting things, and save that nugget for the end.

None of these approaches to endings is exclusive. You may even find that several of them can be combined in a single essay. Whichever approach you take, avoid referring to facts that have not been mentioned in the main body of your essay.

The Editing Stage

Often the best writer is not the one who can dash off a fluent first draft, but the one who is the best editor. To edit well, you need to see your work as the reader will. You have to distinguish between what you meant to say and what is actually on the page. Leave time between drafts so that when you begin to edit, you will be looking at the writing afresh rather than reviewing it from memory. Go to a movie or go for a walk—do anything that will take your mind off your work. Without this distancing, it may be hard to see your paper objectively.

Editing is more than simply checking your work for errors in grammar or spelling. It involves looking at the piece as a whole to see if the ideas are

- well organized,
- well documented, and
- well expressed.

It may mean making changes to the structure of your essay by adding paragraphs or sentences, deleting others, and moving parts around. Experienced writers may be able to check several aspects of their work at the same time, but if you are inexperienced or in doubt about your writing, it's best to look at the organization of the ideas before you tackle sentence structure, diction, style, and documentation.

What follows is a checklist of questions to ask yourself as you begin editing. It focuses on the first step: examining the organization. You can group some questions together and overlook others, depending on your strengths and weaknesses as a writer.

Preliminary editing checklist

☐ Are the purpose and approach of this essay evident from the beginning?
☐ Are all sections of my paper relevant to the topic?

☐ Is the organization logical?

☐ Are my ideas sufficiently developed? Is there enough evidence, explanation, and illustration?

☐ Would an educated person who hasn't read the primary material understand everything I'm saying? Should I clarify some parts or add explanatory material?

☐ In presenting my argument, do I take into account opposing arguments or evidence?

☐ Do my paragraph divisions give coherence to my ideas? Do I use them to cluster similar ideas and signal changes of idea?

☐ Do any parts seem disjointed? Should I add more transitional words or sentences, or logical indicators to make the sequence of ideas easier to follow?

You can devise your own checklist based on comments you have received on previous assignments. This is particularly useful when you move to a closer focus on sentence structure, diction, punctuation, spelling, and style. If you have a particularly weak area—for example, irrelevant evidence, faulty logic, or run-on sentences—you should give it special attention. Keeping a personal checklist will save you from repeating the same mistakes.

Avoiding Plagiarism

If you pass off the work of another, in whole or in part, as your own, or use a source without giving credit to the author, you are plagiarizing (AlSaffar, 2006). Plagiarism is stealing. Within universities and colleges, penalties range from a zero grade for the work to outright expulsion. It is a growing problem, particularly with the rise in the use of online sources, so universities are devoting more resources to combating it (Gullifer and Tyson, 2010). Universities worldwide are increasingly turning to plagiarism-detection software like Turnitin (see Batane, 2010, on its use in Botswana).

Avoid plagiarism by giving credit where it is due. If you are using someone else's idea, acknowledge it, even if you have changed the wording or just summarized the main points. Your work will not seem weaker if you acknowledge the ideas of others. On the contrary, it will be more convincing. Serious academic work is almost always built on the work of preceding scholars, with credit duly given to the earlier work.

Where should you draw the line on acknowledgements? As a rule, you don't need to give credit for anything that's common knowledge. You wouldn't footnote lines from "O Canada," or the date of Confederation, but you should acknowledge any clever turn of phrase that is neither well known nor your own. Always document any unfamiliar fact or claim—statistical or otherwise—or one that's open to question.

Consider the following passage from John Mack Faragher's book *A Great and Noble Scheme*:

> The removal of the Acadians . . . was executed methodically by officers of the government in accordance with a carefully conceived plan many years in the making. It utilized all the available resources of the state. It included the seizure and destruction of Acadian records and registers, the arrest and isolation of community leaders, the separation of men from women and children. In the nineteenth century, operations of that kind would be directed at Indian peoples such as the Cherokees, but before 1755, nothing like it had been seen in North America. Today, the universal condemnation of ethnic cleansing by world opinion makes it difficult to defend what was done. In 2003, Queen Elizabeth II issued a Royal Proclamation acknowledging British responsibility for the decision to deport the Acadian people and regretting its "tragic consequences."
> (Copyright © 2005 by John Mack Faragher. Used by permission of W.W. Norton & Company, Inc.)

Now imagine that a class has been assigned an essay on the expulsion of the French Acadians from Nova Scotia in 1755. One student's essay includes the following passage. It is plagiarized because exact phrasing is taken from the original and no acknowledgement is given:

> ✗ The expulsion of the Acadians in 1755 **included the seizure and destruction of Acadian records and registers, the arrest and isolation of community leaders, the separation of men from women and children.** It was in fact the first instance of **ethnic cleansing** in North America. **In 2003, Queen Elizabeth II issued a Royal Proclamation acknowledging British responsibility for the decision to deport the Acadian people and regretting its "tragic consequences."**

To avoid a charge of plagiarism and its negative consequences, all you need to do is acknowledge your source, either directly in the text ("As Faragher writes . . . ," with an appropriate identification of the source) or in a parenthetical reference. In the correctly documented passage below, words and phrases taken directly from the original are in quotation marks, and a parenthetical text citation is included at the end of the passage. (See Chapter 10 for alternative citation styles.) A bibliography at the end of the essay gives complete publication information for the source.

✔ The expulsion of the Acadians in 1755 "included the seizure and destruction of Acadian records and registers, the arrest and isolation of community leaders, the separation of men from women and children." It was in fact the first instance of "ethnic cleansing" in North America. "In 2003, Queen Elizabeth II issued a Royal Proclamation acknowledging British responsibility for the decision to deport the Acadian people and regretting its 'tragic consequences'" (Faragher, xix).

Remember that plagiarism involves not just the use of someone else's *words* but also the use of someone else's *ideas*. As with other illegal offences, ignorance of the law is no excuse, and "accidental" plagiarism is still plagiarism. When copying material from a book and especially when copying and pasting electronic text from a website, be sure to place the material within quotation marks and record the source. This will help you avoid inadvertently plagiarizing comments you thought were your own.

For more information on documenting sources, please see Chapter 10. Also see the APA (http://www.apastyle.org) or MLA (http://www.mla.org) websites for the most recent updates and new publications available on referencing style.

Writing a Research Proposal

More and more often, students at all levels are being asked to do research projects and write up the findings of their research. Obviously, the size and complexity of a project will depend on the level (and skill) of the student. For example, a first-year student may undertake to observe children at a playground for an hour or interview a half-dozen shoppers at a shopping mall. A fourth-year student may undertake to study how physical disability affects young people's social relationships, or how immigration to a new country affects assimilation into school activities. Out in the work world, an employee may undertake to study how office reorganization affects productivity. But whatever the complexity of the research, it is always desirable to write a research proposal and get the instructor or supervisor to sign off on the project before it begins.

Developing your ideas

Writing a research proposal has its own requirements, but they are not completely unrelated to other types of writing project. For example, just like when you are writing an essay or test answer, you want to begin writing your research proposal by thinking about your audience and the assumptions they may bring to this proposal (and project.) For example, consider how familiar they are with the problem you are studying. If you think about these matters thoroughly, you will realize you must talk about things that are important to the instructor or supervisor (or, after graduation, boss) and talk about them in a way that is readily understandable.

Defining

If your goal is to persuade the reader to allow you to carry out this research, or even to provide funds, you must write the proposal in a way that is attractive and persuasive. You should emphasize the following:

- Why is it important for people to know the answer to the question your research is addressing?
- Why is the answer potentially interesting?
- Why is it socially important?
- Why might it be profitable to your boss's organization?

In this context, you must define your issue of interest. If you are proposing to study shoppers at a shopping mall, you should be ready to consider why people come to a mall and why some people stay and shop for a long time, while others leave quickly. If you are proposing to study physically disabled youth, you should be ready to consider how these youth feel about being disabled and perhaps stigmatized by their disability: whether they feel isolated and lonely, for example. If you are proposing to study office reorganization, you should be ready to talk about employees' fears of change and anxieties about being found inadequate in their new role. By discussing the research issues properly, you start to convince the reader that you will be able to carry out this project and gain useful, even important results. So, in this context, don't bother proposing to study something that is trivial or some question to which everyone already knows the answer.

Solutions and outcomes

Ideally, your research proposal will also supply potential consequences. For example, if you find X in your research, then it may be appropriate to do further research on Y, or to take practical action on Z. To illustrate, if you find that disabled youth are often lonely, depressed, and perhaps even suicidal, you may want to consider (and ask your research subjects) about possible solutions: ways that their situation could be improved. Again, your goal is to persuade the reader—your instructor or supervisor—to give your research the go-ahead. A proposal that both defines a problem *and* offers a solution will often convince readers to support it. But if so, your proposal should also be logical and practical.

With practical goals in mind, think about your research problem-and-solution in terms of objectives—even in terms of "outcomes" and "deliverables." For most student projects, the "deliverable" is an essay or report. At the highest student levels, the deliverable is a thesis, dissertation, or publishable journal article.

The writing stage

Language and writing style

When writing this proposal, use the same elements of good style discussed throughout this book. Don't use casual language, rough language, or jargon; at the same time, don't use language that is unnecessarily formal or complicated. Keep the writing simple, direct, and businesslike. Use strong verbs and avoid the passive voice whenever possible. Passive voice uses forms of "to be" verbs and can make your meaning unclear.

Introduction

Start your proposal with a clear and simple introduction that will get reader interested. Perhaps start with a question you intend to answer. Then state the purpose of your proposal. If you have any important facts that illustrate the importance of the project, show the reader these facts immediately. After the introduction, state your problem:

- What's causing it?
- What effects is it having?
- Is the problem getting worse? If so, why?

Show us why we need to solve this problem as soon as possible. Show how the problem affects everyone, or at least a large portion of the population. Use credible sources to back up your claims: don't rely on emotional appeals.

Setting a schedule

Where appropriate, include a schedule (or timeline) and budget. Being systematic about scheduling and budgeting has two purposes. First, doing so helps to persuade the reader that you know what you are doing and are ready to do it. Second, it ensures that you will have the time and money you need to actually achieve the goals you have set for yourself with this project. Accordingly, you should talk about when you plan to begin, what steps you will take and when each step will be taken, and how much each part of the project will cost. Make sure your proposal makes sense financially. If your proposal is impractical, unaffordable, unpredictable, or likely to take too long, it won't be accepted. Equally bad, the project would bog you down in an endless series of frustrations.

Conclusion

Finish your proposal with a brief conclusion that wraps up your general message. It should summarize the benefits of your project, acknowledge the costs and limitations, and emphasize that the benefits outweigh the costs. Leave the reader feeling like they have read something important and worth thinking about.

The editing stage

Before you submit the proposal, be sure to edit it carefully. Revise it as many times as necessary to make sure it is clear and concise. Ask other people to read it and critique it, so you get some idea how other people—including people like the intended reader—are likely to receive the document. Outside readers may see issues and problems that you didn't think about at all.

Finally, proofread your work one last time. Proofreading will make sure that your document is free of typing errors, grammar errors, punctuation errors, or spelling errors, and that it looks professional. Make sure that your formatting (e.g., type size) is in line with whatever the guidelines require. Failing to deliver a document that looks careful and professional makes you look less credible and reduces the chance that your proposal will get approved.

Writing Exams

Exams call for quick answers to often difficult questions. Writing an exam is like writing an essay, yet the entire process is sped up. The same principles of good thinking and writing apply to exams and essays. To do well on an exam, you need to have mastered the material and—equally important—mastered the skills we have discussed so far. Exams demand memory work, clear and rapid thinking, good organization, and a calm state of mind.

Writing an essay exam—even the open-book or take-home kind—imposes special pressure because the time and the questions are restricted. You can't write and rewrite the way you can in a regular essay, and you must often write on topics not of your choosing. Objective tests, such as multiple-choice tests, may look easier because you don't have to compose the answers. However, objective tests force you to be more decisive about your answers than essay exams do. To do your best you need to stay calm and clear-headed. These general guidelines will help you approach a test or exam with confidence.

Before the exam

Review regularly
A weekly review of lecture notes and readings will help you to remember important material and relate new information to old. If you don't review regularly, at the end of the term you'll be faced with relearning rather than remembering.

Set memory triggers
As you review, condense and focus the material by writing in the margin key words or phrases that will trigger sets of details in your mind. The trigger

might be a word that names or points to an important theory or definition, or a quantitative phrase such as "three causes of the decline in manufacturing" or "five reasons for inflation."

Sometimes you can create an acronym or a nonsense sentence that will trigger a set of facts—something like the acronym HOMES (Huron, Ontario, Michigan, Erie, Superior) for the Great Lakes. Because the difficulty of memorizing increases with the number of items you are trying to remember, any method that will reduce that number will increase your effectiveness.

Ask questions: Try the three-C approach

Think of questions that will get to the heart of the material and force you to examine the relations between subjects or issues; then consider how you would answer them. The three-C approach, discussed in Chapter 8, may help. For example, reviewing the *components* of the subject could mean focusing on the main parts of an issue or on the definitions of major terms or theories. When reviewing *change* in the subject, ask yourself what changes have taken place in the subject, and what the causes or results of these changes are. To review *context* you might consider how certain aspects of the subject—issues, theories, actions, results—compare with others in the course. The three-C approach forces you to look at the material from different perspectives.

Old exams can help you see what kinds of questions you might be asked. If your instructor doesn't make old exams available, get together with classmates and ask each other questions. Brainstorm about what could be asked and how best to prepare for this. The most useful review questions do more than require you to recall facts; they force you to analyze, integrate, or evaluate information.

Allow extra time

Arrive early. Nothing is more nerve-wracking than thinking you're going to be late for your exam. Anticipate any unusual difficulties and allow yourself a good margin.

Writing an essay exam

Read the exam

Take time at the beginning to read through each question, underline key points and instructions ("compare," "outline," "define," etc.), and create a plan. A few minutes spent on thinking and organizing will bring better results than would the same time spent on writing a few more lines and trying to reorganize later.

Apportion your time

Read the instructions carefully to find out how many questions you must answer and if you have any choice. Subtract five minutes or so for the initial planning, then divide the time you have left by the number of questions you have to answer. If possible, allow for a little extra time at the end to reread and edit your work. The "rule of equal thirds" outlined early in this book can be useful. It might be a good idea to spend close to one-third of your time planning your answers, one-third actually writing, and the final third revising. If the instructions indicate that not all questions are of equal value, apportion your time accordingly.

Choose your questions

Decide on the questions that you will do and the order in which you will do them. Sometimes it's a good idea to place your strongest answer first, your weakest answers in the middle, and your second-best answer at the end in order to leave the reader on a high note. If you think you will be rushed, it's wiser to work from best to worst. That way you will be sure to get all the marks you can on your good answers, and you won't have to cut a good answer short at the end.

Keep calm

If your first reaction to the exam is "I can't answer any of these!" force yourself to keep calm; take deep breaths to help yourself relax. Decide which question you can answer best. You can probably find one question that looks manageable: that's the one to begin with. It will help you get rolling and increase your confidence.

Read each question carefully

As you turn to each question, read it again carefully and underline the key words. The wording will suggest the number of parts your answer should have. Don't overlook anything (this is a common mistake when people are nervous). It is important that you interpret the verb used in an exam question correctly because it's usually a guide for the approach to take in your answer. For this reason, it's a good idea to review the following definitions:

outline	state simply, without much development of each point (unless asked).
trace	review by looking back—on stages or steps in a process, or on causes of an occurrence.
explain	show how or why something happens.
discuss	examine or analyze in an orderly way. This allows you considerable freedom, as long as you take into account contrary evidence or ideas.
compare	examine differences as well as similarities—even if the question doesn't say "compare and contrast."
evaluate	analyze strengths and weaknesses to arrive at an overall assessment of worth.

Make notes

To start, jot down—briefly—key ideas and information related to the topic on rough paper or the unlined pages of your answer booklet. These notes will save you the worry of forgetting something by the time you begin writing. Next, arrange your points into a brief plan, using numbers to indicate their order; that way, if you change your mind, it will be easy to reorder them. At the end, be sure to cross out these notes so that the evaluator won't think they are your actual answers.

Be direct

Get to the points quickly and use examples to illustrate them. In an exam, it's best to be direct. Don't worry about composing a graceful introduction: simply state the main points and then get on with developing them. Remember that your paper will likely be one of many marked by someone who has to work quickly—the clearer your answers, the better they will be received. For each main point give specific details that will prove you really know the material. Provide examples whenever possible.

Write legibly

When the marker has to struggle to decipher your ideas, you may get poorer results than you deserve. It's probably better to slow down a bit and print, and write on every other line, to make your writing easier to read. This also leaves you space for changes and additions.

Keep to your time plan

Keep to your plan and don't skip questions. Try to write something on each topic. It's easier to score part marks for a question you don't know much about than it is to score full marks for one you could write pages on. If you find your-self running out of time on an answer and still haven't finished, summarize the remaining points and go on to the next question. Leave a space between questions so that you can go back and add more if you have time.

Reread your answers

Reread your answers at the end, if there's time. Check for clarity of expression. Get rid of confusing sentences and improve your transitions so that the logical connection between your ideas is clear. Revisions that make answers easier to read are worth the effort.

Writing an open-book exam

If you have permission to take your books into the exam do not fall into the trap of relying too heavily on them. You may spend so much time looking things up that you won't have time to write good answers.

Use your books only to check information and look up hard-to-remember details for a topic you already know a good deal about. For instance, if your subject is history, you can look up exact dates or quotations; for a political subject, you can look up voting statistics; for social theory, you can find the authors' exact definitions of key concepts—if you know where to find them quickly. Annotated page markers, labelled flags, or tabs created in advance will help.

You should use the books to make sure your answers are precise and well illustrated. Never use them to replace studying and careful preparation.

Writing a take-home exam

The benefit of a take-home exam is that you have time to plan your answers and consult your texts and other sources, but the time you have to do this is usually less than you would have for an ordinary essay. Don't try to respond with a polished research essay for each question; rather, use the time to create a well-written exam answer. You were likely given this assignment to test your overall command of the course and your ability to understand and assimilate the material.

The guidelines for a take-home exam are therefore similar to those for a regular exam, only you don't need to keep a close eye on the clock:

- Keep your introduction short and get to the point quickly.
- Organize your answer in a straightforward and obvious way so that the reader can easily see your main ideas.
- Use concrete examples to back up your points.

- Where possible, show the range of your knowledge of course material by referring to a variety of sources rather than constantly using the same ones.
- Try to show that you can analyze, evaluate, and synthesize material: that you can do more than simply repeat information.
- If you are asked to acknowledge the sources of any quotations or data you use, be sure to jot them down as you go.

Writing an objective test

Objective tests are common in the social sciences. The questions may be the true/false kind, or, more often, multiple-choice. These questions are designed to confuse the student who is not certain of the correct answers. If you tend to second-guess yourself, or if you are the sort of person who readily sees two sides to every question, you may find objective tests hard at first. Fortunately, practice improves performance.

Preparation for objective tests is the same as for other kinds, though it's important to pay extra attention to definitions and unexpected or confusing pieces of information because these kinds of things are often adapted to make objective-test questions. Although there is no sure recipe for doing well on an objective test—other than knowing the course material completely and confidently—these suggestions may help you to do better:

Find out the marking scheme

If marks are based solely on the number of correct answers, you should pick an answer for every question even if you aren't sure it's the right one. Don't leave any unanswered questions. On the other hand, if there is a penalty for wrong answers—if marks are deducted for errors—you should guess only when you are able to rule out most of the possibilities. Don't make wild guesses.

Do the easy questions first

Go through the test at least twice. On the first round, don't waste time on troublesome questions. Mark these and return to them later. It's best to get all the marks you can on the ones you know. Tackle the more difficult questions on the next round. This approach has two advantages:

1. You won't be forced, because you have run out of time, to leave out any questions that you could easily have answered correctly.

2. When you come back to a difficult question on the second round, you may find that in the meantime you have figured out the answer.

Read the question, mark it up, and think of the answer

It is sometimes useful to read the question and think of the correct answer *before* looking at the response options provided. Having the correct answer in mind makes it far more difficult to confuse you. It is also useful to mark up the questions, underlining or circling key words, and paying close attention to words like *not*: "which of the following was <u>not</u> one of Marx's . . ." Strike out the options that you know are not correct.

Make your guesses educated ones

If you have to guess, you can increase your chance of getting the answers right. Forget about intuition, hunches, and lucky numbers. Forget about so-called patterns of correct answers, like the idea that if there have been two "A" answers in a row, the next one can't possibly be "A." Many test-setters either don't worry about patterns at all or else deliberately elude pattern-hunters by giving the right answer the same letter or number several times in a row.

James F. Shepherd (1979, 1981) has suggested a number of tips that will help you increase your chances of making the right guess:

- Start by weeding out all the answers you know are wrong, rather than looking for the right one.
- Avoid any terms you don't recognize. Some students are taken in by anything that looks like sophisticated terminology and may assume that such answers must be correct. They are usually wrong. The unfamiliar term may well be a red herring, especially if it is close in sound to the correct one.
- Avoid absolutes, especially on questions dealing with people. Few aspects of human life are as certain as is implied by such words as *everyone*, *all*, or *no one; always*, *invariably*, or *never*. Statements containing these words are usually false.
- Avoid jokes or humorous statements.
- Choose the best available answer, even if it is not indisputably true.
- Choose "all of the above" over individual answers when more than two options appear to be correct. Test-setters know that students with a

patchy knowledge of the course material will often fasten on the one fact they know. Only those with a thorough knowledge will recognize that all the answers listed are correct. (Be wary, however, if two answers appear correct and all others are obviously wrong; "all of the above" cannot be correct. Rather, choose the one that seems *most* correct, in this case).

Don't forget to mark up your test sheet, striking out obviously incorrect options. At the very least, if you have to guess, you will end up choosing between two or three options rather than the four or five listed.

Two final tips

If you have time at the end of the exam, go back and reread the questions. Wrong answers caused by misreading can make a significant difference to your score. On the other hand, don't start second-guessing yourself and changing a lot of answers at the last minute. Stick to your decisions unless you are certain you have made a mistake.

Summary

Writing essays and exams are sources of great stress for most students because so much of your course grade depends on your ability to do these in clear and convincing ways. But there are steps you can follow to ease your anxiety and help you develop the skills you need to succeed. Create an outline (and try to stick to it). Craft a rough draft of your answer. Leave yourself plenty of time to edit, polish, and simplify your writing. These strategies will always help you achieve better results. Even for objective tests, study hard; plan your time; stay calm; think logically. Achieving good grades takes time and practice. You can do it.

10 Documentation

In this chapter we will examine

- ways to reference directly quoted material to avoid plagiarism;
- ways to paraphrase or quote indirectly in a proper fashion; and
- ways to use the documentation style most common in your own field.

Introduction

Documenting your sources accurately and completely is essential in academic writing. The purpose of documentation is not only to avoid charges of plagiarism, but also to show the body of knowledge that your work is building on. Academia is based on the premise that researchers are not working in a vacuum and are indebted to those who came before them. By documenting your sources, you are showing that you understand this idea and are ready to make your own contribution to the knowledge pool in your field.

The Evergreen Problem of Plagiarism

Jude Carroll, in *A Handbook for Deterring Plagiarism in Higher Education*, 2nd edition (2013), notes that plagiarism is not understood in the same way by students and staff, so plagiarism must be defined clearly and the penalties for plagiarism also be made clear. As Park (2003) notes, students plagiarize for many reasons. Students, when questioned, often rationalize or justify their cheating behaviour, and downplay the importance of plagiarism by themselves and their peers.

It must be repeated that students will never be permitted to buy essays, borrow essays, or re-use other students' essays and present any parts of these as their own work.

Recall what was being said about plagiarism in the previous chapter: Plagiarism is stealing. You can avoid plagiarism by giving due credit when documenting your sources. As a rule, you don't need to give credit for anything that's common knowledge, but you must always document any fact or claim—statistical or otherwise—that's open to question. To avoid a charge of plagiarism and its negative consequences, make sure you acknowledge your sources, either directly or in the text.

Remember that plagiarism involves not just the use of someone else's *words* but also the use of someone else's *ideas*. When copying material from a book and especially when copying and pasting electronic text from a website, be sure to place the material within quotation marks and record the source. That way, no one will think that you are claiming to have thought or invented these ideas yourself. What follows in this chapter are examples of how to properly document sources to avoid any plagiarizing mishaps.

Quotations

The most direct form of reference, the quotation, is used in all academic writing. Sensible use of quotations can add authority to your writing. Quotations should be used with care, however, and they should not be overused. Never quote a passage just because it sounds impressive; be sure that it adds to your discussion, either by expressing an idea with special force or cogency, or by giving substance to a debatable point. Here are guidelines for incorporating quotations:

1. Integrate the quotation so that it makes sense in the context of your discussion and fits in grammatically:

    ✗   Whether Bill Gates is a visionary is debatable. "640 K ought to be enough for anybody" is now very ironic.

    ✔   Whether Bill Gates is a visionary is debatable. His 1981 prediction that "640 K ought to be enough for anybody" is now considered laughably ironic.

2. If the quotation is no more than four lines long, include it as part of your text, enclosed in quotation marks. If you are quoting four lines or fewer of poetry, these can also be included as part of your text. Use a slash (/) to indicate the end of a line:

In "Newfoundland" Pratt describes the winds as, "Resonant with the hopes of spring, / Pungent with the airs of harvest."

For verse quotations of more than four lines, you should write the words line for line as originally written.

3. A long quotation is usually single-spaced and introduced by a colon, without quotation marks. If the first line of the quotation is the beginning of a paragraph, indent it an extra three spaces:

    In a recent column, a well-known journalist and historian remembered the late prime minister this way:

    > In his prime, Trudeau was exciting, charismatic, sexy. He drove sports cars, wore capes, ascots and floppy hats, and always the signature red rose in his lapel. He slid down banisters, canoed in white-water rapids, did pirouettes behind the Queen's back at Buckingham Palace. He made politics fashionable for the upbeat Sixties generation that emerged from the sleepy 1950s. (Canada History, 2000)

4. For a quotation within a quotation, use single quotation marks:

    One newspaper reports that world leaders "agreed that they need to cooperate to develop 'a long-term global goal for emission reductions' but the statement does not give any specific targets for emissions cuts."

5. Be accurate. Reproduce the exact wording, punctuation, and spelling of the original, including any errors. You can acknowledge a typo or mistake by the original author by inserting the Latin word *sic* in brackets after it. If you want to italicize any part of the quotation for emphasis—amounting to a change to the original text—add "my emphasis" or "emphasis added" in brackets at the end:

    The authors concluded that "flawed data was *not* the reason [*sic*] for the unexpected results" [my emphasis].

6. If you want to insert an explanatory comment into a quotation, enclose it in brackets:

    "He [Mr. Nebbeling] said he has yet to hear from the entire Liberal caucus but is ready for negative and positive responses."

7. If you want to omit something from the original, use ellipsis (. . .) marks:

    "The uprising was the result of indifference on the part of national leaders . . . and mismanagement on the part of civil servants."

Ellipsis marks are discussed further in Chapter 13.

Referencing Your Work

A huge amount of variation exists among accepted formats for referencing your sources. Although different referencing styles have certain general guidelines in common, the specific details surrounding the use of commas, colons, parentheses, quotation marks, and italicization (or underlining) vary widely. In addition, methods of citing electronic sources of information are evolving rapidly as the digital age revolutionizes academic research. Widely accepted practices are outlined below, but always check with your instructor on which format is acceptable.

A note on footnotes

The use of footnotes and endnotes is generally discouraged in social science writing, where the parenthetical-reference style is most often used to identify sources. You may have learned to use footnotes or endnotes to expand on or digress from the main argument of your work, and some academic departments and journals still recommend referencing styles that use a combination of parenthetical references and endnotes or footnotes; however, this practice is falling out of favour in the social sciences. As a rule, if your comments are important, they should be included in the main text of your essay or report; if the information is not immediately relevant, leave it out. You want the reader to be able to focus on the body of your work.

Parenthetical references, or *citations*

The parenthetical-reference (or *scientific*) style, used by most disciplines of social science, has two main features:

1. Brief references (called *citations*) are included in parentheses within the text wherever reference to another person's work is made.
2. At the end of a work, a section entitled *Reference List*, *References*, or *Works Cited* includes the full publication information for those works *directly referred to* in the text; other works that you may have consulted but have not referred to directly in the text should not be listed.

A leading form of this style is known as the Harvard method and is followed, with variations, by the American Psychological Association (APA) and the Modern Language Association of America (MLA). A third variation, the Social Science Style (SSS), is our own system—used throughout this book—which is based on widely accepted conventions followed in many social science journals and books.

These are three models you should consider using. Be aware of the fact that these three models differ widely in places, and, in addition, that each model is constantly undergoing revisions to keep up with new ways of doing research. Many reputable, free online referencing and style guides are available with updates on the latest guidelines (for example, see the Online Writing Lab, or OWL, at Purdue University: http://owl.english.purdue.edu/owl/resource/747/01/ for MLA, or http://owl.english.purdue.edu/owl/resource/560/01/ for APA).

You should also be aware that professors and journals vary widely in their requirements: you may be asked to use one of these methods, or a variation that combines elements of each, or a different style altogether. Make sure you are aware of the preferences and expectations of your department or instructor. If your instructor does not refer you to a particular journal, departmental website, or booklet on style, you will have to make a choice based on the guidelines below. Whatever you do, remember the one "golden rule" for documentation: always be consistent. No matter what style you choose, use it consistently throughout any piece of work; never change midstream.

Guidelines for using citations

1. The citation is inserted in the text at the appropriate point, with the author's surname and, in most cases, the year of publication in parentheses. Note the APA style uses an ampersand (&) to separate authors, whereas the SSS and MLA use "and." Note also that the MLA style omits the year but inserts the relevant page number, and that it does not include a comma between the authors' names and the page number:

    SSS   The most frequent problems changed over the lifespan (Haw and Hawton, 2008).

    APA   The most frequent problems changed over the lifespan (Haw & Hawton, 2008).

    MLA   The most frequent problems changed over the lifespan (Haw and Hawton 139).

2. If reference to the author has already been made within the text, it can be omitted from the citation. In MLA, the page number should still appear in parentheses:

    SSS, APA   Haw and Hawton (2008) tested the findings.

    (or)   In 2008, Haw and Hawton tested the findings.

    MLA   Haw and Hawton tested the findings (139).

    If the reference is to a work as a whole, include the author's name in the text, rather than in a parenthetical reference.

3. In all but the MLA style, if the page reference is not important, all you need to include is the year:

    SSS, APA   Thaler and Plowright (2004) support this hypothesis.

    MLA   Thaler and Plowright support this hypothesis.

    If, however, the citation is to something specific within the source and not just to the work in general, then you must include the specific reference. When referring to a specific page or table, include the number.

Note also that APA includes the abbreviations "p." and "pp." before the page number or numbers:

SSS	(Smyth, 2014: 121–3)
	(Craig, 2009: Table 3)
	(Zakrewski, 2013: Fig. 5.3)
	(Chumak and Chun, 2003: Chap. 3)
APA	(Smyth, 2014, pp. 121–123)
	(Craig, 2009, Table 3)
	(Zakrewski, 2013, Figure 5.3)
	(Chumak & Chun, 2003, Chapter 3)
MLA	(Smyth 121–23)
	(Craig 145; table 3)
	(Zakrewski 78; fig. 5.3)
	(Chumak and Chun 99; ch. 3)

4. When referring to a work with two authors, always use the names of both authors in each citation of the work in the order in which they appear in the publication:

SSS	Analysis of the data (Yang and Kleinman, 2008) revealed . . .
	In their analysis, Yang and Kleinman (2008) revealed . . .
APA	Analysis of the data (Yang & Kleinman, 2008) revealed . . .
	In their analysis, Yang and Kleinman (2008) revealed . . .
MLA	Analysis of the data (Yang and Kleinman 401) revealed . . .
	In their analysis, Yang and Kleinman revealed . . . (401).

In the SSS and APA styles, when there are more than two authors but fewer than six, list all of the authors in the first citation and only the first author followed by "et al." for subsequent citations. When dealing with more than three authors in the MLA style, either give the first author's last name followed by "et al." or list the last names of all authors:

SSS	(Cameron, Jrang, Park, and Allaby, 2003)
	(Cameron et al., 2003)

APA   (Cameron, Jrang, Park, & Allaby, 2003)
(Cameron et al., 2003)

MLA   (Cameron et al. 97)

Remember that if you refer to the authors in the text, their names should be omitted from the citation:

As the study by Cameron et al. (2003) shows . . .

If the work has six or more authors, cite only the name of the first author followed by "et al." for the first and subsequent references.

5. When citing multiple works by different authors in one set of parentheses, use a semicolon to separate the items. In the APA style, items are listed in alphabetical order, but in the SSS and MLA styles, they may also be ranked by order of importance:

   SSS   (Roget, 2014; Miller and Streicher, 1996; Hsuing et al., 2012)

   APA   (Hsuing et al., 2012; Miller & Streicher, 1996; Roget, 2014)

   MLA   (Roget 23; Miller and Streicher 106; Hsuing et al. 71)

6. If authors have the same last names, use initials to distinguish them:

   SSS, APA   (H. Chavez, 2002; P. Chavez, 2004)

   MLA   (A. Best 35; C. Best 107)

7. When using APA or SSS to cite multiple works by the same author, list the surname once, with the dates following in chronological order:

   SSS, APA   (Berberi, 1996, 1998)

   When citing two or more works published within the same year, distinguish them with lower-case letters following the date:

   SSS, APA   (Thompson, 2013a, 2013b)

   This letter is assigned in the reference list, and these kinds of references are ordered alphabetically by title.

When citing one of multiple works by the same author(s) in MLA, include the title, in shortened form, and a relevant page number:

MLA	Smith argued that building blocks are useful tools for child development (*Never Too Soon* 38), though she acknowledged elsewhere that too early exposure leads to . . . (*On Second Thought* 17).

8. When a work has no known or declared author, list the first few words of the reference list entry (usually the title):

SSS, APA	("Drug Dependency a Problem," 2012)
MLA	("Drug Dependency a Problem" 187)

9. If you know that the material you are using will be published soon, use "forthcoming" (SSS and MLA) or "in press" (APA) in place of the publication date. If the work has no listed publication date, use the abbreviation "n.d.":

SSS, MLA	(Levinson, 2001; Norton, forthcoming; Pieter, n.d.)
APA	(Levinson, 2001; Norton, in press; Pieter, n.d.)

10. When citing material that you have not read yourself but have seen cited by others, your citation must show this:

SSS	According to Verschreagen (1995, cited in Kabila, 1998: 62) . . .
APA	According to Verschreagen (1995, as cited in Kabila, 1998, p. 62) . . .
MLA	According to Verschreagen (qtd. in Kabila 62) . . .

In the reference list, give only the secondary source.

11. When citing electronic sources, whenever possible, use the same style as when you are citing any other documents—using the author–date style in SSS and APA or author–page style in MLA:

SSS, APA	Kenneth (2013) explained . . .
MLA	Kenneth explained . . . (234).

When an electronic source does not provide page numbers, you should include information that will help readers find the passage you cited. In cases where the electronic document has numbered paragraphs, use the abbreviation "para." (APA) or "par." (MLA) followed by the paragraph number. In the APA style, if the paragraphs are not numbered but the document has headings, provide the appropriate heading and specify the paragraph number after that heading:

APA   According to Smith (2008), . . . (Mind over Matter section, para. 6).

In the MLA style, give relevant paragraph or section numbers, but do not count unnumbered paragraphs. For sources with no page numbers or any other kind of reference numbers, the work must be cited in its entirety, although an indication of the approximate location can be given.

MLA   Toward the end of his article, Smith claims . . .

MLA   In Smith's introductory paragraph . . .

MLA   In Millar's opposing argument . . .

Remember: never use the page numbers of websites when *you* print them, since different computers often print websites with different pagination.

In the case of electronic sources with unknown authors or unknown dates, use the title in the signal phrase of the text or the first word or two of the title in parentheses; use the abbreviation "n.d." (for "no date"):

APA, SSS   A recent study of tutoring services found . . . ("Tutoring Is Effective," n.d.).

MLA   A recent study of tutoring services found . . . ("Tutoring Is Effective," par. 6).

12. If your style guide does not have an official rule for citing class or lecture notes, you may cite them in text as follows, giving as much detail as possible. For examples of list entries for lectures or other oral presentations, see pages 209–210.

> *MLA*   In a lecture on 18 September 2014, in an undergradu-
> ate course on social research methods, Dr. Irene Smith
> stated, ". . .

13. APA offers suggestions on how to reference personal communication. For interviews, letters, emails, and other person-to-person communication, you should cite, in parentheses, the communicator's initials and surname, the fact that it was personal communication, and the date of the communication. In the APA style, you should not include personal communication in the reference list.

> *APA*   Social research methods can be a lot of fun if done correctly
> (I. Smith, personal communication, October 27, 2014).

> *APA*   Irene Smith claims that social research methods can be
> a lot of fun if done correctly (personal communication,
> October 27, 2014).

The Reference Section

In the reference section (often entitled *Reference List*, *References*, or *Works Cited*) at the end of your work, you will list the complete source information for all of the citations in your text. Be sure to double-check that each citation in your paper has an accompanying reference in this section. Here are general guidelines:

1. List your references alphabetically by (first) author, surname first, followed by given names or initials; do not number them.
2. For a work with multiple authors, do not change the order of the authors' names from the order in which they appear in the text itself.
3. When referencing a work with multiple authors there are marked stylistic differences. In the SSS style, list all authors and reverse only the first author's name. In the APA style, list the names of the first seven authors; for eight or more authors, give the first six names and then insert three ellipsis points and add the last author's name. In the MLA style, list all names in full or, for more than three authors, only the first followed by "et al."; only the first author's name is reversed.

4. When using SSS or APA to cite more than one work by a particular author, list entries in chronological order starting with the earliest (the date should usually follow the author's name); arrange works published in the same year alphabetically by title. When using MLA, list entries alphabetically by title. After the first entry, omit the author's name and insert three hyphens followed by a period, then the rest of the entry.

5. Most styles of referencing include the following information:
   - surname of the author(s) (if no author is given, begin with the first significant word in the title);
   - first name of the author or authors (APA uses only initials);
   - date of publication; and
   - full name of the work being cited.

6. For books, include
   - the location of the publisher (although this has been dropped in the 8th edition of *MLA Handbook*)
   - "ed." or "trans." to indicate an editor or translator respectively;
   - the volume number(s), if any; and
   - the name of the publisher. In most cases, the name of the publisher can be condensed. For example, *Macmillan of Canada Ltd.* can be listed as simply *Macmillan*. Note also that, generally, words like *Inc.*, *Co.*, or *Publisher* are omitted. In APA, the words *Books* and *Press* are retained. The names of university presses, e.g., *Oxford University Press*, are written out in SSS and APA and shortened, e.g., *Oxford UP*, in MLA.

7. For journals, include
   - the author(s);
   - the title;
   - the publication date;
   - the name of the article and the name of the journal;
   - the volume number;
   - the issue number (in all cases for MLA; for APA only if issues are paginated separately); and
   - inclusive page references.

8. For websites, include
   - the author(s);

- the name of the site and/or the organization that maintains the site; and,
- in the APA style, the DOI (digital object identifier) assigned to the site; if none is available, provide the home page URL. MLA recommends including URLs in the citation, using permalinks or DOIs when available; a DOI is preferable. MLA further states that the "http://" or "https://" should not be included.
- APA and MLA styles do not generally include retrieval dates.

Because references to Web-based material vary significantly between styles, consult the examples later in this chapter for specifics.

9. For online databases, SSS and MLA include
   - the name of the database;
   - the date the information was retrieved;
   - for MLA, the medium of publication; and,
   - for SSS, the complete URL of the document being referenced.

   APA does not include database information.

10. For online journal, magazine, and newspaper articles based on a print source, include the documentation information of the print counterparts, modified as appropriate to the electronic source.

Reference examples

There is even more variation in reference style than there is in citation style. You will notice significant differences among styles regarding the use of commas, periods, colons, parentheses, quotation marks, capitalization, and italics. Once again, check with your instructor to see what style is preferred for your course or department. Once you have settled on a style, be sure to use it consistently.

Book by one author

SSS   Manning, Erin. 2003. *Ephemeral Territories: Represent-ing Nation, Home, and Identity in Canada.* Minneapolis: University of Minnesota Press.

APA   Manning, E. (2003). *Ephemeral territories: Represent-ing nation, home, and identity in Canada.* Minneapolis: University of Minnesota Press.

> MLA Manning, Erin. *Ephemeral Territories: Representing Nation, Home, and Identity in Canada*. U of Minnesota P, 2003.

Note that in titles and subtitles, the MLA capitalizes the first word and all remaining words except for articles (*a, an, the*), prepositions (*through, from, of,* etc.), coordinating conjunctions (*and, or,* etc.), and *to* in infinitives. The APA capitalizes all major words and all other words of four letters or more for titles of periodicals only; otherwise, the APA capitalizes only proper nouns and the first letter of the title and subtitle. The SSS follows the MLA convention for capitalizing titles and subtitles of books and journals, but it follows the APA convention for capitalizing shorter works, such as articles or chapters of books.

Book by two authors

> SSS Brown, Jeffrey R., and Ramsay Cook. 1996. *Canada, 1896–1921: A Nation Transformed*. Toronto: McClelland & Stewart.

> APA Brown, J. R., & Cook, R. (1996). *Canada, 1896–1921: A nation transformed*. Toronto, ON: McClelland & Stewart.

> MLA Brown, Jeffrey R., and Ramsay Cook. *Canada, 1896–1921: A Nation Transformed*. McClelland, 1996.

Book with edition number

> SSS Mankiw, Gregory N. 2004. *Principles of Economics*, 3rd ed. Mason, OH: South-Western.

> APA Mankiw, G. N. (2004). *Principles of economics* (3rd ed.). Mason, OH: South-Western.

> MLA Mankiw, Gregory N. *Principles of Economics*. 3rd ed. South-Western, 2004.

Book with one editor

> SSS Osberg, Lars, ed. 2003. *The Economic Implications of Social Cohesion*. Toronto: University of Toronto Press.

> APA Osberg, L. (Ed.). (2003). *The economic implications of social cohesion*. Toronto, ON: University of Toronto Press.

MLA Osberg, Lars, ed. *The Economic Implications of Social Cohesion*. U of Toronto P, 2003.

Book with two editors

SSS Donald, Moira and Linda Hurcombe, eds. 2000. *Representations of Gender from Prehistory to the Present*. New York: St. Martin's.

APA Donald, M., & Hurcombe, L. (Eds.). (2000). *Representations of gender from prehistory to the present*. New York, NY: St. Martin's Press.

MLA Donald, Moira, and Linda Hurcombe, eds. *Representations of Gender from Prehistory to the Present*. St. Martin's, 2000.

Book published in two locations by different presses

SSS Daniels, Simeon. 2001. *A Misuse of Constants*. Toronto: Commercial; London: McChesney.

MLA Daniels, Simeon. *A Misuse of Constants*. Commercial / McChesney, 2001.

APA does not address co-publication.

Chapter in an edited book

SSS Hornyansky, Michael. 1995. "Is your English destroying your image?" *In the Name of Language*. Joseph Gold (ed.). Toronto: Macmillan. 44–78.

APA Hornyansky, M. (1995). Is your English destroying your image? In J. Gold (Ed.), *In the name of language* (pp. 44–78). Toronto, ON: Macmillan.

MLA Hornyansky, Michael. "Is Your English Destroying Your Image?" *In the Name of Language*, edited by Joseph Gold, Macmillan, 1995, pp. 44–78.

Article by one author in a journal

SSS Dodson, Kevin E. 2003. "Kant's socialism: A philosophical reconstruction," *Social Theory and Practice* v 29 no 4, 525–38.

APA   Dodson, K. E. (2003). Kant's socialism: A philosophical re-construction. *Social Theory and Practice, 29*(4), 525–538.

MLA   Dodson, Kevin E. "Kant's Socialism: A Philosophical Reconstruction." *Social Theory and Practice* vol. 29, no. 4, 2003, pp. 525–38.

Article by two or more authors in a journal

SSS   Heath, Deborah, Erin Koch, Barbara Ley, and Michael Montoya. 1999. "Nodes and queries: Linking locations in networked fields of inquiry," *The American Behavioral Scientist* v 43 no 3, 450–63.

APA   Heath, D., Koch, E., Ley, B., & Montoya, M. (1999). Nodes and queries: Linking locations in networked fields of inquiry. *The American Behavioral Scientist, 43*(3), 450–463.

MLA   Heath, Deborah, Erin Koch, Barbara Ley, and Michael Montoya. "Nodes and Queries: Linking Locations in Networked Fields of Inquiry." *American Behavioral Scientist* vol. 43, no. 3, 1999, pp. 450–63.

Signed newspaper article

SSS   Simpson, Jeffrey. "Do we care that Canada is an unequal society?" *Globe and Mail*, 20 July 2011, A14.

APA   Simpson, J. (2011, July 20). Do we care that Canada is an unequal society? *The Globe and Mail*, p. A14.

MLA   Simpson, Jeffrey. "Do We Care That Canada Is an Unequal Society?" *Globe and Mail*, 20 July 2011, p. A14.

Unsigned newspaper article

SSS   "Millions face starvation in southern Somalia," *Globe and Mail*, 19 July 2011, A12.

APA   Millions face starvation in southern Somalia. (2011, July 19). *The Globe and Mail*, p. A12.

MLA   "Millions Face Starvation in Southern Somalia." *Globe and Mail*, 19 July 2011, A12.

Government document

SSS	Human Resources Development Canada. 2013. *Changing Patterns in Women's Employment*. Ottawa: Queen's Printer.
APA	Human Resources Development Canada. (2013). *Changing patterns in women's employment*. Ottawa, ON: Queen's Printer.
MLA	Human Resources Development Canada. *Changing Patterns in Women's Employment*. Ottawa: Queen's Printer, 2013.

Website

When you are documenting websites in your Works Cited or References section, you may have URLs that don't fit on one line. If you must divide a URL over multiple lines, ensure that the line break occurs after a slash, and don't introduce any punctuation (such as a hyphen at a line break or period at the end) into the URL itself; URLs are very specific, so adding punctuation will make the URL invalid.

SSS	Statistics Canada. "Police-reported crime statistics," *The Daily*, 21 July 2011. Retrieved on 23 July 2011 http://www.statcan.gc.ca/daily-quotidien/110721/dq110721-eng.pdf
APA	Statistics Canada. (2011, July 21). Police-reported crime statistics [Online report]. *The Daily*. Retrieved from http://www.statcan.gc.ca/daily-quotidien/110721/dq110721-eng.pdf
MLA	Statistics Canada. "Police-Reported Crime Statistics." *The Daily*, 21 July 2011, http://www.statcan.gc.ca/daily-quotidien/110721/dq110721-eng.pdf.

Entry in an online reference database

SSS	"Social realism," *Encyclopaedia Britannica*. 2013. Retrieved on 19 Oct. 2014 http://www.britannica.com/EBchecked/topic/551374/Social-Realism
APA	Social realism. (2013). In *Encyclopaedia Britannica*. Retrieved from http://www.britannica.com/EBchecked/topic/551374/Social-Realism
MLA	"Social Realism." *Encyclopaedia Britannica*, 2013, www.britannica.com/EBchecked/topic/551374/Social-Realism.

Article in an online journal

When you are citing online journal articles in APA format, you will also have to include a *digital object identifier* (DOI) wherever possible. The DOI system came about because website links can be unreliable. Every article with a DOI is registered and can be easily identified and retrieved electronically, no matter whether the original website you found the article on continues to exist. The DOI is a unique alphanumeric string that begins with a 10 and contains a prefix and a suffix separated by a slash (for example, 10.1037/0096-3445). You will usually find an article's DOI near the copyright notice on the first page.

When referencing an article with a DOI in APA format, you do not need to include the URL. However, if the article does not include a DOI, you should write "Retrieved from" and give the URL of the journal's or publisher's home page. Only provide the exact URL of the article if it will reliably take your reader to the article. Finally, don't add a period after either the DOI or the URL.

In the newest edition of *MLA Handbook*, the recommendation is to include a DOI whenever possible. A DOI is preferred over a regular URL.

Journal article with DOI

> *APA* Jo, B., Asparouhov, T., Muthen, B. O., Ialongo, N. S., & Brown, C. H. (2008). Cluster randomized trials with treatment noncompliance. *Psychological Methods, 13*(1), 1–18. doi:10.1037/1082-989X.13.1.1

> *MLA* Jo, B., T. Asparouhov, B. O. Muthen, N. S. Ialongo, and C. H. Brown. "Cluster randomized trials with treatment noncompliance." *Psychological Methods*, vol. 13, no. 1, 2008, pp. 1–18, doi:10.1037/1082-989X.13.1.1.

Journal article without DOI

> *SSS* Orleans, Myron. 2000. "Introducing low politics: For character, courage and charisma in everyday life," *Journal of Mundane Behavior* v 1 no 3, 5–8. Retrieved on 14 Dec. 2007 http://www.mundanebehavior.org/index.htm

> *APA* Orleans, M. (2000). Introducing low politics: For character, courage and charisma in everyday life. *Journal of Mundane Behavior, 1*(3), 5–8. Retrieved from http://www.mundanebehavior.org/index.htm

MLA   Orleans, Myron. "Introducing Low Politics: For Character, Courage and Charisma in Everyday Life." *Journal of Mundane Behavior*, vol. 1, no. 3, 2000, pp. 5–8, www.mundanebehavior.org/index.htm.

Online newspaper article based on a print source

SSS   Winsa, Patty. "As fundraising gap grows, Toronto's wealthy schools leaving poor schools behind," 11 Apr. 2015. Retrieved on 11 Aug. 2017 https://www.thestar.com/ yourtoronto/education/2015/04/11/as-fundraising-gap-grows-torontos-wealthy-schools-leaving-poor-schools-behind.html

APA   Winsa, P. (2015, April 11). As fundraising gap grows, Toronto's wealthy schools leaving poor schools behind. *Toronto Star*. Retrieved from https://www.thestar.com/ yourtoronto/education/2015/04/11/as-fundraising-gap-grows-torontos-wealthy-schools-leaving-poor-schools-behind.html

MLA   Winsa, Patty. "As fundraising gap grows, Toronto's wealthy schools leaving poor schools behind." *Toronto Star*, 11 Apr. 2015, www.thestar.com/ yourtoronto/education/2015/04/11/as-fundraising-gap-grows-torontos-wealthy-schools-leaving-poor-schools-behind.html.

Lecture or presentation notes

In the MLA style, in cases where you are citing notes that are available online as PDF files or PowerPoint slides on a course site, use the following style:

MLA   Smith, Irene. "SRM101 Week 2: What Is Social Research?" *Social Research Methods 101*. Social Research Methods. Dept. of Sociology, Queen's University. 18 Sept. 2014. Online lecture notes.

In the APA style, when citing online lecture notes, provide the file format in brackets after the lecture title (e.g., PowerPoint slides, Word document).

APA   Smith, I. (2014, September 18). What is social research? [PDF document]. *Social Research Methods 101*. Retrieved from http://www.soc.nonameU.ca/wisr.html

APA   Robins, K. F. C. (2014, June 5). Creating effective presentations [PowerPoint slides]. *Introduction to Public Speaking*. Retrieved from http://great.slides.ca/ppt/cep.html

Summary

As the examples in this chapter show, there is considerable variance in how to document sources, both in the text of an essay or report and in the *References* section. The three referencing methods highlighted here (and remember that these are just three of many methods) vary widely in places, and to complicate matters further, they are constantly changing, as new ways of conducting and publishing research demand updated guidelines for documenting. For example, the DOI system was not in use when we published previous editions of this book, but it is an important facet of APA-style documentation now.

How can you stay on top of the changes? Fortunately, many organizations and journals that recommend a particular referencing style have websites and even Twitter accounts with up-to-date information on new or revised guidelines. In addition, your college or university department or library may have a website with information on how to document sources. It's always a good idea to check there first in case of particular conventions or a particular style preferred by your department.

11   Presenting Your Work

In this chapter we will examine

- strategies for effectively sharing your work with others;
- ways of making the most of your visual aids; and
- suggestions on how to respond effectively to questions about your work.

Introduction

Good research serves little purpose if it is not presented in a clear, convincing manner. This might seem obvious, but making a presentation that is both clear and convincing is perhaps one of the most difficult things for most people. In fact, public speaking may be among the most dreaded of all activities for some people. But there are others who often talk in front of an audience or people who are naturally outgoing, who enjoy giving a presentation, and even find it fun. Regardless of whether you are a professional or a novice, an extrovert or an introvert, a natural performer or a recluse, there are things you can do to help you garner praise and admiration instead of snores and heckles.

Making Presentations

To start, you need to know your topic, your audience, and your own strengths and weaknesses. How you come across will depend on how well you have prepared. You need to seem like someone with expertise, and authority. Your audience needs to think that you know at least as much as they do—preferably more. Otherwise, why should they listen to you?

Know your topic

You need to be confident that you know your topic. You don't want to stand up in front of the group and seem unprepared. Do your research and ask yourself whether you have done everything possible, given the time available. Also ask yourself: "Can I answer any questions that may arise?"

Know your audience

Once you know your topic, make sure you know your audience. Remember, your presentation won't be a success unless you connect with the people who are listening. Are they interested in your topic? Are they generally well informed about the subject matter? Can they understand specialized words? Are they good listeners, or do they act rudely or check their email and send texts? You can't choose or change your audience, but you *can* try to connect with them, on their level, and perhaps inspire their interest and attention.

Plan your presentation

Plan how to deliver your presentation in order to catch your audience's interest. Open with a question or a joke. Whatever you do, don't pull out sloppy notes and start reading in a monotone voice. If needed, make index cards with key ideas, catchphrases, or quotes on them, or create presentation slides with more detailed notes for you to refer to. You can look at these prompters now and then to refresh your memory, but deliver your talk as though you're taking part in a conversation, not reading from notes. Making eye contact with the audience throughout your talk may be the single most valuable thing you can do to keep their attention.

Consider preparing an outline for your audience

It's natural for listeners' attention to wander, even during the best presentations. People have lives outside the classroom—worries about family or work, or thoughts about Saturday night. These thoughts battle for your listeners' attention. To keep your listeners on track (especially if they drifted), provide an outline of your talk. Don't overwhelm them with details: just the main points—key words, in bullet form.

Rehearse your talk

While you may know what you want to say and how you want to say it, no one can perform well without rehearsing. In fact, you have to rehearse your material enough that it sounds as though you haven't rehearsed at all. Frank Sinatra, one of the great singers of the twentieth century, was famous among musicians for the careful way he rehearsed every part of every performance so it would seem natural and dreamy. Rehearse your material in front of a family member, roommate, or friend—anyone who will listen. Rehearse in front of a mirror. If you can't get your material across to a small audience without breaking into a panic, you aren't ready.

Giving Your Talk

Remember, you are presenting *yourself*, as well as your material. Here are a few tips to help you feel comfortable and capture your audience's attention.

Dress comfortably

Naturally, you always look great. However, here's something simple to keep in mind: dress comfortably. You might look great wearing five-inch heels to a club, but in class on presentation day this may not inspire admiration in your classmates. At the same time, in most classroom settings, wearing a suit and tie wouldn't work either. It's always best to dress in a comfortable but professional manner.

When you present material in class, you are putting yourself forward as an authority on your topic. Ask yourself how an expert on climate change (or anorexia, global poverty, domestic violence, racial conflict, and so on) would dress. You want to look professional and serious.

Try to relax

Looking relaxed is easier said than done, especially if you are feeling nervous and unprepared. Assume you will be nervous, and prepare yourself to manage it during your presentation. Some people meditate or listen to music beforehand. Some even think of their audience with no clothes on: that would certainly make them seem less menacing! Remember that they are just people like you and that they too will soon have to present in front of you.

Project your voice

Voice control and voice projection are important in presentations. Don't mumble, or yell, for that matter. Get the message out there. If you saw the 2010 movie *The King's Speech*, you'll remember that even the king of England needed to learn voice control in order to inspire confidence with his voice.

To start, avoid *uptalk*. Uptalking is ending declarative sentences (ones that end with a period) with an upward turn of the voice, as though you are asking a question or seeking permission to say what you are saying. Lamentably, more women than men in our culture are taught to speak this way; but uptalk mainly undermines people's authority, making them seem less knowledgeable and less decisive than those who do not uptalk. Breaking this habit takes time and work, especially because many of us are not aware that we are doing it. However, it will pay off. People will take you more seriously.

Pay attention to the speed at which you speak. If you speak too slowly, you will bore your audience. Speaking quickly will result in you being out of breath, and make it difficult for the class to follow along. Keep the pace comfortable and conversational.

Be confident

Besides voice projection and control, body language is important. When presenting, don't rock back and forth, stare at the ground, wave your hands around frantically, or do other distracting things. One teacher of ours used to shake the coins in his pants pockets when he spoke. This led us to make jokes about how much change he was carrying—a distraction from listening to what he was teaching.

Your body needs to communicate authority, conviction, and ease. Your audience will lose interest if your voice is saying "I am an expert!" but your body is saying "I don't want to be here."

Maintain eye contact with your audience

Some cultures consider it rude to make eye contact when conversing with people, as though you are probing for hidden information. In Canada, most people consider it rude and shifty if you *fail* to look into their eyes when you are speaking, as though you are trying to hide something. You do not want to give the impression you are afraid, embarrassed, or have something to hide (e.g., ignorance of the topic). Be sure to spend more time looking at your listeners than at your notes. Address people in the audience over the course of your presentation. Make them feel engaged in the presentation.

Work with your visual aids

Remember the old saying: a picture is worth a thousand words. Be sure to include visual aids in your presentation. Depending on your topic, this might include photographs, cartoons, graphs, diagrams, charts, video clips, or tables of numbers. Give your audience something to look at while they listen to you: like an outline, it will keep them attentive and even give them another way to grasp what you are saying. Increasingly, presenters distribute or project *infographics*—visual representations of data and information using a combination of charts, images and text—to engage their audience (see Figure 11.1).

Just as reading your notes is boring for listeners, so too is reading off your slides or other visual aids. When making a point that is illustrated on your slide, try to use different words and expand on what is there. Engage your audience using questions. Do not simply read the bullet points on the screen. That style of delivery is tedious and suggests the audience cannot read it for themselves. However, be sure to give your audience time to read through each visual. Many will find it frustrating to see images or text flash by before they've had a chance to take it all in.

If you use figures, diagrams, or graphs, explain them. Describe what the x- and y-axes represent on graphs. Explain what the graph shows. Take the audience through diagrams step by step. Some people are good at reading figures and graphs, but many are not. Some need your help.

Make sure your visual aids are appealing and clear. If an image is too big or too small, too cluttered, or too dull, find another. Imagine how it might look on a big screen. If it is not complementing your presentation, it may be detracting from it—and likely defeating the purpose.

Pace yourself

Most instructors assign a set amount of time for presentations. Use all of your available time: finishing too soon means you didn't do enough research, didn't

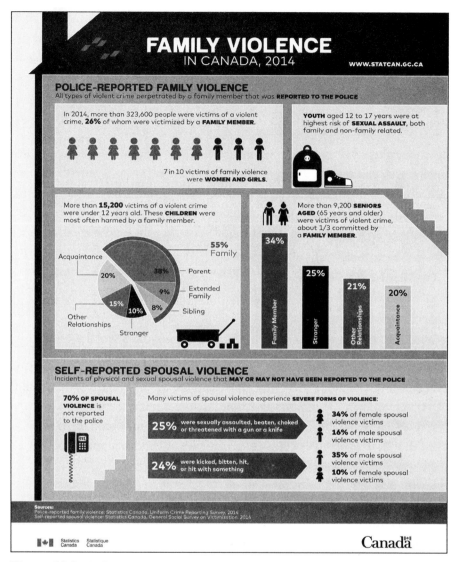

Figure 11.1 Infographic—Family Violence in Canada, 2014

Source: Statistics Canada, 2016 (http://www.statcan.gc.ca/pub/11-627-m/11-627-m2016001-eng.pdf).

have much to say, or went through the material too quickly. But don't go over your allotted time. At worst, you will be cut off in the middle of a sentence. At best, your listeners will be irritated by your presumption that you don't need to follow the same rules they do.

How do you achieve the desirable outcome of not too much or too little material, delivered at a pace that people can follow without getting bored or distracted? The answer, again, is lots of rehearsal. Prepare well and time your-self. Practise your presentation. Above all, watch the clock.

Prepare yourself mentally, and then ease into it. Likely, you will speed up as you get going, so start slowly. Grab the listener with your confidence: be slow and steady, at least at first. Build your argument and impassioned feelings as you go.

Have a strong ending

Listeners are likely to remember different things about a presentation: what you wore, how you spoke, and whether you seemed confident. Above all, you want them to remember your main point: the nugget or take-home message you are trying to put across.

Try to capture your main message in a phrase or short sentence and hammer that message home. As you are finishing your presentation, remind your audience one more time. Tell them, "Here is my point: 'Global warming means a less predictable climate, not always a hotter climate.'" Or, "Wars are never the result of only one cause, and never the doing of one bad country." Or, "We cannot solve the problem of crime in Canada by locking everyone up." Then, give them one more thing to think about—something they haven't heard already that follows from this message and that will make them want to find more information about your topic.

Multimedia Presentations

Increasingly, students are required to share their work with others through multimedia presentations. Instructors ask students to produce multimedia presentations for a number of reasons: to facilitate active learning among students (Rabinowitz, Kernodle, and McKethan, 2010); to diversify students' learning experiences; to help students learn to critically evaluate online re-sources; to encourage students to effectively incorporate different kinds of in-formation; to give students an opportunity to learn new computer skills; and to sharpen students' communication skills (Francek, 2000). Research shows that integrating video clips in multimedia presentations increases students' perception of important information, increases motivation for learning, and helps students better understand and remember key points (Ljubojevic, Vaskovic, Stankovic, and Vaskovic, 2014).

The advent of "slideware" technology such as Microsoft PowerPoint, Apple Keynote, Prezi, and OpenOffice Impress has transformed the classroom experience (Strasser, 2014), but some people, including instructors, continue to use these technologies ineffectively (Tangen et al., 2011). In fact, research has found that how tools like PowerPoint are (mis)used routinely disrupts, dominates, or trivializes the content of a presentation (Gross and Harmon, 2009; Tufte, 2003). These tools should enhance your message rather than detract from it. A good presentation should enhance creativity, assist with visualization of content, and encourage collaboration (Strasser, 2014). A number of experts have put together lists of tips and suggestions on how to do this. We summarize some here.

Pugsley (2010: 51) notes that the aims of visual design are to

- ensure legibility;
- simplify the message;
- increase learner engagement;
- focus learner attention on (a few) important points; and
- provide an alternative channel of communication.

While the quality and structure of your information and argument are of utmost importance, when planning your presentation you need to consider visual and typographical elements as well, including font size and spacing, case (capitals versus lower case), colour, quantity of information on each slide, animation or action, and overall appeal (Pugsley, 2010). Try to avoid pre-set templates. Experiment with slide design, animation, transitions, and fonts. Keep in mind the following advice when preparing visuals for a presentation:

- A sans serif font like Arial is easier to read at a distance than a serif font like Times New Roman (Pugsley, 2010: 52).
- The focal point for capturing attention with images is slightly off centre—therefore, the placement of objects and images is important (Francek, 2000: 202).
- SENTENCES WRITTEN IN CAPITALS ARE DIFFICULT TO READ—because we are accustomed to reading conventions that place a capital letter at the beginning of the sentence only, our ability to process information can be confused by change or excess (Pugsley, 2010: 52).
- Colour choice is crucial: darker colours for backgrounds are more effective than lighter ones (Francek, 2000: 202), pale colours on a white background

should be avoided, and the colours you see on your screen may be altered by the quality of the projector and strength of the bulb during your presentation (Pugsley, 2010: 52). Don't be tempted to use overly bright colours throughout the presentation; while eye-catching, they may become distracting to audiences over the course of the presentation.

Keep your slides clean, clear, and simple. *Never* simply read word for word what appears on your slides. Some people, like Gross and Harmon (2009: 134), warn that "verbal and visual clutter combine to transform the audience's goodwill into bewilderment and hostility." Research assessing the effectiveness of slideware-enhanced presentations has found that the audience is more interested in image-rich slides than bullet points. But be sure that images are relevant to the content of the presentation (Tangen et al., 2011; also see Mackiewicz, 2008).

If you find something relevant, consider inserting *brief* audio or video clips to bring your research to life. The Internet offers many interesting, controversial, and easy-to-use clips. But always assess the relevance, authenticity, and quality of the clip. You may do well to consult with your professor, as you should never let the clips replace important material that you should have covered on your own.

The rules of copyright and plagiarism are as applicable here as they are in regular essay writing (see AlSaffar, 2006). Always cite your sources and give credit where credit is due.

But remember, pretty pictures and bulleted points in eye-catching fonts and colours cannot make up for poor research, unsound and illogical arguments, or lack of confidence. Good presentations are well organized and presented with confidence, and they don't end with the last slide. Usually, presentations are followed by a question period—another opportunity to demonstrate to your audience your knowledge of the topic. For the question period, the basic rules of "be prepared" and "be organized" still apply.

Preparing for Questions

Try to anticipate what your classmates and instructor may ask you. What would you ask if you were in the audience? Having a series of questions—and answers—ready, ahead of time, may help you begin class discussion if nobody actually comes forward with questions.

When you are asked a question, repeat it for all to hear. Remember, you are facing the audience, but those asking the questions typically are not. Repeating the question also gives you a few moments to process what you are being asked before answering it.

If you did not hear or understand a question, ask the person to repeat or rephrase it. There is no point beginning to answer before you know what is being asked. Keep your answers short and to the point. Don't ramble and go off on tangents. At best, you will bore your audience, at worst, you'll look like a know-it-all—in both cases, you will lose the attention and respect of your audience. Finally, if you don't know an answer, say so. It's better to admit not knowing than to bluff your way through and make up a response that at least some members of your audience will know is incorrect. Not knowing an answer may provide an opportunity to open the discussion up to others in the class. Perhaps a classmate can help answer the question and spark further debate. Use your inability to answer as an opportunity to engage more members of your audience.

Do your best to remain calm and maintain your confidence and composure. Remember, answering questions gives you the opportunity to increase your credibility. When you did your background research, you likely found more information than you could use in your presentation. Now may be the time to draw upon that.

Summary

Doing oral presentations, in the classroom and on the job, is an important—but at times daunting—part of sharing your work and knowledge with others. In this chapter we have shared a few strategies and suggestions on how to make presentations less intimidating and how to improve your presentation style. Keep these simple rules in mind and you should be fine: know what you are talking about and to whom you are presenting. Remember that all good performances require work and rehearsal. Be prepared, be organized, and be confident.

12

Common Errors in Grammar and Usage

In this chapter we will examine

- common errors students make when it comes to sentence structure;
- specific challenges, including problems with pronouns, with examples and approaches to overcoming them; and
- troubles students often encounter with modifiers and when dealing with pairs and comparisons.

Introduction

This chapter is not a comprehensive grammar lesson; it's a survey of areas where students often make mistakes. It will help you be aware of weaknesses as you are editing your work. Once you get into the habit of checking your work, it won't be long before you can correct potential problems as you write.

The grammatical terms used here are some of the most basic and familiar ones; if you need to review some of them, see Glossary II. Many excellent grammar books are currently available—your university library or bookstore will have several to choose from, and some institutions may offer free online resources, as well.

Troubles with Sentence Unity

Sentence fragments

To be complete, a sentence must have both a subject and a verb in an independent clause; if it doesn't, it's a fragment. Occasionally a sentence fragment is acceptable, as in the following example:

✔ Will the government try to abolish the gun registry? <u>Not likely</u>.

Here the sentence fragment *Not likely* is intended to be understood as a short form of *It is not likely that it will try.* Unintentional sentence fragments, on the other hand, seem incomplete rather than shortened:

> ✗ Marx had little respect for capitalism. <u>Being a thinker who opposed exploitation</u>.

The last "sentence" is incomplete: where are the subject and verb? (Remember that a participle such as *being* is not a verb; *-ing* words by themselves are only verbals or part-verbs.) The fragment can be made into a complete sentence by adding a subject and a verb:

> ✔ Marx had little respect for capitalism. <u>He was</u> a thinker who opposed exploitation.

Alternatively, you could join the fragment to the preceding sentence:

> ✔ Being a thinker who opposed exploitation, Marx had little respect for capitalism.

> ✔ Marx had little respect for capitalism because he was a thinker who opposed exploitation.

Run-on sentences

A run-on sentence is one that continues beyond the point where it should have stopped:

> ✗ Capitalism is exploitative, but this doesn't stop workers from voting for "establishment" political parties such is the case in England.

This run-on sentence could be fixed by adding a period or semicolon after *parties*:

> ✔ Capitalism is exploitative, but this doesn't stop workers from voting for "establishment" political parties. Such is the case in England.

Another kind of run-on sentence is one in which two independent clauses (phrases that could stand by themselves as sentences) are wrongly joined by a comma:

✗ Marshall McLuhan won international acclaim as a communications theorist, he was a professor of English literature at the University of Toronto.

This error is known as a *comma splice*. Three ways of correcting it include:

1. putting a period after *theorist* and starting a new sentence:

   ✔ . . . as a communications theorist. He . . .

2. replacing the comma with a semicolon:

   ✔ . . . as a communications theorist; he . . .

3. making one of the independent clauses subordinate to the other:

   ✔ Marshall McLuhan, who won international acclaim as a communications theorist, was a professor of English literature at the University of Toronto.

The one exception to the rule that independent clauses cannot be joined by a comma arises when the clauses are short and arranged in a tight sequence:

✔ I examined, I explored, I discovered.

Such instances are not common.

Contrary to what many people think, words such as *however, therefore,* and *thus* cannot be used to join independent clauses:

✗ I would like to finish my essay, however my favourite show is on soon.

This mistake can be corrected either by beginning a new sentence after *essay* or (preferably) by putting a semicolon in the same place:

✔ I would like to finish my essay; however, my favourite show is on soon.

Another option is to join the two independent clauses with a coordinating conjunction—*and*, *or*, *nor*, *but*, *for*, *yet*, or *so*.

> ✔ I would like to finish my essay, but my favourite show is on soon.

Faulty predication

When the subject of a sentence is not grammatically connected to what follows (the predicate), the result is *faulty predication*:

> ✗ The <u>reason</u> he did poorly on the exam <u>was because</u> he watched too much television.

The problem here is that *because* essentially means the same thing as *the reason*. The subject is a noun and the verb *was* needs a noun clause to complete it:

> ✔ The <u>reason</u> he did poorly on the exam <u>was that</u> he watched too much television.

Another solution would be to rephrase the sentence:

> ✔ He did poorly on the exam <u>because</u> he watched too much television.

Faulty predication also occurs with *is when* or *is where* constructions:

> ✗ The critical moment <u>is when</u> the researcher discovers the original source.

You can correct this error in one of two ways:

1. Follow the *is* with a noun phrase to complete the sentence:

    > ✔ The critical moment <u>is the discovery</u> of the original source by the researcher.

    (or)

    > ✔ The critical moment <u>is the researcher's discovery</u> of the original source.

2. Change the verb:

✔ The critical moment <u>occurs</u> when the researcher discovers the original source.

Troubles with Subject–Verb Agreement

Identifying the subject

A verb should always agree in number with its subject. Sometimes, however, when the subject does not come at the beginning of the sentence, or when it is separated from the verb by other information, you may be tempted to use a verb form that does not agree:

✗ The <u>increase</u> in tuition and the cost of books <u>were condemned</u> by the students.

The subject here is *increase*, not *tuition and the cost of books*; therefore the verb should be the singular *was condemned*:

✔ The <u>increase</u> in tuition and the cost of books <u>was condemned</u> by the students.

Either, neither, each

The indefinite pronouns *either*, *neither*, and *each* always take singular verbs:

✗ <u>Neither</u> of the changing rooms <u>have</u> a sauna.
✔ <u>Each</u> of them <u>has</u> a shower.

Compound subjects

When *or*, *either . . . or*, or *neither . . . nor* is used to create a compound subject, the verb should usually agree with the last item in the subject:

✔ Neither she nor <u>her associates are</u> attending the conference.
✔ Either the students or <u>the professor was</u> misinformed.

You may find, however, that sometimes it sounds awkward to use a singular verb when a singular item follows a plural item:

✔ Either my history books or my sociology <u>text</u> <u>is</u> going to gather dust this weekend.

In such instances, it's better to rephrase the sentence:

✔ This weekend, I will be reading either my history books or my sociology text.

Unlike the word *and*, which creates a compound subject and therefore takes a plural verb, the phrases *as well as* and *in addition to* do not create compound subjects; therefore the verb remains singular:

✔ Low pay <u>and</u> a dangerous working environment <u>are</u> causes of employee dissatisfaction.

✔ Low pay, <u>as well as</u> a dangerous working environment, <u>is</u> a cause of employee dissatisfaction.

Collective nouns

A collective noun is a singular noun that includes many members, such as *family*, *army*, or *team*. If the noun refers to the members as a unit, it takes a singular verb:

✔ The football <u>team</u> <u>is</u> playing a home game this weekend.

If, in the context of the sentence, the noun refers to the members as individuals, the verb becomes plural:

✔ The <u>team</u> <u>are</u> receiving their medals after the game.

✔ The <u>majority</u> of immigrants to Canada <u>settle</u> in Montreal, Toronto, or Vancouver.

Titles

The title of a book or a movie is always considered singular, even if it contains plural words; therefore it takes a singular verb:

✔ *Modern Social Theories* was a bestseller.

Tense Troubles

Native speakers of English usually know without thinking which verb tense to use in a given context; however, a few tenses can still be confusing.

The past perfect

If the main verb is in the past tense and you want to refer to something that happened before that time, use the past perfect (*had* followed by the past participle). The time sequence will not be clear if you use the simple past in both clauses:

✘ He <u>hoped</u> that she <u>finished</u> her paper so they could go to the movies.

✔ He <u>hoped</u> that she <u>had finished</u> her paper so they could go to the movies.

Similarly, when you are reporting what someone said in the past—that is, when you are using past indirect discourse—you should use the past perfect tense in the clause describing what was said:

✘ He <u>told</u> the TA that he <u>wrote</u> the essay that week.

✔ He <u>told</u> the TA that he <u>had written</u> the essay that week.

Using *if*

When you are describing a possibility in the future, use the present tense in the condition *(if)* clause and the future tense in the consequence clause:

✔ If she <u>tests</u> us on postmodernism, I <u>will fail</u>.

When the possibility is unlikely, it is conventional—especially in formal writing—to use the subjunctive in the *if* clause, and *would* followed by the base verb in the consequence clause:

> ✔ If she <u>were</u> to cancel the test, I <u>would cheer</u>.

When you are describing a hypothetical instance in the past, use the past subjunctive (it has the same form as the past perfect) in the *if* clause and *would have* followed by the past participle for the consequence. A common error is to use *would have* in both clauses:

> ✗ If the TA <u>would have been</u> clearer, I <u>would have understood</u> him better.

> ✔ If the TA <u>had been</u> clearer, I <u>would have understood</u> him better.

Writing about books

To describe a book in its historical context, use the past tense:

> ✔ John Porter <u>wrote</u> *The Vertical Mosaic* at a time when most people believed all Canadians had a good chance at upward mobility.

To discuss what goes on *within* the work, however, you should use the present tense:

> ✔ Porter <u>sees</u> educational opportunity as important to ordinary Canadians, but not to elites.

When you are discussing an episode or incident in the work and want to refer to a prior or future incident, use past or future tenses accordingly:

> ✔ The author <u>reminds</u> us that, historically, children <u>were</u> employed in light manufacturing; today, we hope for a future in which all children <u>will be prevented</u> from working long hours in dangerous work conditions.

Be sure to return to the present tense when you have finished referring to events in the past or future.

Pronoun Troubles

Pronoun reference

The link between a pronoun and the noun it refers to must be clear. If the noun doesn't appear in the same sentence as the pronoun, it should appear in the preceding sentence:

> ✗ The <u>textbook supply</u> in the bookstore had run out, so we borrowed <u>them</u> from the library.

Because *textbook* is used as an adjective rather than a noun, it cannot serve as referent or antecedent for the pronoun *them*. You must either replace *them* or change the phrase *textbook supply*.

> ✔ The <u>textbook supply</u> in the bookstore had run out, so we borrowed <u>the texts</u> from the library.

> ✔ The bookstore had run out of <u>textbooks</u>, so we borrowed <u>them</u> from the library.

When a sentence contains more than one noun, make sure to avoid ambiguity about which noun the pronoun refers to:

> ✗ The public wants increased <u>social services</u> as well as lower <u>taxes</u>, but the government does not advocate <u>them</u>.

What does the pronoun *them* refer to: the taxes, the social services, or both?

> ✔ The public wants increased social services as well as lower taxes, but the government does not advocate <u>spending increases</u>.

Using *it* and *this*

Using *it* and *this* without a clear referent can lead to confusion:

✗ Although the students wanted to meet in September, <u>it</u> (<u>this</u>) didn't take place until May.

✔ Although the students wanted to meet in September, <u>the gathering</u> didn't take place until May.

Make sure that *it* or *this* clearly refers to a specific noun or pronoun.

Pronoun agreement and gender

A pronoun should agree in number and person with the noun to which it refers. However, an increasing awareness of sexist or biased language has changed what is considered acceptable over the last few decades. In the past, the following sentence would have been considered incorrect:

When a Canadian <u>civil servant</u> retires, <u>their</u> pension is indexed.

It would have been "corrected" to read:

When a Canadian <u>civil servant</u> retires, <u>his</u> pension is indexed.

This is because, traditionally, the word *his* has been used to indicate both male and female. Although some language experts still maintain that *he* and *his* have dual meanings—one for an individual male and one for any human being—today this usage is widely regarded as sexist. Some have addressed this issue by using *he or she* (or *he/she*) and *his or her* (or *his/her*), but these phrases are awkward and cumbersome. For this reason, using *their* or *they* to indicate a single person of either gender is becoming increasingly common, and this trend appears to be gaining acceptance.

As a result, the first sentence above would now be considered correct by many, though some people would still consider it incorrect. To be on the safe side, you may prefer to rephrase the sentence, by switching from the singular to the plural:

✔ When Canadian civil <u>servants</u> retire, <u>their</u> pensions are indexed.

Whichever form you choose, check for agreement between subjects and verbs. Use neutral nouns whenever possible, and, where appropriate, at least try to make clear in your examples and illustrations that you are referring to females as well as males—unless you have a clear need to differentiate.

Using *one*

People often use the word *one* to avoid overusing *I* in their writing. Although in Britain this is common, in Canada and the United States frequent use of *one* may seem too formal and even pretentious:

> If <u>one</u> were to apply for the scholarship, <u>one</u> would find <u>oneself</u> engulfed in so many bureaucratic forms that <u>one's</u> patience would be stretched thin.

In the past, a common way around this problem was to use the third-person *his* or (less often) *her* as the adjectival form of *one*. Today, this usage is regarded with less acceptance. As we saw in the preceding section, you may also be able to substitute the plural *their*; just remember that some people still object to this usage as well. The best solution, again, may be to rephrase the sentence with a plural subject:

> If <u>students</u> were to apply for the scholarship, <u>they</u> would find <u>them-selves</u> engulfed in so many bureaucratic forms that <u>their</u> patience would be stretched thin.

In any case, try to use *one* sparingly, and don't be afraid of the occasional *I*. The major serious error to avoid is mixing the third-person *one* with the second-person *you*.

> ✗   When <u>one</u> studies policies and laws, <u>you</u> are often surprised by their gender bias.

In formal academic writing generally, *you* is not an appropriate substitution for *one*.

Using *me* and other objective pronouns

Remembering that it's wrong to say "Katja and me were invited to present our findings to the class," rather than "Katja and I were invited," many people use the subjective form of the pronoun even when it should be objective:

✘ The professor <u>invited</u> Katja and <u>I</u> to present our findings.

✔ The professor <u>invited</u> Katja and <u>me</u> to present our findings.

The verb *invited* requires an object; *me* is the objective case. Here is a simple hint: read the sentence with only the problem pronoun. You will know by ear which is correct.

✘ The professor invited <u>I</u> to present the findings.

✔ The professor invited <u>me</u> to present the findings.

Prepositions should also be followed by the objective case:

✘ <u>Between</u> you and <u>I</u>, Woody Allen is a bore.

✔ <u>Between</u> you and <u>me</u>, Woody Allen is a bore.

✘ Eating well is a problem <u>for we</u> students.

✔ Eating well is a problem <u>for us</u> students.

Sometimes, however, the correct case can sound stiff or awkward: for example,

✔ <u>To whom</u> was the award given?

Rather than keeping to a correct but awkward form, try to reword the sentence:

✔ <u>Who received</u> the award?

Exceptions for pronouns following prepositions

The rule that a pronoun following a preposition takes the objective case has exceptions. When the preposition is followed by a clause, the pronoun should take the case required by its position in the clause:

✗   The students showed some concern <u>over whom would be selected</u> as class rep.

Although the pronoun follows the preposition *over, whom* is also the subject of the verb *would be selected* and therefore requires the subjective case:

✔   The students showed some concern <u>over who would be selected</u> as class rep.

Similarly, when a gerund (a word that acts partly as a noun and partly as a verb) is the subject of a clause, the pronoun that modifies it takes the possessive case:

✗   Darcy was elated <u>by him winning</u> the most valuable player award.

✔   Darcy was elated <u>by his winning</u> the most valuable player award.

Troubles with Modifiers

Adjectives modify nouns; adverbs modify verbs, adjectives, and other adverbs. Do not use an adjective to modify a verb:

✗   He played <u>good</u>. (adjective with verb)

✔   He played <u>well</u>. (adverb modifying verb)

✔   He played <u>really well</u>. (adverb modifying adverb)

✔   He had a <u>good</u> style. (adjective modifying noun)

✔   He had a <u>really good</u> style. (adverb modifying adjective)

Squinting modifiers

Remember that clarity largely depends on word order: to avoid confusion, the relations between the different parts of a sentence must be clear. Modifiers should, therefore, be as close as possible to the words they modify. A *squinting* modifier is one that, because of its position, seems to look in two directions at once:

> ✗   She expected <u>in the spring</u> a rise in property taxes.

Is *spring* the time of expectation or the time of the property tax increase? Try changing the order of the sentence to make the logical relation clearest:

> ✔   <u>In the spring</u> she <u>expected</u> a rise in property taxes.

> ✔   She expected a <u>spring increase</u> in property taxes.

Other squinting modifiers can be corrected in the same way:

> ✗   Our professor gave a lecture on linear regression, <u>which was well illustrated</u>.

> ✔   Our professor gave a <u>well-illustrated lecture</u> on linear regression.

Dangling modifiers

Modifiers that have no grammatical connection with anything else in the sentence are said to be *dangling*:

> ✗   <u>Walking</u> around the campus in January, the frozen river and snow-covered trees made a picturesque scene.

Who is doing the walking? Here's another example:

> ✗   <u>Reflecting</u> on the results of the opinion polls, it was decided not to call an election for a while.

Who is doing the reflecting? Clarify the meaning by connecting the dangling modifier to a new subject:

✔ <u>Walking</u> around the campus in January, <u>she</u> thought the frozen river and snow-covered trees made a picturesque scene.

✔ <u>Reflecting</u> on the results of the opinion polls, <u>the government</u> decided not to call an election for a while.

Troubles with Pairs (and More)

Comparisons

Make sure that your comparisons are complete. The second element in a comparison should be equivalent to the first, whether the equivalence is stated or merely implied.

✘ Today's students have a greater understanding of new technology than some of their professors.

This sentence suggests the two things being compared are *technology* and *professors*. Adding a second verb (*have*) that is equivalent to the first one shows that the two things being compared are *professors' understanding* and *students' understanding*:

✔ Today's students <u>have</u> a greater understanding of new technology than some of their professors <u>have</u>.

A similar problem arises in the following comparison:

✘ That cabinet minister is <u>a tiresome man</u> and so are his press conferences.

Press conferences may be tiresome, but they are not *a tiresome man*; to make sense, the two parts of the comparison must be parallel:

✔ That cabinet minister is <u>tiresome</u> and so are his press conferences.

Correlatives

Constructions such as *both . . . and*, *not only . . . but*, and *neither . . . nor* are especially tricky. The coordinating term must not come too early or else one of the parts that comes after will not connect with the common element. For the implied comparison to work, the two parts that come after the coordinating term must be grammatically equivalent:

✘   He <u>not only</u> uses social networking <u>but</u> microblogging services too.

✔   He uses <u>not only</u> social networking <u>but</u> microblogging services too.

✘   He <u>neither</u> plays soccer <u>nor</u> basketball.

✔   He plays <u>neither</u> soccer <u>nor</u> basketball.

Parallel phrasing

A series of items in a sentence should be phrased in parallel wording. Make sure that all the parts of a parallel construction are in fact equal:

✘   Stephen Harper loves <u>his</u> job, <u>his</u> country, and wife.

✔   Stephen Harper loves <u>his</u> job, <u>his</u> country, and <u>his</u> wife.

The sentence can be modified by using the pronoun *his* before the first element only; however, once you have decided to include the pronoun *his* with the first two elements, the third element must have it too.

For clarity as well as stylistic grace, keep similar ideas in similar form:

✘   He <u>failed</u> economics and <u>barely passed</u> statistics, but political science <u>was</u> a subject he did well in.

✔   He <u>failed</u> economics and barely <u>passed</u> statistics, but he <u>did well</u> in political science.

13 Punctuation

In this chapter we will examine

- rules of punctuation and why we need them;
- ways to use commas, periods, semicolons, and colons; and
- ways to use punctuation marks in sentences of varying complexity.

Introduction

Punctuation, anyone? If we all wrote like Ernest Hemingway, we could avoid a chapter on punctuation. Or we could make do with a short chapter saying something like this: First, finish every thought-bite (or *sentence*) with a period. Second, if the thought-bite asks a question, finish it with a question mark. End of story. However, we don't all write like Ernest Hemingway, in short bursts of simple thought. Most people's sentences are closer to 20 words, and in academic writing, the norm is closer to 30 words or more.

Short sentences are punchy and attention-grabbing, but they get tiresome if overused. In most writing, sentences are longer because they need to contain clauses. These clauses elaborate on the key ideas in the sentence. If the sentence is written poorly, this elaboration can slow down the flow, making it harder to interpret. Well-written, well-punctuated writing, on the other hand, can speed the reader along by introducing one thought after another, almost seamlessly. To do this—to hold the reader's attention in the face of long and complicated thoughts—you need to punctuate your sentences properly. You need to show the reader where to pause briefly (as after a comma), where to pause a slightly longer time (as after a semicolon), and where to pause even longer and start the next bit with renewed emphasis (as after a colon).

There's no way around this: if your punctuation is faulty, your readers will be confused. Worse still, they may be tempted to skip over rough spots. You will lose their interest; and, as you may suspect, poor punctuation can result in lower grades. Punctuation marks are the traffic signals of writing: use them with precision to keep readers moving smoothly through your work.

There is no easy way to learn about punctuation. You just have to expose yourself to the rules. Punctuation marks in this chapter are arranged alphabetically: *apostrophe, brackets, colon, comma, dash, ellipsis, exclamation mark, hyphen, parentheses, period, quotation marks,* and *semicolon.*

Apostrophe [']

The apostrophe forms the possessive case for nouns and some pronouns.

1. **Add an apostrophe followed by *s* to**
   - all singular and plural nouns *not* ending in *s*:

     cat's meow; women's studies

   - singular *proper* nouns ending in *s*:

     Keats's poetry; Carlos's ball

   Note, however, that the final *s* can be omitted if the word has a number of them already and would sound awkward, as in *Sisyphus'*, or if a name in French ends with a silent *s*, as in *Descartes'*.

   - indefinite pronouns:

     someone's; anybody's

2. **Add an apostrophe to plural nouns ending in *s*:**

   our families' pets; the lawyers' arguments

3. **Use an apostrophe to show contractions of words:**

   isn't; can't; winter of '16

   Caution: don't confuse *it's* (the contraction of *it is*) with the possessive of *it* (*its*), which has no apostrophe.

Brackets [ ]

Brackets are square enclosures, not to be confused with parentheses (which are curved; see p. 249).

Use brackets to set off a remark of your own within a quotation:

> Fox maintains, "Obstacles to Western unification [in this decade] are as numerous as they are serious."

Brackets are sometimes used to enclose *sic*, which is used after an error, such as a misspelling, to show that the mistake was in the original. *Sic* may be italicized or underlined:

> The politician, in his letter to constituents, wrote about "these parlouse [*sic*] times of economic difficulty."

Colon [:]

A colon indicates that something is to follow.

1. **Use a colon before a formal statement or series:**

   ✔ The winners are the following: Diana, Peter, Susan, and Hwan.

   Do not use a colon if the words preceding it do not form a complete sentence:

   ✘ The winners are: Diana, Peter, Susan, and Hwan.

   ✔ The winners are Diana, Peter, Susan, and Hwan.

   Occasionally, however, a colon is used if the list is arranged vertically:

   ✔ The winners are: Diana
   Peter
   Susan
   Hwan

2. **Use a colon for formality before a direct quotation:**

> ✔ The leaders of the anti-nuclear group repeated their message: "The world needs bread before bombs."

Comma [,]

Commas are the trickiest of all punctuation marks; even the experts differ on when to use them. Most agree, however, that too many commas are as bad as too few because too many make writing choppy and awkward to read. Recent writers use fewer commas than earlier writers did. When in doubt, let simplicity and clarity be your guide. If you are not sure, some of the most widely accepted conventions are these:

1. **Use a comma to separate two independent clauses joined by a coordinating conjunction (*and, but, for, or, nor, yet, so*).** By signalling that there are two clauses, the comma will prevent the reader from confusing the beginning of the second clause with the end of the first:

   > ✘ She went out for dinner with her sister and her roommate joined them later.

   > ✔ She went out for dinner with her sister, and her roommate joined them later.

   When the second clause has the same subject as the first, you have the option of omitting both the second subject and the comma:

   > ✔ He can make a convincing argument, but he can't put it in writing.

   > ✔ He can make a convincing argument but can't put it in writing.

   If you mistakenly punctuate two sentences as if they were one, the result will be a *run-on sentence*; if you use a comma but forget the coordinating conjunction, the result will be a *comma splice*:

✘ She went to the library, it was closed.

✔ She went to the library, <u>but</u> it was closed.

Remember that words such as *however, therefore,* and *thus* are conjunctive adverbs, not conjunctions: if you use one of them the way you would use a conjunction, the result will again be a *comma splice*:

✘ He was accepted into law school, <u>however</u>, he took a year off to earn money for his tuition.

✔ He was accepted into law school; <u>however</u>, he took a year off to earn money for his tuition.

Conjunctive adverbs are often confused with conjunctions. You can distinguish between the two if you remember that a conjunctive adverb's position in a sentence can be changed:

✔ He was accepted into law school; he took a year off, <u>however</u>, to earn money for his tuition.

The position of a conjunction, on the other hand, is invariable: it must be placed between the two clauses:

✔ He was accepted into law school, <u>but</u> he took a year off to earn money for his tuition.

When, in rare cases, the independent clauses are short and closely related, they may be joined by a comma alone:

✔ I came, I saw, I conquered.

A *fused sentence* is a run-on sentence in which independent clauses are slapped together with no punctuation at all:

✘ He watched the hockey game all afternoon the only exercise he got was going to the kitchen between periods.

A fused sentence sounds like breathless babbling—and it's a serious error. This example could be fixed by adding a period or semicolon after the word *afternoon*.

✔ He watched the hockey game all afternoon. The only exercise he got was going to the kitchen between periods.

2. **Use a comma between items in a series** (place a coordinating conjunction before the last item):

✔ She finally found an apartment that was large, bright, and clean.

✔ Then she had to scrounge around for dishes, pots, cutlery, and a kettle.

The comma before the conjunction is optional:

✔ She adopted a cat, a dog and a budgie.

Sometimes, however, the final comma can help to prevent confusion:

✗ For breakfast, I had coffee, cinnamon toast and yoghurt.

In this case, a comma can prevent the reader from thinking that *cinnamon toast* and *yoghurt* are a single item or that both the toast and yoghurt are cinnamon flavoured:

✔ For breakfast, I had coffee, cinnamon toast, and yoghurt.

3. **Use a comma to separate adjectives preceding a noun when they modify the same element:**

✔ It was a cold, dark night.

When the adjectives *do not* modify the same element, however, you should not use a comma:

✗ It was a pleasant, winter outing.

Here *winter* modifies *outing*, but *pleasant* modifies the whole phrase *winter outing*. A good way of checking whether or not you need a comma is to see if you can reverse the order of the adjectives. If you can reverse it (*cold, dark night* or *dark, cold night*), use a comma; if you can't (*winter pleasant outing*), omit the comma:

✔ It was a pleasant winter outing.

4. **Use commas to set off an interruption (or "parenthetical element"):**

✔ My tutor, however, couldn't answer the question.

✔ The film, I hear, isn't nearly as good as the book.

✔ The music, they say, was adapted from a piece by Mozart.

Remember to put commas on *both sides* of the interruption:

✘ The film I hear, isn't nearly as good as the book.

✘ The music, they say was adapted from a piece by Mozart.

5. **Use commas to set off words or phrases that provide additional but non-essential information:**

✔ Our president, Sue Stephens, does her job well.

✔ The golden retriever, his closest companion, went with him everywhere.

In these examples, *Sue Stephens* and *his closest companion* are *appositives*: they give additional information about the nouns they refer to (*president* and *golden retriever*), but the sentences would still make sense without them. Here's another example:

✔ My oldest friend, who lives in Halifax, was married last week.

The phrase *who lives in Halifax* is called a *non-restrictive modifier*, because it does not limit the meaning of the word it modifies (*friend*). Without that modifying clause the sentence would still specify who was married. Because the information the clause provides is not necessary to the meaning of the sentence, you must use commas on both sides to set it off.

In contrast, a *restrictive modifier* is one that provides essential information; therefore, it must not be set apart from the element it modifies, and commas should not be used:

✔ The woman who came over to my place was my cousin.

Without the clause *who came over to my place*, the reader would not know which woman was the cousin. To avoid confusion, be sure to distinguish carefully between essential and additional information. The difference can be important:

✘ Students, who are not willing to work, should not receive grants.

The commas tell the reader that the writer meant, "Students should not receive grants." The commas set off "who are not willing to work"—the non-restrictive modifier—as additional information and non-essential. If the phrase was a restrictive modifier, indicating only those students who do not want to work, it would *not* be set off with commas:

✔ Students who are not willing to work should not receive grants.

6. **Use a comma after an introductory phrase when omitting it would cause confusion:**

✘ On the balcony above the singers entertained the diners.

✔ On the balcony above, the singers entertained the diners.

✘ When he turned away the prisoner disappeared.

✔ When he turned away, the prisoner disappeared.

7. **Use a comma to separate elements in dates and addresses:**

> February 2, 2015. (*Commas are often omitted if the day comes first:* *2 February 2015.*)

> 109 Hudson Bay Drive, Edmonton, Alberta.

> They lived in St. John's, Newfoundland.

8. **Use a comma before a quotation in a sentence:**

> ✔ He said, "Life is too short to worry."

> ✔ "The children's safety," he warned, "is in your hands."

For more formality, you may instead use a colon (see p. 239).

9. **Use a comma with a name followed by a title:**

> D. Patel, Ph.D.

> Pauline Lareau, M.D.

Dash [—]

A dash (also called an *em dash* because it's about the same width as a letter *m*) creates an abrupt pause, emphasizing the words that follow. Never use dashes as casual substitutes for other punctuation: overuse can detract from the calm, well-reasoned effect you want.

1. **Use a dash to stress a word or phrase:**

> The Egyptians—as a matter of honour—vowed to retake the islands.

> Ramirez was well received in the legislature—at first.

2. **Use a dash in interrupted or unfinished dialogue:**

"It's a matter—to put it delicately—of personal hygiene."

"I just thought—" Deborah began to explain, but Susan cut her off.

You can type two hyphens together, with no spaces on either side, to show a dash. Your software will likely automatically convert this to a dash for you as you continue typing. Alternatively, you can insert an em dash from the list of special characters in your word-processing software.

En dash [–]

An en dash is shorter than a full dash and slightly longer than a hyphen, approximately the width of a letter *n*. It denotes that there is a range from one thing to another.

Use an en dash rather than a hyphen to separate parts of inclusive numbers or dates:

The years 1812–1914

pages 7–12

See the **Hyphen** section on page 247 for guidelines on when to use a hyphen.

Ellipsis [. . .]

1. **Use an ellipsis (three spaced dots) to show an omission from a quotation:**

He reported that "the drought in the thirties, to many farming families in the West . . ., resembled a biblical plague, with locusts and all" (Fenn, 2013: 33).

If the omission comes at the beginning or end of the quotation, an ellipsis is not typically used:

He reported that the drought "resembled a biblical plague, with locusts and all" (Fenn, 2013: 33).

However, ellipsis points may be included to prevent misinterpretation or to emphasize that the quotation begins or ends in midsentence:

He reported that the drought "resembled a biblical plague . . ." (Fenn, 2013: 33).

2. **Use an ellipsis to show that a series of numbers continues indefinitely:**

1, 3, 5, 7, 9 . . .

Exclamation Mark [!]

An exclamation mark helps to show emotion or feeling. It is usually found in dialogue:

"No way!" she declared.

In academic writing, you should only use an exclamation mark in those rare instances when you want to give a point an emotional emphasis:

He predicted that his band would make a comeback. Some forecast!

Hyphen [-]

1. **Use a hyphen if you must divide a word at the end of a line.** When a word is too long to fit at the end of a line, it's best to start a new line rather than break it. If you must divide, however, remember these rules:

- Divide between syllables.
- Never divide a one-syllable word.
- Never leave one letter by itself.
- Divide double consonants except when they come before a suffix, in which case divide before the suffix:

ar-rangement; embar-rassment; fall-ing; pass-able

- When a consonant has been doubled to form the suffix, keep the second consonant with the suffix:

  refer-ral; begin-ning

2. **Use a hyphen to separate the parts of certain compound words:**

- compound nouns:

  sister-in-law; vice-consul

- compound verbs:

  freeze-dry; water-ski

- compound nouns and adjectives used as modifiers preceding nouns:

  a well-considered plan; twentieth-century attitudes

Note that when these compounds do not precede the noun they modify, they are not hyphenated:

  The plan was well considered.

  Those were attitudes of the twentieth century.

Many hyphenated nouns and verbs have been losing their hyphen over time. When in doubt, check a dictionary.

3. **Use a hyphen with certain prefixes (*all-*, *self-*, *ex-*, and those prefixes preceding a proper name):**

  all-party; self-imposed; ex-jockey; anti-nuclear; pro-Canadian

4. **Use a hyphen to emphasize contrasting prefixes:**

  The coach agreed to give both pre- and post-game interviews.

5. **Use a hyphen for written-out compound numbers from one to ninety-nine and compound fractions:**

  eighty-one years ago; two-thirds of a cup

Parentheses [( )]

1. **Use parentheses to enclose an explanation, example, or qualification.** Parentheses show that the enclosed material is of incidental importance to the main idea. They denote an interruption that is more subtle than one marked off by dashes but more pronounced than one set off by commas:

    > My brother (who is older than I am) is a superb cook and carpenter.

    > His latest plan (according to neighbours) is to dam the creek.

    Remember that punctuation should not precede parentheses, but it may follow them if required for the sentence to make sense:

    > I like coffee in the morning (if it's not instant), but she prefers tea.

    If the parenthetical statement comes between two complete sentences, it should be punctuated as a sentence, with the period, question mark, or exclamation point *inside* the parentheses:

    > I finished my last essay on Tuesday. (It was on Freud's theory of repression.) Fortunately, I had three weeks left to study for the exam.

    > They're out playing baseball. (Who plays baseball in February?) They should be back soon.

2. **Use parentheses to enclose references:** see Chapter 10 for details.

Period [.]

1. **Use a period at the end of a sentence.** A period indicates a full stop, not a pause.
2. **Use a period with abbreviations.** British style omits the period in certain cases, but North American style usually requires it for abbreviated titles (Mrs., Dr., Rev., Ph.D., etc.). It is becoming more common in North America to omit periods for place names (BC, NWT, etc.). Although the abbreviations and acronyms for some organizations include periods, the most common ones generally do not (CARE, CIDA, CBC, RCMP, etc.).

3. **Use a period at the end of an indirect question.** Do *not* use a question mark:

✘ He asked if I wanted a sandwich?

✔ He asked if I wanted a sandwich.

Quotation Marks [" " or ' ']

Quotation marks are usually double in American style and single in British practice. In Canada double quotation marks are more common, but either style is accepted as long as you are consistent.

1. **Use quotation marks to signify direct discourse (the actual words of a speaker):**

   I asked: "What is the matter?"

   "I have a pain in my big toe," he replied.

2. **Use quotation marks to show that words themselves are the issue:**

   The term "love" in tennis comes from the French word for "egg."

   Alternatively, you may italicize or underline the terms in question.
   Sometimes quotation marks are used to mark a slang word or an inappropriate usage, to show that the writer is aware of the difficulty:

   Hitler's "final solution" was the most barbaric act of the twentieth century.

   Use this device only when necessary. In general, it's better to let the context show your attitude, or to choose another term.

3. **Use quotation marks to enclose the titles of poems, short stories, songs, and articles in books or journals.** In contrast, titles of books, films, paintings, and longer musical works are italicized or underlined:

   The story I like best in Robert Weaver's *Canadian Short Stories* is "Bernadette," by Mavis Gallant.

4. **Use quotation marks to enclose quotations within quotations (single or double, depending on your primary style):**

> He said, "Hitler's 'final solution' was the most barbaric act of the twentieth century."

When the material being quoted is four lines or longer, it should be indented and single-spaced. No quotation marks should be used. If the block quotation is from the beginning of a paragraph, the normal indentation of the first word should be included.

Placement of punctuation with quotation marks

British and American methods of punctuating quotations differ. Again, both practices are accepted in Canada as long as you are consistent (it is also prudent to check with your instructor). British style usually places the punctuation outside the quotation marks, unless it is actually part of the quotation. The American practice, which is followed in this book, is increasingly common in Canada:

- A comma or period always goes inside the quotation marks:

  > He said, "Give me another chance," but I replied, "You've had enough chances."

- A semicolon or colon always goes outside the quotation marks:

  > Mary wants to watch "The Journal"; I'd rather watch the basketball game.

- A question mark, dash, or exclamation mark goes inside quotation marks if it is part of the quotation, but outside if it is not:

  > He asked, "What's for dinner?"

  > Did he really call the boss a "lily-livered hypocrite"?

  > His speech was hardly an appeal for "blood, sweat, and tears"!

  > I was just whispering to Louisa, "That instructor is a—" when suddenly he glanced at me.

- When a reference is given parenthetically (in round brackets) at the end of a quotation, the quotation marks precede the parentheses and the sentence punctuation follows them:

> Lamarche suggests that we should "abandon the Foreign Investment Review Agency" (*Globe Weekly*, 12 April 2007).

Semicolon [;]

A semicolon indicates a degree of separation, intermediate between a comma and a period.

1. **Use a semicolon to join independent clauses (complete sentences) that are closely related:**

> For five days he worked non-stop; by Saturday he was exhausted.

> His lecture was confusing; no one could understand the terminology.

A semicolon is especially useful when the second independent clause begins with a conjunctive adverb such as *however, moreover, consequently, nevertheless, in addition*, or *therefore* (usually followed by a comma):

> He brought in a box of doughnuts; however, no one touched it.

Some grammarians may disagree, but it's usually acceptable to follow a semicolon with a coordinating conjunction if the second clause is complicated by other commas:

> Cheryl, my dear friend, is a keen jogger in all weather; but sometimes, especially in winter, I think it does her more harm than good.

2. **Use a semicolon to mark the divisions in a complicated series when individual items themselves need commas.** Using a comma to mark the subdivisions and a semicolon to mark the main divisions will help to prevent mix-ups:

> ✗ He invited Maria DaSilva, the vice-principal, Marvin Goldman, and Christine Lai.

Is the vice-principal a separate person?

✔ He invited Maria DaSilva, the vice-principal; Marvin Goldman; and
Christine Lai.

In a case such as this, the elements separated by the semicolon do not
need to be independent clauses.

Summary

As we noted in the opening, punctuation marks are the traffic signals of writing. They guide your reader through your written work, helping them keep pace and avoid confusion. There are no simple tricks to learning the rules. That said, the more you write, the easier it gets.

14 Misused Words and Phrases

In this chapter we will examine

- words and phrases that are often misused;
- examples of word pairs that are incorrectly used interchangeably; and
- how to avoid needless (and sometimes silly) mistakes.

Introduction

If you find yourself unsure of whether to use the term *accept* or *except*, you are not alone. TAs and professors grading essays and exams find dozens of words that students struggle with and misuse on a regular basis. This chapter contains examples of common errors, as well as tips and suggestions on how to avoid them. A periodic read-through of this material will refresh your memory and help you avoid needless mistakes.

accept, except. Accept is a verb meaning to *receive affirmatively*; **except**, when used as a verb, means to *exclude*:

> I <u>accept</u> your apology.

> The professor <u>excepted</u> him from the late penalties.

> All courses <u>except</u> this one are full.

accompanied by, accompanied with. Use **accompanied by** for people; use **accompanied with** for objects:

He was <u>accompanied by</u> his lawyer.

The textbook arrived, <u>accompanied with</u> a discount coupon.

advice, advise. Advice is a noun, **advise** a verb:

He was <u>advised</u> to ignore his mother's <u>advice</u>.

affect, effect. Affect is a verb meaning to *influence*; **effect** can be either a noun meaning *result* or a verb meaning to *bring about*.

The quality of his textbook <u>affects</u> his ability to understand course content.

The <u>effect</u> of higher government spending is higher inflation.

Students lack confidence in their ability to <u>effect</u> change in the classroom.

all ready, already. To be **all ready** is simply to be ready for something; **already** means *beforehand* or *earlier*:

The students were <u>all ready</u> for the term to end.

The professor had <u>already</u> returned the essays by the time Blair submitted his late paper.

all right. Write as two separate words: *all right*. This can mean *safe and sound, in good condition, okay*; *correct*; *satisfactory*; or *I agree*.

Are you <u>all right</u>?

The student's answers were <u>all right</u>.

(Note the ambiguity of the second example: does it mean that the answers were all correct or simply satisfactory? In this case, it might be better to use a clearer, more precise word.)

all together, altogether. All together means *in a group*; **altogether** is an adverb meaning *entirely*:

> He was altogether certain that the children were all together.

allusion, illusion. An allusion is an indirect reference to something; an **illusion** is a false perception:

> Martin Luther King's allusion to the Gettysburg Address is well documented by historians.

> An optical illusion is also known as a mind game.

a lot. Write as two separate words: *a lot*.

alternate, alternative. Alternate means *every other* or *every second* thing in a series; **alternative** refers to a *choice* between options:

> The two sections of the class attended tutorials on alternate weeks.

> The students could do a multimedia presentation as an alternative to writing the exam.

among, between. Use **among** for three or more persons or objects, **between** for two:

> Between you and me, there's trouble among the student leaders.

amount, number. Amount indicates quantity when units are not discrete and not absolute; **number** indicates quantity when units are discrete and absolute:

> A large amount of timber.

> A large number of students.

See also **less, fewer.**

analysis. The plural is **analyses.**

anyone, any one. Anyone is written as two words to give numerical emphasis; otherwise write it as one word:

Any one of us could pass that easy exam.

Anyone could do that.

anyways. This is non-standard English: use *anyway.*

as, because. As is a weaker conjunction than **because** and may be confused with *when*:

✗ As I was working, I ate at my desk.

✔ Because I was working, I ate at my desk.

✗ He arrived as I was leaving.

✔ He arrived when I was leaving.

as to. This is a common feature of bureaucratese. Replace it with a single-word preposition such as *about* or *on*:

✗ She was concerned as to the range of disagreement.

✔ She was concerned about the range of disagreement.

✗ The reporter recorded his comments as to the treaty.

✔ The reporter recorded his comments on the treaty.

bad, badly. Bad is an adjective meaning *not good*:

The sushi tastes bad.

He felt bad about giving her the wrong answers.

Badly is an adverb meaning *not well*; when used with the verbs **want** or **need**, it means *very much*:

The critics said she played the villain's part badly.

I badly need to pass the exam.

beside, besides. Beside is a preposition meaning *next to*:

She worked beside her dear friend until all the cookies were sold.

Besides has two uses: as a preposition it means *in addition to*; as a conjunctive adverb it means *moreover*:

> Besides recommending the changes, the consultants are implementing them.

> Besides, it was hot and we wanted to rest.

between. See **among.**

bring, take. One **brings** something to a closer place and **takes** it to a farther one:

> Next time you come to study, bring your textbook along.

> Take it with you when you go.

can, may. Can means to *be able*; **may** means to *have permission*:

> Can you explain the difference?

> May I have another hour to complete the essay?

In speech, **can** is used to cover both meanings; in formal writing, however, you should observe the distinction.

can't hardly. A faulty combination of the phrases **can't** and **can hardly.** Use one or the other of them instead:

> He can't read French.

> He can hardly read French.

Literally speaking, this becomes a double negative, which ultimately means the opposite. Another example would be the phrase "I didn't do nothing." Thus, **can't hardly** literally means *can*.

cite, sight, site. To **cite** something is to *quote* or *mention* it as an example or authority; **sight** can be used in many ways, all of which relate to the ability to *see*; **site** refers to a specific *location*, a particular place at which something is located.

This was the <u>site</u> of the Battle of the Plains of Abraham.

Is it true that eating carrots improves your <u>eyesight</u>?

Your professor told you to <u>cite</u> your sources!

complement, compliment. The verb to **complement** means to *complete*; to **compliment** means *to praise*.

Her ability to analyze data <u>complements</u> her excellent research skills.

I <u>complimented</u> her on her outstanding report.

compose, comprise. Both words mean *to constitute* or *make up*, but **compose** is preferred. **Comprise** is correctly used to mean *consist of* or *be composed of*. Using **comprise** in the passive ("is comprised of")—as you might be tempted to do in the second example below—is usually frowned on in formal writing:

These students <u>compose</u> the group which will receive the scholarships.

Each paragraph <u>comprises</u> an introduction, an argument, and a conclusion.

continual, continuous. Continual means *repeated over a period of time*; **continuous** means *constant* or *without interruption*:

The weather caused <u>continual</u> delays at the airport.

Five days of <u>continuous</u> rain ruined our holiday.

could of. This construction is incorrect, as are **might of, should of,** and **would of.** Replace *of* with *have*:

✘ He <u>could of</u> passed the test but didn't.

✔ He <u>could have</u> passed the test, but didn't.

✔ They <u>might have</u> been there, but I didn't see them.

✔ He <u>should have</u> known she'd be late for the rehearsal.

✔ We <u>would have</u> left earlier had she warned us.

council, counsel. Council is a noun meaning an *advisory* or *deliberative assembly.* **Counsel** as a noun means *advice* or *lawyer;* as a verb it means to *give advice.*

> The student <u>council</u> meets on Mondays.

> We respect her <u>counsel because</u> she's seldom wrong.

> As an academic <u>counsellor</u>, you will likely <u>counsel</u> students who are on probation.

criterion, criteria. A **criterion** is a standard for judging something. **Criteria** is the plural of **criterion** and thus requires a plural verb:

> The committee's ethical <u>criteria</u> set the standard for the university's research programs.

data. Data is the plural of **datum**. It refers to the set of information, usually in numerical form, which is used for analysis as the basis for a study. Informally, **data** is often used as a singular noun, but in formal contexts it should be treated as a plural:

> These <u>data were</u> gathered by students for use in their essays.

> John reported that <u>his data are</u> exactly what he needs to prove his argument.

deduce, deduct. To **deduce** something is to *work it out by reasoning;* to **deduct** means to *subtract* or *take away* from something. The noun form of both words is **deduction.**

> Using this evidence, we can <u>deduce</u> that he was cheating.

> Once you get your grade, you should <u>deduct</u> the late marks.

delusion, illusion. A **delusion** is a belief or perception that is distorted; an **illusion** is a false perception:

> Some claim that Napoleon had <u>delusions</u> of grandeur.

> The oasis he thought he saw was an <u>illusion</u>.

dependent, dependant. Dependent is an adjective meaning *contingent on* or *subject to*; **dependant** is a noun.

> Addie's graduation is <u>dependent</u> upon her passing statistics.

> Addie is a <u>dependant</u> of her father.

device, devise. The word ending in -**ice** is the noun; the word ending in -**ise** is the verb.

> We <u>devised</u> a plan after we figured out how to use the new <u>device</u>.

different than, different from. Use *different from* to compare two persons or things; use *different than* with a full clause:

> You are different from me.

> This landscape is different than it used to be.

diminish, minimize. To **diminish** means to *make* or *become smaller*; to **minimize** is to *reduce* something to the smallest possible amount or size.

> <u>Minimize</u> the font and watch their attention <u>diminish</u>.

disinterested, uninterested. Disinterested implies impartiality or neutrality; **uninterested** implies a lack of interest:

> As a <u>disinterested</u> observer, he was in a good position to judge the issue fairly.

> <u>Uninterested</u> in the proceedings, he yawned repeatedly.

due to. Although increasingly used to mean *because of*, **due** is an adjective and therefore needs to modify something:

> ✗ Due to his incompetence, we lost the contract. [Due is dangling.]

> ✔ The loss was <u>due</u> to his incompetence.

e.g., i.e. E.g. stands for *exempli gratia* and means *for example* (typically not a finite list of options); **i.e.** stands for *id est* and means *that is* (provides clarification; should be able to be replaced with *in other words*). The two are incorrectly used interchangeably.

> She takes part in all kinds of activities, e.g., (for example) the debating team, the school newspaper, and the drama club.

> She's a very active student, i.e., (in other words) she is involved in many extracurricular activities.

entomology, etymology. Entomology is the study of insects; **etymology** is the study of the derivation and history of words.

> "From the Greek, meaning that which is cut in pieces" is the etymology of the term entomology.

exceptional, exceptionable. Exceptional means *unusual* or *outstanding*, whereas **exceptionable** means *open to objection* and is generally used in negative contexts.

> Her accomplishments are exceptional, and her grades reflect this.

> After reviewing the evidence, we found nothing exceptionable in his behaviour.

farther, further. Farther refers to distance, **further** to extent:

> He paddled farther than his friends did.

> She explained the plan further.

focus (noun). The plural may be either **focuses** (also spelled **focusses**) or **foci.**

good, well. Good is an adjective that modifies a noun; **well** is an adverb that modifies a verb.

> She is good at math, so she does well in her statistics courses.

> The experiment went well.

hanged, hung. Hanged means *executed by hanging.* **Hung** means *suspended* or *clung to*:

> Some heretics were first <u>hanged</u> and then burned for their beliefs.
>
> He <u>hung</u> his degree on the wall for all to see.
>
> She <u>hung</u> on to her professor's every word.

hereditary, heredity. Heredity is a noun; **hereditary** is an adjective. **Heredity** is the biological process whereby characteristics are passed from one generation to the next; **hereditary** describes those characteristics.

> <u>Heredity</u> has determined that you have brown hair.
>
> Your asthma may be <u>hereditary</u>.

hopefully. Use **hopefully** as an adverb meaning *full of hope*:

> She scanned the auditorium <u>hopefully</u>, waiting for the TA to appear.

In formal writing, using **hopefully** to mean *I hope* is still frowned upon, although increasingly common; it's better to use *I hope*:

> ✘ <u>Hopefully</u> you'll write a better essay next term.
>
> ✔ <u>I hope</u> you'll write a better essay next term.

i.e. *Not* the same as **e.g.**! See **e.g.** above.

illusion. See **allusion, delusion.**

incite, insight. Incite is a verb meaning to *stir up*; **insight** is a noun meaning (often sudden) *understanding.*

> <u>Inciting</u> a riot is against the law.
>
> After reading the court documents, she gained <u>insight</u> on the matter.

infer, imply. To **infer** means to *deduce* or *conclude by reasoning*. People often confuse it with **imply**, which means to *suggest* or *insinuate*.

> We can infer from the large population density that there is a high demand for services.

> The large population density implies that there is a high demand for services.

inflammable, flammable, non-flammable. Despite its *in-* prefix, **inflammable** is not the opposite of **flammable**: both words describe things that are easily set on fire. The opposite of flammable and inflammable is **non-flammable**. To prevent any possibility of confusion, it's best to avoid **inflammable** altogether.

irregardless. This word is redundant; use *regardless*.

its, it's. Its is a form of possessive pronoun; **it's** is a contraction of *it is*. Many people mistakenly put an apostrophe in **its** in order to show possession.

> ✗ The cub wanted it's mother. [This means it is.]

> ✔ The cub wanted its mother.

> ✔ It's time to leave.

less, fewer. Less is used when units are *not* discrete and *not* absolute (*less information*). **Fewer** is used when the units *are* discrete and absolute (*fewer marbles*).

> She got fewer points because she provided less information than the professor required.

lie, lay. To **lie** means to *assume a horizontal position*; to **lay** means to *put down*. The changes of tense often cause confusion:

Present	Past	Past participle	Present participle
lie	lay	lain	lying
lay	laid	laid	laying

During the rescue, the soldier yelled: "<u>lay</u> down your arms and <u>lie</u> face down."

like, as. Like is a preposition, but people often use it wrongly as a conjunction. To join two independent clauses, use the conjunction **as**:

> ✘ I want to progress <u>like</u> you have this year.

> ✔ I want to progress <u>as</u> you have this year.

> ✔ My politics professor is <u>like</u> my old school principal—firm but fair.

might of. See **could of.** Both are incorrect.

minimize. See **diminish.**

mitigate, militate. To **mitigate** means to *reduce the severity* of something; to **militate** against something means to *oppose* it.

myself, me. Myself is an intensifier of, not a substitute for, *I* or *me*:

> ✘ He gave it to Maria and <u>myself</u>.

> ✔ He gave it to Maria and <u>me</u>.

> ✘ Jane and <u>myself</u> are invited.

> ✔ Jane and <u>I</u> are invited.

> ✔ <u>Myself</u>, I would prefer not to be invited.

> ✔ I wish I hadn't done that to <u>myself</u>.

nor, or. Use **nor** with **neither**; use **or** by itself or with **either**:

> He is <u>neither</u> overworked <u>nor</u> underfed.

> The plant is <u>either</u> diseased <u>or</u> dried out.

off of. Remove the unnecessary **of**:

> ✘ The fence kept the children <u>off of</u> the premises.

> ✔ The fence kept the children <u>off</u> the premises.

phenomenon. A singular noun: the plural is **phenomena**.

plaintiff, plaintive. A **plaintiff** is a person who brings a case against someone else to court; **plaintive** is an adjective meaning *sorrowful*.

populace, populous. **Populace** is a noun meaning the *people* of a place; **populous** is an adjective meaning *thickly inhabited*.

> The populace of Countryside village is not well educated.

> With so many people in such a small area, Countryside village is a populous place.

practice, practise. **Practice** can be a noun or an adjective; **practise** is always a verb. Note, however, that in the United States and sometimes in Canada, the spelling of the verb is **practice**:

> Gaining a working knowledge of statistics takes practice. (noun)

> That was only a practice test, so study harder next time. (adjective)

> The players need to practise (or practice) their skills. (verb)

precede, proceed. To **precede** is to *go before* (earlier) or *in front of* others; to **proceed** is to *go on* or *ahead*:

> During convocation, the faculty will precede the students into the hall.

> The award winners will proceed to the front of the hall.

prescribe, proscribe. These words are sometimes confused, although they have quite different meanings. **Prescribe** means *to advise the use of* or *impose authoritatively*. **Proscribe** means to *reject, denounce*, or *ban*:

> The professor prescribed the conditions under which the equipment could be used.

> The university senate proscribed the publication of unsigned editorials in the newspaper.

principle, principal. Principle is a noun meaning a *general truth* or *law*; **principal** can be used as either a noun or an adjective, meaning *chief.*

> Dr. Dobbs was the principal investigator in the study.
>
> Some say the school principal was tough as nails.
>
> Others say he was a principled man.

rational, rationale. Rational is an adjective meaning *logical* or *able to reason.* **Rationale** is a noun meaning *explanation*:

> Dropping the course was not a rational decision.
>
> The professor sent an email explaining the rationale for his decision.

real, really. Real, an adjective, means *true* or *genuine*; **really**, an adverb, means *actually, truly, very,* or *extremely.*

> The professor was a real gem.
>
> His lectures were really informative.

seasonable, seasonal. Seasonable means *usual* or *suitable for the season*; **seasonal** means *of, depending on,* or *varying with the season*:

> The temperature is seasonably high.
>
> When packing your clothes, you must take into account seasonal changes in the weather.

should of. See **could of**. Both are incorrect.

their, there, they're. Their is the possessive form of the third-person plural pronoun. **There** is usually an adverb, meaning *at that place* or *at that point.* **They're** is a contraction of *they are*:

> There is no point in arguing with them.
>
> They're angry because their grades don't reflect their efforts.
>
> They parked their bikes there, by the tree.

tortuous, torturous. The adjective **tortuous** means *full of twists and turns* or *circuitous*. **Torturous**, derived from *torture*, means *involving torture* or *excruciating*:

> To avoid heavy traffic, they took a <u>tortuous</u> route home.

> The concert was a <u>torturous</u> experience for the audience.

turbid, turgid. **Turbid**, with respect to a liquid or colour, means *muddy, not clear*, or (with respect to literary style) *confused*. **Turgid** means *swollen, inflated*, or *enlarged*, or (again with reference to literary style) *pompous* or *bombastic*.

unique. This word, which means *of which there is only one* or *unequalled*, is both overused and misused. Lacking degrees of comparison—one thing cannot be "more unique" than another—expressions such as *very unique* are incorrect.

while. To avoid misreading, use **while** only when you mean *at the same time that*. Do not use *while* as a substitute for *although, whereas*, or *but*:

> ✗ <u>While</u> she's getting good grades, she's likely not going to apply to grad school.

> ✗ I headed for home, <u>while</u> she decided to stay.

> ✔ He fell asleep <u>while</u> he was reading.

-wise. Never use **-wise** as a suffix to form new words when you mean *with regard to*:

> ✗ <u>Grades-wise</u>, he could have done better this year.

> ✗ <u>Sales-wise</u>, the company did better last year.

> ✔ The company's sales increased last year.

your, you're. **Your** is a pronominal adjective used to show possession; **you're** is a contraction of *you are*:

> <u>You're</u> likely to miss <u>your</u> exam if you don't leave soon.

Glossary I
Social Science

achievement. The gaining of social position or social status as the outcome of personal effort, in competition with others.

actual intervention. An action or program aimed at changing an existing social condition.

agency. The power of actors to operate independently of the determining constraints of social structure.

aggregate data. Statistics produced for large groups or categories of people, in which the characteristics of individual respondents are no longer identifiable.

altruism. Concern for the welfare of others rather than oneself.

analysis of variance. A procedure used to test whether differences between the means of several groups are likely to be found in the population from which those groups were drawn.

anomaly. A finding that does not fit the thinking within a paradigm.

applied research. Research intended to provide decision makers with practical, action-oriented recommendations to solve a problem.

authority. A highly regarded scholar who is referenced to support a line of argument.

baseline. A measure of conditions or behaviour before experimental manipulation is carried out.

basic research. Research intended to make and test theories about some aspect of real life.

bias. See **researcher bias**.

bureaucracy. A type of organization in which administration is based on impersonal, written rules and a hierarchy of offices.

conditioning variable. A characteristic that determines whether an independent variable will have a strong or weak effect on the dependent variable.

conditions, control. An absence of treatments (i.e., experimental conditions), predicted to not change the attitudes or behaviours of experimental subjects.

conditions, experimental. Treatments that are predicted to change the attitudes or behaviour of experimental subjects.

constant. A characteristic or condition (of a person, group, or society) that does not change over time. (Compare **variable**.)

construct validity. A high degree of correlation among items believed to measure the same thing.

control (for). Examine the influence on the dependent variable of changes in one independent variable while holding constant (i.e., *controlling for*) other independent variables.

data. Facts or evidence, based on observation, experience, or experimentation, that can be checked or verified.

deduce. Infer by reasoning from known facts.

demography. The statistical study of human populations with regard to size, structure, and composition.

dependent variable. A characteristic or condition that results from change in another characteristic or condition; a variable assumed to be the effect of an independent variable.

disconfirmatory finding. An observed relationship that fails to prove a hypothesis.

distribution. The way in which a condition or characteristic is spread over members of a group or category of people.

experiment. A study of groups or individuals carried out in an environment controlled by the researcher, who manipulates some variables to see their effects on other variables.

face validity. The accuracy with which an indicator measures the variable it is meant to represent.

folkways. Norms that are cause for only mild or informal punishment when violated. (Compare **mores**.)

frequency distribution. The number of times each value of a variable occurs in a set of observations.

hypothesis. An untested statement of an expected relationship between two or more variables.

identity. The fluid/dynamic, socially constructed conception, qualities, beliefs, and expressions that make a person or group who or what they are.

ideology. A system of ideas or ideals that forms the basis of economic or political theory and policy. A body of ideas underlying and informing social and political action.

imagined intervention. An action or program, imagined but not carried out, that would aim to change an existing social condition.

independent variable. A characteristic or condition that causes change in another characteristic or condition; a causal or explanatory variable presumed to be the cause of a dependent variable.

infographic. Brief for information graphic; a representation of information in graphic format, designed to make data/information understandable at a glance. This process (and others like it) is sometimes referred to as data visualization.

interval measure. The level or type of measurement that is based on numeric categories that are an equal distance, or interval, from one another, with no absolute zero.

intervening variable. A characteristic or condition that explains the link between a cause and an effect; a variable through which the independent variable acts on the dependent variable.

intervention. An action or manipulation whose effect on a group of people is to be studied.

longitudinal study. A study that involves collecting data from the same population at intervals (two or more points) over time.

mean. The mathematical average of a set of numbers; a calculated central value of a set of numbers.

median. The value or quantity lying at the midpoint of a frequency distribution of observed values such that the observations fall half above and half below it.

model. A theoretical "picture" of the relations among causes and effects.

mores. Norms that carry moral significance, which are therefore cause for severe punishment when violated. (Compare **folkways**.)

negative relationship. A relationship between two variables, in which an increase in one produces a decrease in the other. (Compare **positive relationship**.)

nominal measure. The level or type of measurement that places people into named categories (e.g., male/female).

norms. Rules or expectations about proper behaviour in particular situations, which serve as guidelines for an individual's actions.

operationalize. Devise measures to accurately represent the concepts or variables in a theory.

ordinal measure. The level or type of measurement that places people in order from most to least in respect to some characteristic.

paradigm. A theoretical perspective or way of viewing the world.

policy instrument (or **policy tool**). An organizational resource (e.g., the right to legislate and enforce a policy) that can be used to influence social problems.

policy research. See **applied research**.

positive relationship. A relationship between two variables, in which an increase in one produces an increase in the other. (Compare **negative relationship**.)

positivism. A philosophical system that holds that rationally justifiable assertions can and should be scientifically verified, or are capable of logical or mathematical proof.

power. The ability to do or act in a particular way, despite resistance; the capacity or ability to influence the behaviour of others.

proposition. See **hypothesis**.

pure research. See **basic research**.

qualitative data. Data that cannot be satisfactorily described by numbers and must be described in words.

quantitative data. Data that can be satisfactorily described by numbers.

quasi-experiment. A modified experiment, in which the experimenter cannot exercise complete control over sampling or the research environment.

ratio measure. The level or type of measurement used to measure phenomena where absolute zero exists (e.g., height or weight).

reactivity. A condition in which research subjects behave differently from usual because they are aware that they are being studied (i.e., Hawthorne Effect).

relationship. An association or connection between variables, such that a change in one produces a change in the other.

reliability. The extent to which a measuring procedure produces consistent results over time or with different investigators.

researcher bias. The way in which a researcher's beliefs or expectations affect or influence the findings of a study.

scale. A set of measured items combined to provide a single overall measure of some concept or variable.

semiotics. A theory or study of signs and symbols as elements of communicative behaviour, involving the analysis of systems of communication, including language, gestures, or clothing.

significance (or **statistical significance**). The likelihood that an observed relationship has occurred by chance alone.

sociogram. A diagram of relationships among members of a group that shows who interacts with whom, and who are the most popular, influential, or otherwise "central" people.

socio-economic status. An economic or sociological measure of a person's overall standing as measured by their level of education, work experience, and personal and family's economic and social position in relation to others; a measure usually based on income, education, and occupation.

speculative study (or **thought experiment**). An attempt to predict the effects of an independent variable on a dependent variable, based on a combination of imagined and real data.

state. A nation or territory considered as an organized political community under one government.

strong relationship. A relationship between two variables, in which a large change in one variable produces a large change in the other. (Compare **weak relationship**.)

test (or **verify**). Examine the correctness of a theory by matching predicted against observed findings.

theory. A set of interconnected statements or propositions that attempts to explain a causal relationship.

unobtrusive measure. Any method of data collection in which research subjects are not aware they are being studied and therefore do not change their behaviour.

validity. The ability of an indicator or measure to accurately represent the variable it is meant to represent.

value neutrality. A way of conducting research that seeks to ensure a fair and objective hearing for what the data actually show.

variable. A characteristic or condition that can differ from one person, group, or situation to another. (Compare **constant**.)

verify. (or **validate**). See **test**.

weak relationship. A relationship between two variables, in which a large change in one variable produces a small change in the other. (Compare **strong relationship**.)

xenophobia. An exaggerated hostility or fear of foreigners.

zeitgeist. The spirit of a particular age.

Glossary II
Grammar

abstract. A summary accompanying a formal scientific report or paper, briefly outlining the contents.

abstract language. Language that deals with theoretical, intangible concepts or details: e.g., *justice, goodness, truth*. (Compare **concrete language**.)

acronym. A pronounceable word made up of the first letters of the words in a phrase or name: e.g., *NATO* (from *North Atlantic Treaty Organization*). A group of initial letters that are pronounced separately is an **initialism**: e.g., *CBC, NHL*.

active voice. See **voice**.

adjectival phrase (or **adjectival clause**). A group of words modifying a noun or pronoun: e.g., *the dog that belongs to my brother*.

adjective. A word that modifies or describes a noun or pronoun: e.g., *red, beautiful, solemn*.

adverb. A word that modifies or qualifies a verb, adjective, or adverb, often answering a question such as *how? why? when?* or *where?*: e.g., *slowly, fortunately, early, abroad*. (See also **conjunctive adverb**.)

adverbial phrase (or **adverbial clause**). A group of words modifying a verb, adjective, or adverb: e.g., *The dog ran with great speed*.

agreement. Consistency in tense, number, or person between related parts of a sentence: e.g., between subject and verb, or noun and related pronoun.

ambiguity. Vague or equivocal language; meaning that can be taken two ways.

antecedent (or **referent**). The noun for which a following pronoun stands: e.g., *cats* in *Cats are happiest when they are sleeping*.

appositive. A word or phrase that identifies a preceding noun or pronoun: e.g., *Mrs. Jones, my aunt, is sick*. The second phrase is said to be **in apposition to** the first.

article. See **definite article, indefinite article**.

assertion. A positive statement or claim: e.g., *The data are inconclusive*.

auxiliary verb. A verb used to form the tenses, moods, and voices of other verbs: e.g., *am* in *I am swimming*. The main auxiliary verbs in English are *be, do, have, can, could, may, might, must, shall, should*, and *will*.

bibliography. (1) A list of works used or referred to in writing an essay or report. (2) A reference book listing works available on a particular subject.

case. Any of the inflected forms of a pronoun. (See **inflection**.)
   Subjective case: *I, we, you, he, she, it, they*.
   Objective case: *me, us, you, him, her, it, them*.
   Possessive case: *my/mine, your/yours, our/ours, his, her/hers, its, their/theirs*.

circumlocution. A roundabout or circuitous expression, often used in a deliberate attempt to be vague or evasive: e.g., *in a family way* for *pregnant; at this point in time* for *now*.

clause. A group of words containing a subject and predicate. An **independent clause** can stand by itself as a complete sentence: e.g., *I had lunch*. A **subordinate** (or **dependent**) **clause** cannot stand by itself but must be connected to another clause: e.g., *Because I was hungry, I had lunch.*

cliché. A phrase or idea that has lost its impact through overuse and betrays a lack of original thought: e.g., *slept like a log; gave 110 per cent.*

collective noun. A noun that is singular in form but refers to a group: e.g., *family, team, jury.* It may take either a singular or plural verb, depending on whether it refers to individual members or to the group as a whole.

comma splice. See **run-on sentence.**

complement. A completing word or phrase that usually follows a linking verb to form a **subjective complement**: e.g., (1) *He is my father;* (2) *That cigar smells terrible.* If the complement is an adjective it is sometimes called a **predicate adjective.** An **objective complement** completes the direct object rather than the subject: e.g., *We found him honest and trustworthy.*

complex sentence. A sentence containing a dependent clause as well as an independent one: e.g., *I bought the ring, although it was expensive.*

compound sentence. A sentence containing two or more independent clauses: e.g., *I saw the accident and I reported it.* A sentence is called **compound-complex** if it contains a dependent clause as well as two independent ones: e.g., *When the fog lifted, I saw the accident and I reported it.*

conclusion. The part of an essay in which the findings are pulled together or the implications revealed so that the reader has a sense of closure or completion.

concrete language. Specific language that communicates particular details: e.g., *red corduroy dress, three long-stemmed roses.* (Compare **abstract language.**)

conjunction. An uninflected word used to link words, phrases, or clauses. A **coordinating conjunction** (e.g., *and, or, but, for, yet*) links two equal parts of a sentence. A **subordinating**

conjunction, placed at the beginning of a subordinate clause, shows the logical dependence of that clause on another: e.g., (1) *Although I am poor, I am happy;* (2) *While others slept, he studied.* **Correlative conjunctions** are pairs of coordinating conjunctions (see **correlatives**).

conjunctive adverb. A type of adverb that shows the logical relation between the phrase or clause that it modifies and a preceding one: e.g., (1) *I sent the letter; it never arrived, however.* (2) *The battery died; therefore the car wouldn't start.*

connotation. The range of ideas or meanings suggested by a certain word in addition to its literal meaning. Apparent synonyms, such as *poor* and *underprivileged*, may have different connotations. (Compare **denotation.**)

context. The text surrounding a particular passage that helps to establish its meaning.

contraction. A word formed by combining and shortening two words: e.g., *isn't* from *is not; we're* from *we are.*

coordinate construction. A grammatical construction that uses correlatives. (See **correlatives.**)

coordinating conjunction. Each of a pair of correlatives. (See **correlatives.**)

copula verb. See **linking verb.**

correlatives (or **coordinates**). Pairs of coordinating conjunctions: e.g., *either/or; neither/nor; not only/but also.*

dangling modifier. A modifying word or phrase (often including a participle) that is not grammatically connected to any part of the sentence: e.g., *Walking to school, the street was slippery.*

definite article. The word *the*, which precedes a noun and implies that it has already been mentioned or is common knowledge. (Compare **indefinite article.**)

demonstrative pronoun. A pronoun that points out something: e.g., (1) _This is his reason_; (2) _That_ looks like my lost earring. When used to modify a noun or pronoun, a demonstrative pronoun becomes a kind of **pronominal adjective**: e.g., _this_ hat, _those_ people.

denotation. The literal or dictionary meaning of a word. (Compare **connotation**.)

dependent clause. See **clause**.

diction. The choice of words with regard to their tone, degree of formality, or register. Formal diction is the language of orations and serious essays. The informal diction of everyday speech or conversational writing can, at its extreme, become slang.

direct object. See **object**.

discourse. Talk, either oral or written. **Direct discourse** (or **direct speech**) gives the actual words spoken or written: e.g., _Donne said, "No man is an island."_ In writing, direct discourse is put in quotation marks. **Indirect discourse** (or **indirect speech**) gives the meaning of the speech rather than the actual words. In writing, indirect discourse is not put in quotation marks: e.g., _He said that no one exists in an island of isolation._

ellipsis. Three spaced periods indicating an omission from a quoted passage. At the end of a sentence use four periods.

essay. A literary composition on any subject. Some essays are descriptive or narrative, but in an academic setting most are expository (explanatory) or argumentative.

euphemism. A word or phrase used to avoid some other word or phrase that might be considered offensive or too harsh or blunt: e.g., _pass away_ for _die_.

expletive. (1) A word or phrase used to fill out a sentence without adding to the sense: e.g., _To be sure_, it's hot today! (2) A swear word.

exploratory writing. The informal writing done to help generate ideas before formal planning begins.

fused sentence. See **run-on sentence**.

general language. Language that lacks specific details; abstract language.

gerund. A verbal (part-verb) that functions as a noun and is marked by an _-ing_ ending: e.g., _Swimming_ can help you become fit.

grammar. The study of the forms and relations of words, and of the rules governing their use in speech and writing.

hypothesis. A supposition or trial proposition made as a starting point for further investigation.

hypothetical instance. A supposed occurrence, often indicated by a clause beginning with _if_.

indefinite article. The word _a_ or _an_, which introduces a noun and suggests that it is nonspecific. (Compare **definite article**.)

independent clause. See **clause**.

indirect discourse (or **indirect speech**). See **discourse**.

indirect object. See **object**.

infinitive. A type of verbal not connected to any subject: e.g., _to ask_. The **base infinitive** omits the _to_: e.g., _ask_.

inflection. The change in the form of a word to indicate number, person, case, tense, or degree.

initialism. See **acronym**.

integrate. Combine or blend together.

intensifier (or **qualifier**). A word that modifies and adds emphasis to another word or phrase: e.g., _very_ tired, _quite_ happy, I _myself_.

interjection. An abrupt remark or exclamation, usually accompanied by an exclamation mark: e.g., *Oh dear! Alas!*

interrogative sentence. A sentence that asks a question: e.g., *What is the time?*

intransitive verb. A verb that does not take a direct object: e.g., *fall, sleep, talk.* (Compare **transitive verb**.)

introduction. A section at the start of an essay that tells the reader what is going to be discussed and why.

italics. Slanting type used for emphasis or to indicate the title of a book or journal.

jargon. Technical terms used unnecessarily or in inappropriate places: e.g., *peer-group interaction* for *friendship.*

linking verb (or **copula verb**). A verb such as *be, seem,* or *feel,* used to join subject to complement: e.g., *The apples <u>were</u> ripe.*

literal meaning. The primary, or denotative, meaning of a word.

logical indicator. A word or phrase—usually a conjunction or conjunctive adverb—that shows the logical relation between sentences or clauses: e.g., *since, furthermore, therefore.*

misplaced modifier. A word or group of words that can cause confusion because it is not placed next to the element it should modify: e.g., *I <u>only</u> ate the pie.* [Revised: *I ate <u>only</u> the pie.*]

modifier. A word or group of words that describes or limits another element in the sentence: e.g., *The man <u>who came to dinner</u> was my uncle.*

mood. (1) As a grammatical term, the form that shows a verb's function.
    Indicative mood: *She is going.*
    Imperative mood: *Go!*

    Interrogative mood: *Is she going?*
    Subjunctive mood: *It is important that she go.*
(2) When applied to literature generally, the atmosphere or tone created by the author.

non-restrictive modifier (or **non-restrictive element**). See **restrictive modifier**.

noun. An inflected part of speech marking a person, place, thing, idea, action, or feeling, and usually serving as subject, object, or complement. A **common noun** is a general term: e.g., *dog, paper, automobile.* A **proper noun** is a specific name: e.g., *Martin, Sudbury, Ski-Doo.*

object. (1) A noun or pronoun that completes the action of a verb is called a **direct object**: e.g., *He passed <u>the puck</u>.* An **indirect object** is the person or thing receiving the direct object: e.g., *He passed <u>the puck</u>* (direct object) *<u>to Markus</u>* (indirect object). (2) The noun or pronoun in a group of words beginning with a preposition: e.g., *at the <u>house</u>, about <u>her</u>, for <u>me</u>.*

objective complement. See **complement**.

objectivity. A position or stance taken without personal bias or prejudice. (Compare **subjectivity**.)

outline. With regard to an essay or report, a brief sketch of the main parts; a written plan.

paragraph. A unit of sentences arranged logically to explain or describe an idea, event, or object. The start of a paragraph is usually marked by indentation of the first line.

parallel wording. Wording in which a series of items has a similar grammatical form: e.g., *At her wedding, my grandmother promised <u>to love</u>, <u>to honour</u>, and <u>to obey</u> her husband.*

paraphrase. Restate in different words.

parentheses. Curved lines enclosing and setting off a passage; not to be confused with square brackets.

parenthetical element. A word or phrase inserted as an explanation or afterthought into a passage that is grammatically complete without it: e.g., *My musical career, if it can be called that, consisted of playing the triangle in kindergarten.*

participle. A verbal (part-verb) that functions as an adjective. Participles can be either **present**—usually marked by an -*ing* ending—(e.g., *taking*), or **past** (e.g., *having taken*); they can also be **passive** (e.g., *being taken* or *having been taken*).

part of speech. Each of the major categories into which words are placed according to their grammatical function. Some grammarians include only function words (nouns, verbs, adjectives, and adverbs); others also include pronouns, prepositions, conjunctions, and interjections.

passive voice. See **voice**.

past participle. See **participle**.

periodic sentence. A sentence in which the normal order is inverted or in which an essential element is suspended until the very end: e.g., *Out of the house, past the grocery store, through the school yard, and down the railway tracks raced the frightened boy.*

person. In grammar, the three classes of personal pronouns referring to the person speaking (**first person**), the person spoken to (**second person**), and the person spoken about (**third person**). With verbs, only the third-person singular has a distinctive inflected form.

personal pronoun. See **pronoun**.

phrase. A unit of words lacking a subject-predicate combination, typically forming part of a clause. The most common kind is the **prepositional phrase**—a unit consisting of a preposition and an object: e.g., *They are waiting at the house*.

plural. Indicating two or more in number. Nouns, pronouns, and verbs all have plural forms.

possessive case. See **case**.

prefix. An element placed in front of the root form of a word to make a new word: e.g., *pro-, in-, sub-, anti-*. (Compare **suffix**.)

preposition. A short word heading a unit of words containing an object, thus forming a **prepositional phrase**: e.g., *under the tree, before my time.*

pronoun. A word that stands in for a noun. A **personal pronoun** stands for the name of a person: *I, he, she, we, they,* etc.

punctuation. A conventional system of signs (comma, period, semicolon, etc.) used to indicate stops or divisions in a sentence and to make meaning clearer.

reference works. Sources consulted when preparing an essay or report.

referent. See **antecedent**.

reflexive verb. A verb that has an identical subject and object: e.g., *Isabel taught herself to skate.*

register. The degree of formality in word choice and sentence structure.

relative clause. A clause introduced by a relative pronoun: e.g., *The man who came to dinner is my uncle.*

relative pronoun. *Who, which, what, that,* or their compounds, used to introduce an adjective or noun clause: e.g., *the house that Jack built; whatever you say.*

restrictive modifier (or **restrictive element**). A phrase or clause that identifies or is essential to the meaning of a term: e.g., *The book that my aunt gave me is missing.* It should not be set off by commas. A **non-restrictive modifier** is not needed to identify the term and is usually set off by commas: e.g., *This book, which my aunt gave me, is one of my favourites.*

rhetorical question. A question posed and answered by a writer or speaker to draw attention to a point; no response is expected on the part of the audience: e.g., *How significant are these findings? In my opinion, they are extremely significant, for the following reasons . . .*

run-on sentence. A sentence that goes on beyond the point where it should have stopped. The term covers both the **comma splice** (two sentences incorrectly joined by a comma) and the **fused sentence** (two sentences incorrectly joined without any punctuation).

sentence. A grammatical unit that includes both a subject and a predicate (verb). The end of a sentence is marked by a period.

sentence fragment. A group of words lacking either a subject or a verb; an incomplete sentence.

simple sentence. A sentence made up of only one clause: e.g., *Joaquim climbed the tree.*

slang. Colloquial speech considered inappropriate for academic writing; it is often used in a special sense by a particular group: e.g., *stoked* for *excited, dis* for *show disrespect for.*

split infinitive. A construction in which a word is placed between *to* and the base verb: e.g., *to completely finish.* Many still object to this kind of construction, but splitting infinitives is sometimes necessary when the alternatives are awkward or ambiguous.

squinting modifier. A kind of misplaced modifier that could be connected to elements on either side, making meaning ambiguous: e.g., *When he wrote the letter finally his boss thanked him.*

standard English. The English currently spoken or written by literate people and widely accepted as the correct and standard form.

subject. In grammar, the noun or noun equivalent with which the verb agrees and about which the rest of the clause is predicated: e.g., *They swim every day when the pool is open.*

subjective complement. See **complement.**

subjectivity. A stance that is based on personal feelings or opinions and is not impartial. (Compare **objectivity**.)

subjunctive. See **mood**.

subordinate clause. See **clause**.

subordinating conjunction. See **conjunction**.

subordination. Making one clause in a sentence dependent on another.

suffix. An element added to the end of a word to form a derivative: e.g., *prepare, preparation; sing, singing.* (Compare **prefix**.)

synonym. A word with the same dictionary meaning as another word: e.g., *begin* and *commence.*

syntax. Sentence construction; the grammatical arrangement of words and phrases.

tense. A set of inflected forms taken by a verb to indicate the time (i.e., past, present, future) of the action.

theme. A recurring or dominant idea.

thesis statement. A one-sentence assertion that gives the central argument of an essay.

topic sentence. The sentence in a paragraph that expresses the main or controlling idea.

transition word. A word that shows the logical relation between sentences or parts of a sentence and thus helps to signal the change from one idea to another: e.g., *therefore, also, however.*

transitive verb. A verb that takes an object: e.g., *hit, bring, cover.* (Compare **intransitive verb**.)

usage. The way in which a word or phrase is normally and correctly used; accepted practice.

verb. That part of a predicate, expressing an action, state of being, or condition, that tells what a subject is or does. Verbs are inflected to show tense (time). The principal parts of a verb are the three basic forms from which all tenses are made: the base infinitive, the past tense, and the past participle.

verbal. A word that is similar in form to a verb but does not function as one: a participle, a gerund, or an infinitive.

voice. The form of a verb that shows whether the subject acted (**active voice**) or was acted upon (**passive voice**): e.g., _He stole the money_ (active). _The money was stolen by him_ (passive). Only transitive verbs (verbs taking objects) can be passive.

References

Ackerly, Brooke, Maria Stern, and Jacqui True. 2006. *Feminist Methodologies for International Relations*. Cambridge: Cambridge University Press.

Acocella, Ivana. 2012. "The focus groups in social research: Advantages and disadvantages," *Quality & Quantity* v 46 no 4, 1125–36.

Adorno, T. W., Else Frenkel-Brunswik, Daniel J. Levinson, and R. Nevitte Sanford. 1969. *The Authoritarian Personality*. New York: W.W. Norton.

AlSaffar, Jackie. 2006. "Copyright concerns in online education: What students need to know," *Journal of Library Administration* v 45 no 1/2, 1–16.

Al-Shehab, Ali J. 2008. "Gender and racial representation in children's television programing in Kuwait: Implications for education," *Social Behavior & Personality: An International Journal* v 36 no 1, 49–63.

American Sociological Association. 1999. "American Sociological Association Code of Ethics." Retrieved on 5 Oct. 2010 http://www.asanet.org/images/asa/docs/pdf/CodeofEthics.pdf

Anthony, Denise, Sean Smith, and Tim Williamson. 2005. "Explaining quality in Internet collective goods: Zealots and good Samaritans in the case of *Wikipedia*." Paper presented at Fall 2005 Innovation and Entrepreneurship seminar at MIT. Retrieved on 5 July 2008 http://web.mit.edu/iandeseminar/Papers/Fall2005/anthony.pdf

Avins, Andrew L. 1998. "Can unequal be more fair? Ethics, subject allocation, and randomized clinical trials," *Journal of Medical Ethics* v 24 no 6, 401–8.

Babbie, Earl, and Lucia Benaquisto. 2010. *Fundamentals of Social Research*. Toronto: Nelson Education.

Bacon, Francis. 1620. *Novum Organum*. n.p.

Baker, Sheridan. 1981. *The Practical Stylist*, 5th ed. New York: Harper and Row.

———, and Lawrence B. Gamache. 1998. *The Canadian Practical Stylist*, 4th ed. Don Mills: Addison-Wesley.

Bandura, Albert. 1973. *Aggression: A Social Learning Analysis*. Englewood Cliffs: NJ Prentice-Hall.

———. 1977. *Social Learning Theory*. Englewood Cliffs, NJ: Prentice-Hall.

Barron, Ian. 2013. "The potential and challenges of critical realist ethnography," *International Journal of Research & Method in Education* v 36 no 2, 117–30.

Batane, Tshepo. 2010. "Turning to Turnitin to fight plagiarism among university students," *Journal of Educational Technology & Society* v 13 no 2, 1–12.

Becker, Betsy Jane. 1990. "Coaching for the Scholastic Aptitude Test: Further synthesis and appraisal," *Review of Educational Research* v 60 no 3, 373–417.

Benhabib, Seyla. 2002. *The Claims of Culture: Equality and Diversity in the Global Era*. Princeton, NJ: Princeton University Press.

Benson, Kari. 2010. "Avoiding the blank screen blues," *Teaching Professor* v 24 no 9, 3.

Bergmann, Reinhard, John Ludbrook, and Will P. J. M. Spooren. 2000. "Different outcomes of the Wilcoxon-Mann-Whitney test from different statistics packages," *The American Statistician* v 54 no 1, 72–7.

Berlin, Isaiah. 1953. *The Hedgehog and the Fox: An Essay on Tolstoy's View of History*. London: Weidenfeld & Nicolson.

Berman, Helene, Gloria Alvernaz Mulcahy, Cheryl Forchuk, Kathryn Ann Edmunds, Amy Haldenby, and Rachel Lopez. 2009. "Uprooted and displaced: A critical narrative study of homeless, aboriginal, and newcomer girls in Canada," *Issues in Mental Health Nursing* v 30 no 7, 418–30.

Black, Erik. 2008. "Wikipedia and academic peer review: Wikipedia as a recognized medium for scholarly publication?" *Online Information Review* v 32 no 1, 73–88.

Blackburn, Robin. 2002. "The imperial presidency, the war on terrorism, and the revolutions of modernity," *Constellations* v 9 no 4, 3–33.

Blane, D. B. 1996. "Collecting retrospective data: Development of a reliable method and a pilot study of its use," *Social Science and Medicine* v 42 no 5, 751–7.

Blumenthal, Daniel S., and Ralph J. DiClemente, eds. 2004. *Community-Based Health Research: Issues and Methods.* New York: Springer.

Grant, Ruth W and Jeremy Sugarman. 2004. "Ethics in human subjects research: Do incentives matter?" *The Journal of medicine and philosophy,* vol 29 no 6, 717–38.

Brewer-Smyth, Kathleen. 2008. "Ethical, Regulatory, and Investigator Considerations in Prison Research," *Advances in Nursing Science* v 31 no 2, 119–27.

Briggs, John. 2013. "Indigenous knowledge: A false dawn for development theory and practice?" *Progress in Development Studies* v 13 no 3, 231–43.

British Sociological Association. 1999. "Statement of Professional Ethics." Retrieved on 5 Oct. 2000 http://www.britsoc.org.uk

Brody, Janet L., and Holly B. Waldron. 2000. "Ethical issues in research on the treatment of adolescent substance abuse disorders," *Addictive Behaviors* v 25 no 2, 217–28.

Brunt, Lodewijk. 1999. "Thinking about ethnography," *Journal of Contemporary Ethnography* v 28 no 5, 500–9.

Bryman, Alan, Edward Bell, and James J. Teevan. 2012. *Social Research Methods,* 3rd Canadian ed. Don Mills: Oxford University Press.

Cahill, Caitlin. 2007. "The personal is political: Developing new subjectivities through participatory action research," *Gender, Place & Culture: A Journal of Feminist Geography* v 14 no 3, 267–92.

Calahan, Charles A., and Walter R. Schumm. 1995. "An exploratory analysis of family social science mail survey response rates," *Psychological Reports* v 76 pt 2, 1379–88.

Canada History. 2000. "Pierre Trudeau." Retrieved on 30 Oct. 2010 http://www .canadahistory.com/sections/politics/pm/ pierretrudeau.htm

Canadian Sociology and Anthropology Association. 1994. "Statement of Ethical Practice."

Retrieved on 5 Oct. 2000 http://www.unb .ca/web/anthropology/csaa/csaa.html

Carroll, Joyce Armstrong. 2012. "Teaching the thesis," *School Library Monthly* v 29 no 2, 18–20.

Carroll, Jude. 2013. *A Handbook for Deterring Plagiarism in Higher Education,* 2nd ed.). Oxford, UK: Oxford Centre for Staff and Learning Development.

Chojnacka, Helena. 2000. "Early marriage and polygyny: Feature characteristics of nuptiality in Africa," *Genus* v 56 no 3–4, 179–208.

Cluett, Robert, and Lee Ahlborn. 1965. *Effective English Prose.* New York: L. W. Singer.

Comte, Auguste. 1855. *The Positive Philosophy.* Harriet Martineau (trans.). 3 vols. New York: Calvin Blanchard.

Cooper, H. M. 1984. *The Integrative Research Review: A Systematic Approach.* Newbury Park, CA: Sage.

Couper, Mick, and Linda L. Stinson. 1999. "Completion of self-administered questionnaires in a sex survey," *The Journal of Sex Research* v 36 no 4, 321–30.

Creswell, John W. 1992. *Qualitative and Quantitative Approaches.* Thousand Oaks, CA: Sage

———. 2013. *Qualitative Inquiry and Research Design: Choosing among Five Approaches,* 3rd ed. Los Angeles: Sage.

Crighton, Eric J., C. Brown, Jamie Baxter, Louise Lemyre, Jeffrey Masuda, and F. Ursitti. 2013. "Perceptions and experiences of environmental health risks among new mothers: A qualitative study in Ontario, Canada," *Health, Risk & Society* v 15 no 4, 295–312.

Cunningham, John A., Donna Ansara, and T. Cameron Wild. 1999. "What is the price of perfection? The hidden costs of using detailed assessment instruments to measure alcohol consumption," *Journal of Studies on Alcohol* v 60 no 6, 756–8.

Curtis, Karen A. 1999. "'Bottom-up' poverty and welfare policy discourse: Ethnography to the rescue?" *Urban Anthropology and Studies of Cultural Systems and World Economic Development* v 28 no 2, 103–40.

Curtis, Penny. 2008. "The experiences of young people with obesity in secondary school: Some implications for the healthy school agenda," *Health and Social Care in the Community* v 16 no 4, 410–18.

Daily, Catherine M., and Janet P. Near. 2000. "CEO satisfaction and firm performance in family firms: Divergence between theory and practice," *Social Indicators Research* v 51 n 2, 125–70.

Dalton, Dan R., James C. Wimbush, and Catherine M. Daily. 1996. "Candor, privacy and 'legal immunity' in business ethics research: An empirical assessment of the randomized response technique (RRT)," *Business Ethics Quarterly* v 6, 87–99.

Davey, Rachel. 2007. "Making an effective bid: Developing a successful research proposal," *Clinician in Management* v 15 no 3/4, 137–44.

Davis-Delano, Laurel, and Todd Crosset. 2008. "Using social movement theory to study outcomes in sport-related social movements," *International Review for the Sociology of Sport* v 43 no 2, 115–34.

de Finney, Sandrina. 2010. "'We just don't know each other': Racialised girls negotiate mediated multiculturalism in a less diverse Canadian city," *Journal of Intercultural Studies* v 31 no 5, 471–87.

Dennis, Barbara. 2009. "Acting up: Theater of the oppressed as critical ethnography," *International Journal of Qualitative Methods* v 8 no 2, 65–96.

Denzin, Norman K. 1998. "The new ethnography: Review article," *Journal of Contemporary Ethnography* v 27 no 3, 405–15.

———. 1999. "Interpretive ethnography for the next century," *Journal of Contemporary Ethnography* v 28 no 5, 510–19.

DeVriese, Leila. 2013. "Paradox of globalization: New Arab publics? New social contract?" *Perspectives on Global Development and Technology* v 12 no 1–2, 114–34.

Dodge, Bernadine. 2006. "Re-imag(in)ing the past," *Rethinking History* v 10 no 3, 345–67.

Durkheim, Émile. 1951. *Suicide: A Study in Sociology*. John A. Spaulding and George Simpson (trans.). New York: Free Press of Glencoe.

Duxbury, Alec. 2008. "The tyranny of the thesis statement," *English Journal* v 97 no 4, 16–18.

Easton, Alyssa, James H. Price, and Susan K. Telljohann. 1997. "An informational versus monetary incentive in increasing physicians' response rates," *Psychological Reports* v 81 no 3 pt 1, 968–70.

Eder, Donna, and William Corsaro. 1999. "Ethnographic studies of children and youth: Theoretical and ethical issues," *Journal of Contemporary Ethnography* v 28 no 5, 520–31.

Edgerly, Stephanie, Emily Vraga, Kajsa Dalrymple, Timothy Macafee, and Timothy Fung. 2013. "Directing the dialogue: The relationship between YouTube videos and the comments they spur," *Journal of Information Technology & Politics* v 10 no 3, 276–92.

Eichler, Margrit. 2014. "The past of the future and the future of families," *Canadian Families Today: New Perspectives,* 3rd ed. David Cheal and Patrizia Albanese (eds.). Toronto: Oxford University Press.

Enloe, Cynthia. 2007. *Globalization & Militarism: Feminists Make the Link*. Lanham, MD: Rowman & Littlefield.

Evans, Geoffrey, and Colin Mills. 1999. "Are there classes in post-communist societies? A new approach to identifying class structure," *Sociology* v 33 no 1, 23–46.

Eytan, Ariel. 2011. "Religion and mental health during incarceration: A systematic literature review," *Psychiatric Quarterly* v 82, 287–95.

Faragher, John Mack. 2005. *A Great and Noble Scheme: The Tragic Story of the Expulsion of the French Acadians from Their American Homeland*. New York: W. W. Norton.

Ferris, Jackie and Harold Wynne (2001). *The Canadian problem gambling index: Final report*. Canadian Centre on Substance Abuse (CCSA), Canadian Consortium for Gambling Research. Retrieved from: http://www.ccgr.ca/en/projects/resources/CPGI-Final-Report-English.pdf

Fine, Gary Alan. 1999. "Field labor and ethnographic reality," *Journal of Contemporary Ethnography* v 28 no 5, 532–9.

Fisher, Celia B., Ann D'Alessandro-Higgins, and Jean Marie B. Rau. 1996. "Referring and reporting research participants at risk: Views from urban adolescents," *Child Development* v 67, 2086–100.

Flick, Uwe. 2006. *An Introduction to Qualitative Research*, 3rd ed. London: Sage.

Flink, Herb. 2007. "Essential communication skills for engineers: Tell it like it is," *Industrial Engineer* v 39 no 3, 44–8.

Fontes, Lisa Aronson. 1998. "Ethics in family violence research: Cross-cultural issues," *Family Relations* v 47 no 1, 53–61.

Fox, Bonnie. 2009. *When Couples Become Parents: The Creation of Gender in the Transition to Parenthood*. Toronto: University of Toronto Press.

Fraenkel, Jack R., and Norman E. Wallen. 1996. *How to Design and Evaluate Research in Education*. New York: McGraw-Hill.

Francek, Mark. 2000. "Multimedia term papers in introductory earth science classes," *Journal of College Science Teaching* v 29 no 3, 199–204.

Frank, Steven. 2005. "I'll show you my underwear (or how to tackle the dreaded thesis statement)," *Writing* v 27 no 4, 14–17.

Freud, Sigmund. 1963. *Civilization and Its Discontents*. Joan Riviere (trans.). London: Hogarth Press.

Gaber, Ivor. 1996. "Hocus-pocus polling: The use of focus groups by political parties," *New Statesman* v 125 Aug. 16, 20–1.

Galloway, Kristin L. 2011. "Focus groups in the virtual world: Implications for the future of evaluation." *New Directions for Evaluation* vol 2011 no 131, 47–51.

Gans, Herbert J. 1999. "Participant observation in the era of 'ethnography'," *Journal of Contemporary Ethnography* v 28 no 5, 540–8.

Geertzen, Jan H., Corine G. Van Es, and Pieter U. Dijkstra. 2009. "Sexuality and amputation: A systematic literature review," *Disability and Rehabilitation* v 31 no 7, 522–7.

Ghassib, Hisham. 2012. "A theory of the knowledge industry," *International Studies in the Philosophy of Science* v 26 no 4, 447–56.

Gibaldi, Joseph. 1999. *MLA Handbook for Writers of Research Papers*, 5th ed. New York: The Modern Language Association of America.

Glaser, Barney G. 1978. *Theoretical Sensitivity: Advances in the Methodology of Grounded Theory*. Mill Valley, CA: The Sociology Press.

Gondolf, Edward, and Ellen R. Fisher. 1988. *Battered Women as Survivors: An Alternative to Treating Learned Helplessness*. Lexington, MA: Lexington Books.

Gothberg, June, Brooks Applegate, Patricia Reeves, Paula Kohler, Linda Thurston, and Lori Peterson. 2013. "Is the medium really the message? A comparison of face-to-face, telephone, and Internet focus group venues," *Journal of Ethnographic & Qualitative Research* v 7 no 3, 108–27.

Gouin, Rachel R., Karen Cocq, and Samantha McGavin. 2011. "Feminist participatory research in a social justice organization," *Action Research* v 9 no 3, 261–81.

Grant, Ruth W., and Jeremy Sugarman. 2004. "Ethics in human subjects research: Do incentives matter?" *The Journal of medicine and philosophy*, vol 29 no 6, 717–38.

Gross, Alan, and Joseph Harmon. 2009. "The structure of PowerPoint presentations: The art of grasping things whole," *IEEE Transactions on Professional Communication* v 52 no 2, 121–37.

Gubrium, Jaber F., and James A. Holstein. 1997. *The New Language of Qualitative Method*. New York: Oxford University Press.

—— and ——. 1999. "At the border of narrative and ethnography," *Journal of Comparative Ethnography* v 28 no 5, 561–73.

Guendouzi, Jackie. 2006. "'The guilt thing': Balancing domestic and professional roles," *Journal of Marriage and Family* v 68 no 4, 901–9.

Gullifer, Judith, and Graham Tyson. 2010. "Exploring university students' perceptions of plagiarism: A focus group study," *Studies in Higher Education* v 35 no 4, 463–81.

Haluska, Jan Charles. 2006. "In defense of the formula essay," *Academic Questions* v 20 no 1, 46–55.

Hammersley, Martyn. 1999. "Not bricolage but boatbuilding: Exploring two metaphors for thinking about ethnography," *Journal of Contemporary Ethnography* v 28 no 5, 574–85.

Hampton, Keith, and Barry Wellman. 1999. "Netville online and offline: Observing and surveying a wired suburb," *The American Behavioral Scientist* v 43 no 3, 475–92.

Hare, Sheri, James H. Price, and Michael G. Flynn. 1998. "Increasing return rates of a mail survey to exercise professionals using a modest monetary incentive," *Perceptual and Motor Skills* v 86 no 1, 217–18.

Heckelman, Jac C. 1997. "Determining who voted in historical elections: An aggregated logic approach," *Social Science Research* v 26, 121–34.

Hegelund, Allan. 2005. "Objectivity and subjectivity in the ethnographic method," *Qualitative Health Research* v 15 no 5, 647–68.

Hesse-Biber, Sharlene Nagy, Patricia Leavy, and Michele L. Yaiser. 2004. "Feminist approaches to research as a process: Reconceptualizing epistemology, methodology, and method," *Feminist Perspectives on Social Research*. Sharlene Nagy Hesse-Biber and Michelle L. Yaiser (eds.). New York: Oxford University Press.

Himmelfarb, Samuel. 2008. "The multi-item randomized response technique," *Sociological Methods and Research* v 36 no 4, 495–514.

Hu, Meiqun, Ee-Peng Lim, Aixin Sun, Hady W. Lauw, and Ba-Quy Vuong. 2007. "Measuring article quality in Wikipedia: Models and evaluation," *Proceedings of the Sixteenth Association of Computing Machinery (ACM) Conference on Information and Knowledge Management*, Lisbon, Portugal, 243–52. Retrieved 5 July 2008 http://delivery.acm .org/10.1145/1330000/1321476/p243-hu .pdf?key1=1321476&key2=0239535121& coll=GUIDE&dl=GUIDE&CFID= 76963643&CFTOKEN=68899462

Interagency Advisory Panel on Research Ethics. 2005. *Tri-Council Policy Statement: Ethical Conduct for Research Involving Humans*. Retrieved on 4 July 2008 http://www.pre .ethics.gc.ca/english/index.cfm

International Federation of Library Associations and Institutions. n.d. "Citation guides for electronic documents." Retrieved on 30 Sept. 1999 http://www.ifla.org/I/training/citation/ citing.htm

Israel, B. A., A. J. Schultz, E. A. Parker, and A. B. Becker. 1998. "Review of community-based research: Assessing partnership approaches to improve public health," *Annual Review of Public Health* v 19, 173–202.

Jaidka, Kokil, Christopher Khoo, and Jin-Cheon Na. 2013. "Literature review writing: How

information is selected and transformed," *Aslib Proceedings* v 65 no 3, 303–25.

Johnson, Noel D. and Alexandra A. Mislin. 2011. "Trust games: A meta-analysis," *Journal of Economic Psychology* v 32 no 5, 865–89.

Johnson, R. Burke and Anthony J. Onwuegbuzie. 2004. "Mixed methods research: A research paradigm whose time has come," *Educational Researcher,* v 33 no 4, 14–26.

Johnston, Charlotte, and Sheila Woody. 2008. "Ethical challenges in community-based research: Introduction to the series," *Clinical Psychology: Science and Practice* v 15 no 2, 115–17.

Jortner, Adam. 2003. "The Thesis Statement," *Literary Cavalcade* v 55 no 6, 34–5.

Kasper, Anne. 1994. "A feminist, qualitative methodology: A study of women with breast cancer," *Qualitative Sociology* v 17 no 3, 263–81.

Kaye, Sanford. 1998. *Writing under Pressure: The Quick Writing Process*. New York: Oxford University Press.

Kellsey, Charlene. 2005. "Writing the literature review," *College & Research Libraries News* v 66 no 7, 526–34.

Kenyon, Gary M. 1996. "Ethical issues in ageing and biography," *Ageing and Society* v 16, 659–75.

Kupek, Emil. 1999. "Estimation of the number of sexual partners for the nonrespondents to a large national survey," *Archives of Sexual Behavior* v 28 no 3, 23–42.

Lal, Vinay. 1997. "Discipline and authority: Some notes on future histories and epistemologies of India," *Futures* (London, England) v 29 no 10, 985–1000.

Levy, C. Michael, and Sarah Ransdell. 1995. "Is writing as difficult as it seems?" *Memory and Cognition* v 23 no 6, 767–79.

Li, Peter. 1986. "Methods of sociology research," *The Social World: An Introduction to Sociology*. Lorne Tepperman and R. Jack Richardson (eds.). Toronto: McGraw-Hill Ryerson.

Library and Archives Canada. 2014. "Index to federal Royal Commissions." Retrieved on 10 Sept. 2014 http://www.bac-lac.gc.ca/eng/ discover/royal-commissions-index/Pages/ index-federal-royal-commissions.aspx

Limmer, Mark. 2010. "Young men, masculinities and sex education," *Sex Education* v 10 no 4, 349–58.

Lipset, Seymour Martin. 1956. *Union Democracy: The Internal Politics of the International Typographical Union [by] Seymour Martin Lipset, Martin A. Trow [and] James S. Coleman*. Glencoe, IL: Free Press.

Lockyer, Sharon. 2006. "Heard the one about … applying mixed methods in humour research?" *International Journal of Social Research Methodology* v 9 no 1, 41–59.

Ljubojevic, Milos, Vojkan Vaskovic, Srecko Stankovic, and Jelena Vaskovic. 2014. "Using supplementary video in multimedia instruction as a teaching tool to increase efficiency of learning and quality of experience," *International Review of Research in Open and Distance Learning* v 15 no 3, 275–91.

Maas, Cora J. M., Joop J. Hox, and Gerty J. L. M. Lensvelt-Mulders. 2004. "Longitudinal meta-analysis," *Quality & Quantity* v 38 no 4, 381–9.

Mackiewicz, Jo. 2008. "Comparing Powerpoint experts' and university students' opinions about Powerpoint presentations," *Journal of Technical Writing & Communication* v 38 no 2, 149–65.

Madden, Amy, Ian Ruthven, and David McMenemy. 2013. "A classification scheme for content analyses of YouTube video comments," *Journal of Documentation* v 69 no 5, 693–714.

Mahoney, James. 1999. "Nominal, ordinal, and narrative appraisal in macrocausal analysis," *American Journal of Sociology* v 104 no 4, 1154–96.

Malthus, T.R. 1958 [1798]. *An Essay on the Principle of Population*. Toronto: Dent.

Mann, Susan A., Michael D. Grimes, and Alice Abel Kemp. 1997. "Paradigm shifts in family sociology? Evidence from three decades of family textbooks," *Journal of Family Issues* v 18, 315–49.

Marshall, C., and G.B. Rossman. 1989. *Designing Qualitative Research*. Newbury Park, CA: Sage.

Marshall, Emily, Sabrina Wong, Jeannie Haggerty, Jean-Fréderic Levesque. 2010. "Perceptions of unmet healthcare needs: What do Punjabi and Chinese-speaking immigrants think? A qualitative study," *BMC Health Services Research* v 10, 46–53.

Marx, Karl. 1961. *Economic and Philosophical Manuscripts of 1844*. Moscow: Foreign Languages Publishing House.

Maynard, Michael L. 1996. "Effectiveness of 'begging' as a persuasive tactic for improving response rate on a client/agency mail survey," *Psychological Reports* v 78, 204–6.

McAuliffe, William E., Stephanie Geller, and Richard LaBrie. 1998. "Are telephone surveys suitable for studying substance abuse? Cost, administration, coverage and response rate issues," *Journal of Drug Issues* v 28 no 2, 455–81.

McCrady, Barbara S., and Donald A. Bux, Jr. 1999. "Ethical issues in informed consent with substance abusers," *Journal of Consulting and Clinical Psychology* v 67 no 2, 186–93.

McCullough, B.D. 1998. "Assessing the reliability of statistical software: Part I," *The American Statistician* v 52 no 4, 358–66.

———. 1999. "Assessing the reliability of statistical software: Part II," *The American Statistician* v 53 no 2, 149–59.

Merriam, Sharan B. 1988. *Case Study Research in Education: A Qualitative Approach*. San Francisco, CA: Jossey-Bass Publishers.

Meter, Karl M. van. 1994. "Sociological methodology," *International Social Science Journal* v 46, 15–25.

Michael, John. 2003. "Beyond us and them: Identity and terror from an Arab American's perspective," *The South Atlantic Quarterly* v 102 no 4, 701–28.

Michelson, Ethan. 2008. "Dear Lawyer Bao: Everyday problems, legal advice and state power in China," *Social Problems* v 55 no 1, 43–71.

Mill, John Stuart. 1859. *On Liberty*. n.p.

Milner, Stephen J. 1999. "Partial readings: Addressing a Renaissance archive," *History of the Human Sciences* v 12 no 2, 89–105.

Mintz, Sidney W. 2000. "Sows' ears and silver linings: A backward look at ethnography," *Current Anthropology* v 41 no 2, 169–77, 188–9.

Modern Language Association of America. 1998. *MLA Style Manual and Guide to Scholarly Publishing*, 2nd ed. New York: Modern Language Association of America.

Molfese, Victoria, Karen Karp, and Linda Siegel. 2002. "Recommendations for writing successful proposals from the reviewer's perspective," *Journal of Research Administration* v 33 no 3, 21–4.

Montante, Sarah. 2004. "Crafting a thesis for an expository essay," *Literacy Cavalcade* v 56 no 5, 36–7.

Morgan, David L. 1996. "Focus groups," *Annual Review of Sociology* v 22, 129–52.

Moshiri, Saeed. 1999. "Producing quality graphs with econometrics and statistics software," *The Economic Journal* v 109, F756–71.

Myers, G., and Phil Macnaghten. 1998. "Rhetorics of environmental sustainability: Commonplaces and places," *Environment and Planning A* v 30 no 2, 333–53.

Nelder, Mary, and Susan J. Snelling. 2000. *Women Speak: Research on Women Abuse*. Ottawa, ON: Ministry of Justice Canada.

Novick, Alvin. 1996. "One small ethical issue arising in ethnographic research," *AIDS and Public Policy Journal* v 11, 115–17.

Oakley, Ann. 1981. "Interviewing women: A contradiction in terms," *Doing Feminist Research*. H. Roberts (ed.). London: Routledge & Kegan Paul.

Oden, Lorette, and James H. Price. 1999. "Effects of a small monetary incentive and follow-up mailings on return rates of a survey to nurse practitioners," *Psychological Reports* v 85 no 3 pt 2, 1154–6.

O'Mahony, Joyce Maureen, Tam Truong Donnelly, Dave Este, and Shelley Raffin Bouchal. 2012. "Using critical ethnography to explore issues among immigrant and refugee women seeking help for postpartum depression," *Issues in Mental Health Nursing* v 33 no 11, 735–42.

Oster, Robert A. 1998. "An examination of five statistical software packages for epidemiology," *The American Statistician* v 52 no 3, 267–80.

Park, Chris. 2003. "In other (people's) words: Plagiarism by university students—literature and lessons," *Assessment & Evaluation in Higher Education* vol 28 no 5, 471–88.

Pascale, Celine-Marie. 2010. "Epistemology and the politics of knowledge," *Sociological Review* (Supplement) v 58 no s2, 154–65.

Paulos, John Allen. 1998. *Once Upon a Number: The Hidden Mathematical Logic of Stories*. New York: Perseus (Basic Books).

Pavlik, Volory N., David J. Hyman, and Carlos Vallbona. 1996. "Response rates to random digit dialing for recruiting participants to an onsite health study," *Public Health Reports* v 111, 444–50.

Pearson, Geoff. 2009. "The researcher as hooligan: Where 'participant' observation means breaking the law," *International Journal of Social Research Methodology* v 12 no 3, 243–55.

Pearson, Stephen, and Panganai Makadzange. 2008. "Help-seeking behaviour for sexual-health concerns: A qualitative study of men in Zimbabwe," *Culture, Health & Sexuality* v 10 no 4, 361–76.

Peñuelas, Ana Belén Cabrejas. 2008. "A comparison of an effective and an ineffective writer's mental representations of their audience, rhetorical purpose and composing strategies," *RaeL: Revista Electrónica de Lingüística Aplicada* no 7, 90–104.

Plotnick, Robert D., and Saul D. Hoffman. 1999. "The effect of neighbourhood characteristics on young adult outcomes: Alternative estimates," *Social Science Quarterly* v 80 no 1, 1–18.

Pourjaili, Hamid, and Janet Kimbrell. 1994. "Effects of four instrumental variables on survey response," *Psychological Reports* v 75, 895–8.

Pratt, E. J. 2001. "Newfoundland," *15 Canadian Poets X 3*. Gary Geddes (ed.). Toronto: Oxford University Press.

Price, Bronwyn. 2010. "Teaching effective literature use skills for research reports in geography," *Journal of Geography in Higher Education* v 34 no 2, 247–64.

Pugsley, Lesley. 2010. "Design an effective PowerPoint presentation," *Education for Primary Care* v 21 no 1, 51–3.

Rabinowitz, Erik, Michael Kernodle, and Robert McKethan. 2010. "The effective use of PowerPoint to facilitate active learning," *JOPERD: The Journal of Physical Education, Recreation & Dance* v 81 no 5, 12–16.

Raby, Rebecca. 2010. "Public selves, inequality, and interruptions: The creation of meaning in focus groups with teens," *International Journal of Qualitative Methods* v 9 no 1, 1–15.

Rajan, S. Ravi. 2002. "Disaster, development and governance: Reflections on the 'lessons' of Bhopal," *Environmental Values* v 11 no 3, 169–94.

Raymer, Robert. 2010. "Getting started with pre-writing techniques," *Writer* v 123 no 5, 24–5.

Reichardt, Charles S., and Thomas D. Cook. 1979. "Beyond qualitative versus quantitative methods," *Qualitative and Quantitative Methods in Evaluation Research*. Charles S. Reichardt and Thomas D. Cook (eds.). Beverly Hills, CA: Sage Publications.

Reinharz, Shulamit. 1992. *Feminist Methods in Social Research*. New York: Oxford University Press.

Rendall, Michael S., Lynda Clarke, and H. Elizabeth Peters. 1999. "Incomplete reporting of men's fertility in the United States and Britain: A research note," *Demography* v 36 no 1, 135–44.

Roberta, Marie, Robert Pauzé, and Louise Fournier. 2005. "Factors associated with homelessness of adolescents under supervision of the youth protection system," *Journal of Adolescence* v 28 no 2, 215–30.

Robinson, Katherine Morton. 2001. "Unsolicited narratives from the Internet: A rich source of qualitative data. *Qualitative Health Research* vol 11 no 5, 706–14.

Roelfs, David J., Eran Shor, Louise Falzon, Karina W. Davidson, and Joseph E. Schwartz. 2013. "Meta-analysis for sociology—A measure-driven approach," *Bulletin of Sociological Methodology* v 117 no 1, 75–92.

Ryan, Vernon D., Kerry A. Agnitsch, Lijun Zhao, and Rehan Mullick. 2005. "Making sense of voluntary participation: A theoretical synthesis," *Rural Sociology* v 70 no 3, 287–313.

Santangelo, Tanya, and Natalite G. Olinghouse. 2009. "Effective writing instruction for students who have writing difficulties," *Focus on Exceptional Children* v 42 no 4, 1–20.

Scarce, Rik. 1994. "(No) trial (but) tribulations: When courts and ethnography conflict," *Journal of Contemporary Ethnography* v 23, 123–49.

———. 2005. *Contempt of Court: A Scholar's Battle for Free Speech from behind Bars*. Lanham, MD: Alta-Mira Press.

Schweitzer, N. J. 2008. "Wikipedia and psychology: Coverage of concepts and its use by undergraduate students," *Teaching of Psychology* v 35 no 2, 81–5.

Shaffer, Victoria and Hal Arkes. 2009. "Preference reversals in evaluations of cash versus non-cash incentives," *Journal of Economic Psychology* v 30 no 6, 859–72.

Shaw, Lori Anne. 2010. "Divorce mediation outcome research: A meta-analysis," *Conflict Resolution Quarterly* v 27 no 4, 447–66.

Shepherd, James F. 1979. *College Study Skills*. Boston: Houghton Mifflin.

———. 1981. *RSVP: The Houghton Mifflin Reading, Study, and Vocabulary Program*. Boston: Houghton Mifflin.

Smith, Dorothy E. 2008. "From the 14th floor to the sidewalk: Writing sociology at ground level," *Sociological Inquiry* v 78 no 3, 417–22.

Sprague, Joey, and Mary Zimmerman. 1993. "Overcoming dualisms: A feminist agenda for sociological methodology," *Theory on Gender/Feminism on Theory*. Paula England (ed.). New York: Aldine.

Statistics Canada. 2016. Family Violence in Canada, 2014. Ottawa: Statistics Canada. Retrieved from http://www.statcan.gc.ca/pub/11-627-m/11-627-m2016001-eng.pdf

Steinberg, Alan M., Robert S. Pynoos, and Armen K. Goenjian. 1999. "Are researchers bound by child abuse reporting laws?" *Child Abuse and Neglect* v 23 no 8, 771–7.

Stone, Emma, and Mark Priestley. 1996. "Parasites, pawns and partners: Disability research and the role of non-disabled researchers," *The British Journal of Sociology* v 47, 699–716.

Strasser, Nora. 2014. "Using Prezi in higher education," *Journal of College Teaching & Learning* (Online) v 11 no 2, 94–8.

Stringer, Ernie. 1997. *Community-Based Ethnography: Breaking Traditional Boundaries of Research, Teaching, and Learning*. New York, NY: Lawrence Erlbaum Associates.

Subramanian, S. V., Kelvyn Jones, Afamia Kaddour, and Nancy Krieger. 2009.

"Revisiting Robinson: The perils of individualistic and ecologic fallacy," *International Journal of Epidemiology* v 38 no 2, 342–60.

Sugiman, Pamela. 2009. "'Life is sweet': Vulnerability and composure in the wartime narratives of Japanese Canadians," *Journal of Canadian Studies* v 43 no 1, 186–218.

Sullivan, Cris M., Maureen H. Rumptz, and Rebecca Campbell. 1996. "Retaining participants in longitudinal community research: A comprehensive protocol," *The Journal of Applied Behavioral Science* v 32, 262–76.

Summers, Jodi, and James H. Price. 1997. "Increasing return rates to a mail survey among health educators," *Psychological Reports* v 81, 551–4.

Tangen, Jason, Merryn Constable, Eric Durrant, Chris Teeter, Brett Beston, and Joseph Kim. 2011. "The role of interest and images in slideware presentations," *Computers & Education* v 56 no 3, 865–72.

Tashakkori, Abbas, and Charles Teddlie (eds.). 2002. *Handbook of Mixed Methods in Social and Behavioral Research*. Thousand Oaks, CA: Sage.

Teare, John F., Karen Authier, and Roger Peterson. 1994. "Differential patterns of post-shelter placement as a function of problem type and severity," *Journal of Child and Family Studies* v 3 no 1, 7–22.

Thomas, Francis-Noel, and Mark Turner. 2011. *Clear and Simple as the Truth: Writing Classic Prose*, 2nd ed. Princeton, NJ: Princeton University Press.

Thompson, A. J., and A. V. Martinet. 1980. *A Practical English Grammar*, 3rd ed. Oxford: Oxford University Press.

Timmins, Fiona, and Catherine McCabe. 2005. "How to conduct an effective literature search," *Nursing Standard* v 20 no 11, 41–7.

Tobias, Joshua, Chantelle Richmond, and Isaac Luginaah. 2013. "Community-based participatory research (CBPR) with Indigenous communities: Producing respectful and reciprocal research," *Journal of Empirical Research on Human Research Ethics* v 8 no 2, 129–40.

Tolhurst, Rachel, Beryl Leach, Janet Price, Jude Robinson, Elizabeth Ettore, Alex Scott-Samuel, Nduku Kilonzo, Louis Sabuni, Steve Robertson, Anuj Kapilashrami, Katie Bristow, Raymond Lang, Francelina Romao, and Sally Theobald. 2012. "Intersectionality and gender mainstreaming in international health: Using a feminist participatory action research process to analyse voices and debates from the global south and north," *Social Science & Medicine* v 74 no 11, 1825–32.

Tufte, Edward R. 2003. *The Cognitive Style of PowerPoint*. Cheshire, CT: Graphics Press.

Turabian, Kate. 1967. *A Manual for Writers of Term Papers, Theses, and Dissertations*, 3rd ed. revised. Chicago: University of Chicago Press.

Turney, Lyn, and Catherine Pocknee. 2005. "Virtual focus groups: New frontiers in research," *International Journal of Qualitative Methods* v 4 no 2, 1–10.

Unger, Rhoda K. 1999. "Comments on 'focus groups': Comment on S. Wilkinson," *Psychology of Women Quarterly* v 23 no 2, 245–6.

Visser, Penny S., Jon A. Krosnick, and Jesse Marquette. 1996. "Mail surveys for election forecasting? An evaluation of the Columbus dispatch poll," *The Public Opinion Quarterly* v 60 Summer, 181–227.

Vivar, Cristina G, Anne McQueen, Dorothy Whyte, and Navidad Canga Armayor. 2007. "Getting started with qualitative research: Developing a research proposal," *Nurse Researcher* v 14 no 3, 60–73.

Waldram, James B. 1998. "Anthropology in prison: Negotiating consent and accountability with a 'captured' population," *Human Organization* v 57 no 2, 238–44.

Warren, Ron, Jan LeBlanc Wicks, Robert H. Wicks, Ignatius Fosu, and Donghung Chung. 2007. "Food and beverage advertising to children on US televisions: Did national food advertisers respond?" *Journalism & Mass Communication Quarterly* v 84 no 4, 795–810.

Warriner, Keith, John Goyder, and Heidi Gjertsen. 1996. "Charities, no; lotteries, no;

cash, yes: Main effects and interactions in a Canadian incentives experiment," *The Public Opinion Quarterly* v 60, 542–62.

Weaver, Andrew J., Jakob D. Jensen, Nicole Martins, Ryan J. Hurley, and Barbara J. Wilson. 2011. "Liking violence and action: An examination of gender differences in children's processing of animated content," *Media Psychology* v 14 no 1, 49–70.

Webb, Christine. 1984. "Feminist methodology in nursing research," *Journal of Advanced Nursing* v 9, 249–56.

Webb, Wilse B. 1998. "Writing history and accident reports: A metaphorical analysis," *Perceptual and Motor Skills* v 86 no 2, 631–41.

Weinberger, Morris, Jeffrey A. Ferguson, and Glenda Westmoreland. 1998. "Can raters consistently evaluate the content of focus groups?" *Social Science and Medicine* v 46 no 7, 929–33.

Wenger, Neil S., Stanley G. Korenman, and Richard Berk. 1999. "Reporting unethical research behavior," *Evaluation Review* v 23 no 5, 553–70.

White, Adrian, and Katja Schmidt. 2005. "Systematic literature reviews," *Complementary Therapies in Medicine* v 13, 54–60.

Wiederman, Michael W., David L. Weis, and Elizabeth Rice Allegeier. 1994. "The effect of question preface on response rates to a telephone survey of sexual experience," *Archives of Sexual Behavior* v 23, 203–15.

Williams, Matthew. 2007. "Policing and cybersociety: The maturation of regulation within an online community," *Policing & Society* v 17 no 1, 59–82.

Willmack, Diane K., Howard Schuman, and Beth Ellen Pennell. 1995. "Effects of a prepaid nonmonetary incentive on response rates and response quality in a face-to-face survey," *The Public Opinion Quarterly* v 59, 78–92.

Wöhner, T. and R. Peters. 2009. "Assessing the quality of Wikipedia articles with lifecycle based metrics," *International Symposium on Wikis and Open Collaboration*, New York: NY.

Wood, Marilynn J. 2003. "Systematic literature reviews," *Clinical Nursing Research* v 12, 3–7.

Yoshikawa, Hirokazu, Thomas Weisner, Ariel Kalil, and Niobe Way. 2008. "Mixing qualitative and quantitative research in developmental science: Uses and methodological choices," *Developmental Psychology* v 44 no 2, 344–54.

Index

The Making Sense Series

Margot Northey with Joan McKibbin
MAKING SENSE
A Student's Guide to Research and Writing
Eighth Edition

Margot Northey, Dianne Draper, and David B. Knight
MAKING SENSE IN GEOGRAPHY AND ENVIRONMENTAL SCIENCES
A Student's Guide to Research and Writing
Sixth Edition

Margot Northey, Lorne Tepperman, and Patrizia Albanese
MAKING SENSE IN THE SOCIAL SCIENCES
A Student's Guide to Research and Writing
Seventh Edition

Margot Northey and Judi Jewinski
MAKING SENSE IN ENGINEERING AND THE TECHNICAL SCIENCES
A Student's Guide to Research and Writing
Fourth Edition

Margot Northey and Patrick von Aderkas
MAKING SENSE IN THE LIFE SCIENCES
A Student's Guide to Research and Writing
Third Edition

Margot Northey, Bradford A. Anderson, and Joel N. Lohr
MAKING SENSE IN RELIGIOUS STUDIES
A Student's Guide to Research and Writing
Third Edition

Margot Northey and Brian Timney
MAKING SENSE IN PSYCHOLOGY
A Student's Guide to Research and Writing
Second Edition

Margot Northey, Kristen Ferguson, and Jon G. Bradley
MAKING SENSE IN EDUCATION
A Student's Guide to Research and Writing
Second Edition